TOMLIN

TOMLIN

THE SOUL OF A FOOTBALL COACH

JOHN HARRIS

FOREWORD BY
TONY DUNGY

SPORTS PUBLISHING

Sports Publishing books may be purchased in bulk at special discounts for sales promotion, corporate gifts, fund-raising, or educational purposes. Special editions can also be created to specifications. For details, contact the Special Sales Department, Sports Publishing, 307 West 36th Street, 11th Floor, New York, NY 10018 or sportspubbooks@skyhorsepublishing.com.

Sports Publishing® is a registered trademark of Skyhorse Publishing, Inc.®, a Delaware corporation.

Visit our website at www.sportspubbooks.com.

10 9 8 7 6 5 4 3 2 1

Library of Congress Cataloging-in-Publication Data is available on file.

Jacket design by Brian Peterson
Jacket photograph: Getty Images

Print ISBN: 978-1-68358-475-9
Ebook ISBN: 978-1-68358-476-6

Printed in the United States of America

To my family for their love and support: Dr. Yulanda McCarty-Harris Esq., Courtney-Rose, Myles, Langston, and John Morris

To the memory of my grandfather George Lilley, who introduced me to *Black Boy* and *Native Son*

To the memory of Ralph Wiley

CONTENTS

FOREWORD

BY TONY DUNGY

THE first time I met Mike Tomlin was when he walked into my office at One Buc Place in February of 2001. I was the head coach of the Tampa Bay Buccaneers and Mike was a twenty-eight-year-old college secondary coach at the University of Cincinnati. My assistant head coach, Herm Edwards, had just left our staff to become the head coach of the New York Jets and I was looking for someone to coach our defensive backs. Several members of our scouting staff had recommended this young coach from Cincinnati, saying he was a bright, energetic, teacher who was a great communicator.

After hearing the same type of accolades about Mike from several people, I called him and asked him to come to Tampa to interview with our defensive staff. We were about fifteen minutes into the interview when I knew that I was going to hire him. For a young coach he was very composed. He wasn't awed by the situation at all and he knew his craft. He was confident in what he wanted to teach and how he would get it across to our players. And our scouts were absolutely right about one thing—he was a great communicator!

At that moment I felt Mike Tomlin was going to be a very good defensive backfield coach for us. I could see he had some special qualities but I never imagined that less than six years later he would be named head coach of one of the most iconic franchises in the NFL, the Pittsburgh Steelers.

When Mike joined us, our defense was loaded with All-Pros and future Hall of Fame players, including John Lynch who was six months older than Mike. But from day one he had total control of his meeting room and it didn't take long for him to earn the respect of every player. He was instrumental in helping make that defense better and in raising the level of play of the entire secondary. That's when I first heard him use the phrase "The standard is the standard," and it was clear Mike Tomlin set very high standards.

Mike and I were only together for that one season. I was fired after a playoff loss to the Philadelphia Eagles and eight days later the Indianapolis Colts hired me to be their coach. I asked the Bucs to let me take Mike with me to be my defensive coordinator but they would not let him out of his contract. The Bucs knew they had something special in Mike, and I did, too. I would have to watch the rest of his career from afar but there would be some moments where our stories intertwined.

The Bucs went on to win the Super Bowl in 2002 and one of their young defensive backs, Dexter Jackson, was named MVP of the game. I was proud of Mike and thrilled to see how that secondary was progressing. Others in the NFL were noticing too and in 2006 the Minnesota Vikings hired him to be their defensive coordinator. At the end of that season our paths would indirectly cross again.

In late January of 2007 our Colts team was preparing to face the New England Patriots in the AFC Championship Game when I got a call from my old boss, Steelers owner Dan Rooney.

I thought he was calling to wish me luck on our effort to get to the Super Bowl but he had something else on his mind. "What can you tell me about this young coach in Minnesota, Mike Tomlin? We've talked to him and he seems phenomenal," Dan said. I could tell from his voice that Dan was very interested in hiring Mike. He was calling me because he knew Mike had been on my staff but also because I had worked with and for the two previous Steeler head coaches, Chuck Noll and Bill Cowher. I told Dan I thought Mike had a lot of the same qualities as those two and that he would be just as successful.

That Sunday we beat the Patriots to earn the right to play in Super Bowl XLI. The next day Mike Tomlin was announced as the new head coach of the Pittsburgh Steelers. That was an awesome weekend for me and I was obviously excited about going to the Super Bowl. But I was just as excited for Mike, and for the Steelers, because I knew my old team was getting a great young coach.

While my coaching career was winding down Mike's was just beginning. For the next seventeen years he would lead the Steelers to some great moments. In the 2008 season, my final year of coaching, we beat the Steelers in Pittsburgh. It was the only time I coached against Mike and it was gratifying to see him on the other sideline. Two months later I retired from coaching and joined the NBC *Football Night in America* team. My first broadcast was the Steelers' Super Bowl XLIII win over the Arizona Cardinals. Incredible!

Mike Tomlin has maintained those high standards his entire career. What is his secret? What makes him special? There are a few things—intelligence, hard work, dedication, and preparation—for sure. But there's something else. There's the special sauce that winners have and I think in reading this book you'll find out more about what has made Mike Tomlin so great. I am so proud of Mike not just for his record and his ability to put winning teams together, but for his ability to shape men. I believe that as you read this book you'll learn just how he has done both.

INTRODUCTION

ON January 22, 2007, Michael Pettaway Tomlin was named as the new head coach of the Pittsburgh Steelers. Replacing the future Hall of Famer Bill Cowher—who had won Super Bowl XL just two seasons earlier—he would become the sixteenth coach in the franchise's history and only the third the organization had known in thirty-nine years.

At only thirty-four years of age, Tomlin had just completed a season as the defensive coordinator for the Minnesota Vikings. In fact, it was his *only* season as defensive coordinator, with five previous years as the defensive backs coach for the Tampa Bay Buccaneers.

So the storied Steelers had brought in the young Tomlin, with just six years of coaching experience on the NFL level, to be the new leader of the franchise.

The question on many people's minds—both those in Pittsburgh and across the NFL—was, *Who is Mike Tomlin?* On the surface, he was young, black, and had only a few years of professional coaching experience. What did the Rooney family know that nobody else did?

Now going into his seventeenth season at the helm, Tomlin brought a championship to Pittsburgh in just his second year as head coach (in Super Bowl XLIII), led the team to Super Bowl

XLV two years later, and has never suffered a losing season. Yet the same question asked in 2007 still rings true:

Who is Mike Tomlin?

To understand Tomlin is to read through his "Tomlinisms" to the type of person he is, the obstacles he's faced, and the mindset that has allowed him to fight off the constant barrage of doubters to his success—both on and off the field.

Five years after the creation of the "Rooney Rule"—named after former Steelers chairman Dan Rooney, which stated that every franchise was to interview at least one minority candidate for their open head coaching position—Tomlin's hiring was only the tenth of a black man in league history, and the first since the Cleveland Browns tabbed Romeo Crennel in 2005. It was also the same year that two black head coaches— Tony Dungy of the Indianapolis Colts and Lovie Smith of the Chicago Bears—made history when they faced off in Super Bowl XLI.

More than twenty years later, the issue of race in football still casts a shadow over the NFL (as well as, it is to be assumed, some of the ire and criticism directed toward Tomlin).

While that's not the goal of this book, it must be noted, as it's a part of his story.

From day one, he had skeptics questioning his age and experience level; perhaps focusing on his skin color instead of respecting his ability to communicate, teach, motivate, and connect. Maybe they were just reading his book by its cover.

Yet, at the end of the day, the NFL is a results-driven league. If you win, you stay. If you lose, you're out. So it goes without saying that Tomlin's tenure in Pittsburgh could have gone sideways if he didn't connect with his veterans.

There had to be something there for it to work; for those players to regain their Super Bowl mojo from two years earlier. How much change would there really have been if the Steelers had gone another way? Maybe the holdovers would have continued to play the way they did when the team went 8–8 in Cowher's final season. Meet the new coach, same as the old coach?

When you're talking about a football team—the players in the locker room—they are the ones putting their bodies on the line for the greater good of the team. And to have somebody you want to go to bat for? Well, that has to be earned. Is this person a leader of men for these Pro Bowlers, All Pros, and Super Bowl ring–wearing players earning millions, regardless of who's standing in front of them delivering the message?

"When Coach T walked in the building for the first time, I saw this young face, Afro, he definitely had a swagger about him," said former Steeler Willie Colon, who played tackle for six seasons under Tomlin. "He was very direct. Very honest. When you're in a Coach T meeting, he doesn't just stand in front of the podium. He walks the aisles. Kind of like that old-school teacher. And he's not afraid to call somebody out. There was a sense of order, a sense of direction. There was a sense of there was a standard. Like, 'I'm not coming here to be the token black coach. I'm coming here not to drop the torch. If anybody's not a part of what I'm trying to do or the culture, I think you know where the exit is.'"

For the Steelers to go to battle for a rookie coach they may have not been familiar with (as most weren't) and buy in the way they did? Well, that's special.

Perhaps he was in the right place at the right time. Perhaps he benefitted from the Rooney Rule. Perhaps he knew the right people. Perhaps all of those things are true. But making those assumptions would be unfair to Tomlin the man, and especially Tomlin the coach.

* * *

When you take into account the criticism of a coach who has never had a losing season and led his team to a Super Bowl victory, it seems that the same lines are used to discount his success. "He won the Super Bowl with Cowher's team." "He had a Hall of Fame quarterback." "He wouldn't have had the same success had he joined a losing team." "What has he done lately?"

We understand how the coaching carousel works, how coaches come and go, how they may have success in one place but not another. And then you have Tomlin, who has been a mainstay in a top football market—and succeeded—for a decade and a half.

Knowing all this, he has worked to keep his thoughts close to his chest, avoiding the opportunity for the media to use his words against him or his team. A coach who has had strong personalities in his locker room and worked to keep all the situations—both good and bad—handled behind closed doors. And not only to be selfless, but work to understand human beings—whether that be his players, coaches, those in the front office, and even team employees—and be a constant for them all in whatever capacity they might need, both on and off the field.

In speaking on the *Pivot* podcast, hosted by former Steeler Ryan Clark, along with Fred Taylor and Channing Crowder, Tomlin talked specifically about "intimacy" in terms of the relationships he has with his players.

I'm open to intimacy but at the same time I realize that I'm not gonna have intimate relationships with everybody, everybody don't want intimate relationships with me, everybody's not comfortable with intimate relationships with me, but everybody knows I'm open and some people take advantage of it and so then we end up with something that's cool, that's beyond our professional relationship that lasts a lifetime like me and my bro right here but it doesn't always come to that and it doesn't have to, but as a leader, I better let it be known that I'm open because you can't do ordinary stuff man and expect unique results that don't make sense. We can't have ordinary relationships. I coach, you play do this good job, bad job and expect like the end of our journey for the confetti to be raining down on us. No man what we're chasing is scarcity to that, like its scarcity to that and so you better be willing to do unique things in order to expect unique results and that's just life and so I'm always like as a leader, how do I wear that responsibility? How do I, how do I create that, How do I create an atmosphere where that happens, I gotta be vulnerable, I gotta be open, I gotta be open to intimacy. I can help these dudes with every aspect of their life football and otherwise I got to let them see me, my successes, my failures, everything like that's, that's the only way. That's what it is.

* * *

Every coach has his own way of leading. Some are loud, while others are quiet. At the end of the day—as previously mentioned—each franchise is looking for a leader of men. Someone who understands the numerous personalities that are in a single locker room and that not everyone is created equal. Not everyone responds to coaching the same way and that you must adapt and adjust to reach each person to get the most out of their potential.

Tomlin has shown the persona of someone whose goal is not to "change" a player, but rather learn who they are and how to work with them, get the best out of each and every one of them—not for his personal benefit, but rather the team.

During the same interview on the *Pivot* podcast, Tomlin verbalized one way in which he looks to connect with those in the facility, leading as both a coach and a human being:

> I better be sensitive to the needs of the group and I better work to meet them. And that's what I mean when I say, I better be what they need me to be. So it's gonna be different things at different times, and I'm open to that part of coming ready. Like I talked about coming ready and coming in. The spirit in which I come is just that because, day to day, I don't know what they need me to be. I better have my ear to the ground. I better get a feel for it. I think that's one of the reasons why I established the routine that I do right. You ever noticed there's a certain point in the morning when I'm walking around on the first floor with a cup of coffee? I come in early, I get all my necessary business out of

the way, because I want to get a feel for the group as they come into the building.

That gives me a directive in terms of what maybe I need to be for them that day. And so how the hell am I gonna get a feel for that if I'm upstairs hiding behind my desk or something to that nature. So I have established little routines that provide me the information that I need to be that.

From the players to the coaches to even the staff, he's cognizant of everyone in the building.

"Coach T would get his cup of coffee. He called it his 'daily lap,'" said West Virginia tight ends coach Blaine Stewart, whose late father Bill Stewart hired Tomlin for his first coaching job at VMI. Blaine was an assistant on Tomlin's staff from 2018 to 2022. "If a guy had a professional routine, whether it'd be cold tubs or treatment or weight room or breakfast, that was kind of a measuring stick to make sure the guys were doing well. Coach T was used to seeing a guy at a certain time and a certain place. If a guy wasn't there, that may be an indicator that something's going on in his life. It gave him kind of a one-on-one relationship with guys."

Imagine you're a rookie or a ten-year veteran, and you're having a really bad day. You enter the team facility not in the best of moods. For you not to say a word, and your head coach says, "I saw you this morning. How are you feeling? You want to talk? Let me know what I can do." Knowing a player can talk to his head coach about football or anything else going on in their lives, and that they're going to do what they can for that player because they read their body language and have worked to understand them as a person . . . well, those types of people (and coaches) are few and far between.

* * *

When I came up with the idea to write this book in the fall of 2022, Tomlin appeared to be headed toward his first losing season as an NFL head coach. The question I kept asking myself was, *Would this affect his legacy?*

Writing a book about Tomlin, one of the winningest coaches in NFL history, made perfect sense. After all, I covered his early years in Pittsburgh for the *Pittsburgh Tribune-Review.* I attended all his press conferences and watched all his games in person. I listened to his cliches and tried my best to decipher them. Back then, I thought I knew him. But after doing research for this book, I realized I didn't really know him at all.

You may have preconceived ideas about who Mike Tomlin is, as I once did. As someone whose job it was to interview him at least once a week during the season, whose job it was to speak with him and get quotes from him, I often left frustrated because he would only give me what *he* wanted or needed me to hear, but that's not what *I* wanted or needed.

Through interviews with colleagues, coaches, teammates, players, and family members, my eyes have been opened. I now have a far greater understanding of the "real" Mike Tomlin—the man, the coach, the teacher, the strategist, the motivator, and, yes, the future Hall of Famer.

Looking back to when the Steelers were 2–6 last season going into their bye week, I realized Tomlin's story needed to be written—even if the team finished with a losing record.

As anyone knows, you often learn more about a person when they are faced with adversity than when things are going right.

This I know to be true about Tomlin, whose team won seven of its final nine games to finish 9–8 and keep his record intact. Yet, with all that said, he hasn't been spoiled by success.

Tomlin still coaches with the same vigor and wide-eyed hunger, the need to prove himself despite all the accolades he's received, that he had when he first joined the Steelers.

If nothing else, 2022 was the year to discover if Tomlin still had that "it" factor he displayed the first time he met Dan Rooney, who flew to Minneapolis to meet Tomlin before inviting him to Pittsburgh for an official interview.

Tomlin didn't have a loaded roster like he had on his Super Bowl teams, but to quote one of his all-time favorite sayings, "The standard is still the standard."

"Mike Tomlin is the Coach of the Year, end of story," former NFL general manager and three-time Super Bowl winner Michael Lombardi said on Twitter at season's end, "One of the best coaching jobs ever."

But now that I know him better, as you will within these pages, it's obvious that wasn't good enough, and a new year brings new challenges he must face for the betterment of himself and the Pittsburgh Steelers.

1

HUMBLE BEGINNINGS

WILLIAM & MARY
(WIDE RECEIVER, 1991–94)

"It's not what you're capable of, it's about what you're willing to do."

DAN Quinn, who by his job description was in his first year as a college football assistant coach, felt more like a college *student* when the team's star wide receiver approached him with a bold, almost audacious, invitation: "Q, I'm picking you up. We're going to a fraternity party."

"I was like, 'OK,'" said Quinn. "We just kind of hit it off. I'm a year older than him, so, I'm thinking, *That's my dude.*"

"Q, I'll pick you up around nine o'clock."

"I'll be ready."

"I didn't even think about saying 'no,'" said Quinn.

The player extending the frat party invitation to Quinn was Mike Tomlin, future head coach of the Pittsburgh Steelers.

The year was 1994.

"We were around each other when we were all doing that stuff at that age," Quinn said. "We were at frat parties before there were cell phones with pictures on them. We had a good time together."

Tomlin was a senior on a William & Mary football team that finished the season 8–3 and tied for the Yankee Conference Mid-Atlantic Division title. A three-year starter, Tomlin (1991–94) finished his career with 101 receptions for 2,052 yards and 20 touchdowns. He established a school record with a 20.2 yards per catch average.

"I believe leaders aren't born. They're made," said Quinn, who led the Atlanta Falcons against the New England Patriots in Super Bowl LI two decades later and has been the Dallas Cowboys' defensive coordinator since 2021. "I'd say Mike T was damn near born with a 'C' on his chest. He was the captain out there."

In '94, Tomlin was twenty-three, Quinn twenty-four.

Quinn was struck by Tomlin's fearlessness to navigate the divide between player and coach. Tomlin's confidence level and poise was uncommon for a college student-athlete.

"His last year playing in college was my first year in coaching," said Quinn. "Two weeks in, he's inviting me to a party."

Tomlin played wide receiver. It was obvious that Tomlin was strong, fast and tough. He was a born leader whose nonstop motor and competitiveness was contagious.

In one of William & Mary's early games that season, the Tide put together a scoring march that could break the will of an opponent. "It was Mike making the catch for another first down, or making the big block," said Quinn.

On a football team, most wide receivers are the prima donnas in the locker room. The best wideouts with Type-A personalities like Tomlin often have a "just give me the damn ball" mentality that can divide a roster. Not Tomlin, who was a leader for *all* positions on both sides of the ball.

"Mike was a person that bridged position groups, offense to defense. It's rare on a football team to see that happen," Quinn said. "Most guys might be the leader of the offense or the leader of the defense. It's only been a few times in my career where a player was the team leader.

"What I saw in the early '90s with Mike," continued Quinn, "was his ability to instantly connect with the receivers, quarterbacks, defensive guys, the GA (graduate assistant), me, to anybody else there."

Tomlin was popular away from the football field in the small college town of Williamsburg, Virginia, with a population around 12,000 people. He was always on the move—working, talking, meeting people, studying, playing football. Included among his several jobs: checking IDs at Paul's Deli, a popular student hangout across the street from Zable Stadium where the football team played its home games.

"From the first day he walked through that door, he was a guy you could talk to," Paul's Deli owner Peter Isipas told the *Pittsburgh Tribune-Review*.

Shawn Knight was Tomlin's roommate for three of his four years at William & Mary. The Tribe's record-setting quarterback, had rare insight into Tomlin the football player and Tomlin the person.

"Mike had the ability to connect with and relate to people no matter what their background," Knight said. "Virginia's an interesting state. You've got urban areas. You've got very rural areas. You've got densely populated areas. So when you bring people and bring players together from very different parts of the state, and then adding to that players from different parts of the country with the various cultures and subcultures, Mike connected with people no matter where they were from. That was one of the reasons he was voted a captain."

Tomlin's engaging personality and magnetism broke down barriers and opened lines of communication with teammates.

"Sometimes people can relate to others who can't always relate to them," Knight said. "Mike always had that personality that, no matter where people were from, they could relate to him and connect with him.

"Mike's sensitivity to people, to personalities, to building chemistry, he was always very, very reflective, very introspective in terms of assessing his own performance, assessing team chemistry and understanding people from different backgrounds, being able to relate to them and understanding what different people needed."

In Tomlin's big, wide world, everyone on his football team was the same. On every team, white players mingle with white players and black players hang out with black players. In Tomlin's case, there were no limits to the company he kept on the team. It's naïve to say that Tomlin didn't see color; *everybody* sees color in some form or fashion. Growing up playing sports with kids from different races and backgrounds, Tomlin became a product of his environment in a literal sense.

"We came up in a pretty much diverse area in Newport News," said older brother Ed Tomlin, who played safety at the University of Maryland. "We played ball and went to elementary school and played Little League with white kids. Unlike some of my teammates when I got to Maryland, there were guys who came from a lot of urban areas. It was their first time being on a team with white kids. It was less of an adjustment for us.

"We had white Little League coaches," Ed Tomlin continued. "They loved you up . . . We were pretty good so they treated you good anyway if you were the 'guy.' We had those influences in our lives that were white, black . . . One of our coaches was Greek. He told us a lot about his culture.

"Mike was a product of his environment. There were some rough parts of Newport News. We didn't have any white neighbors. We went to white schools. There was a pool that wasn't technically segregated that was right across the street from my grandmother's house that no black people could use. We used to walk past this school every day from K through 6. Walked past the swimming pool that in the summertime we could not swim in. I went to Mallory Elementary. It was the Mallory pool."

Ed was four years older and three and a half grades ahead of Mike. When they weren't attending school and doing homework, their world revolved around sports. One of their favorite hangouts was the Peninsula Boys and Girls Club in downtown Newport News. Julia Copeland dropped her sons off on her way to work in the shipyards along the James River coastline when they weren't staying with their grandparents.

"I was a Boys Club kid," Mike Tomlin said on the *Footbahlin with Ben Roethlisberger* podcast. "We weren't a day care family. My mom was a single parent. At the Boys Club, it was two dollars for a summer pass. Mom dropped you off on her way to work. That was day care. It shaped us."

Mike Tomlin was too young to remember when his parents separated; he was ten months old. Julia and Leslie Copeland married when Mike was six. Leslie Copeland was a former semi-pro baseball player around Hampton Roads who taught his stepsons how to play. Mike was a quick learner; his team won the district championship in his first baseball season.

"To tell you the truth, I used to feel sorry for Michael," Julia Copeland told the *Pittsburgh Post-Gazette*. "He'd have to come home after the games with the coach. He'd have to listen to everything that was done wrong and not to repeat that anymore."

"We grew up in a situation where we didn't necessarily have a dad—understand?" said Ed Tomlin, who said their stepfather taught them the mental aspect of sports. "We both pride ourselves on the type of fathers we wanted to be."

No big fan of football due to a mother's instinctive fear of injury, Julia Copeland wasn't pleased when the boys' uncle, Howard Pettaway, signed up both of her sons to play youth football when they turned eight. Two years after Mike signed up, his team won the Pee Wee city championship. His performance earned a mention in the *Newport News Daily Press*.

"We kind of got, not necessarily the best of both worlds, but a diverse cut of both worlds," Ed Tomlin said. "I think a lot of that had to do with athletics. Our upbringing wouldn't have been nearly as diverse had we not participated in organized sports and interacted with white kids and coaches on that level. There's a lot of guys who grew up in our neighborhood from some of the projects that we grew up in who didn't necessarily participate in sports and didn't have that experience and probably don't have those skill sets either."

Mike Tomlin loved to talk. A sociology major with the pipes of a Motown lead singer, he sized you up and analyzed how to push your buttons.

He invited assistant coaches to frat parties. He talked up teammates and opponents alike, and he did it all with a natural swag. Talking smack to an opposing defensive back was as satisfying to Tomlin as pumping up or challenging a teammate.

"Talk about a vocal leader. He did it in practice. But he also would talk a lot in games. He got in a lot of DBs' heads," former William & Mary strength and conditioning coach John Sauer told the *Pittsburgh Tribune-Review*. "Looking back on it all now, *everybody* gravitated to him."

"There was stuff going on in the locker room all the time," former William & Mary assistant Matt Kelchner, who recruited Tomlin, told the *Newport News Daily Press*.

Kelchner recalled one-on-one battles between Tomlin and fellow wide receiver and Kappa Alpha Psi fraternity brother Terry Hammons—who referred to themselves as "The Bomb Squad"—and the defense.

Tomlin and Hammons wore cut-off shirts to show off their abs during pregame warmups. They even had a slogan: *We might not be the best wide receiving corps in the nation, but we think we are.*

"He wasn't a fast wide receiver, but he was a long strider," Buffalo Bills head coach Sean McDermott, who played safety at William & Mary and was Tomlin's college teammate for two seasons, told CBS Sports. "He had length and he was willing to go over the middle to make great catches."

There was one unforgettable day at practice when Tomlin, after catching a long pass against McDermott, flipped the ball at assistant coach Russ Huesman, who swore aloud. McDermott gritted his teeth.

"Terry Hammons and Mike, they'd come in [the locker room] after wiping out the defense in a one-in-one drill," Kelchner said. "They'd put their helmets on with their ear pads upside down, like horns coming out of their ears, just their jockstraps on, and go parading down to the defensive back corner just to abuse . . . those guys."

* * *

How Mike Tomlin ended up at William & Mary was a story unto itself.

The Tomlin brothers attended former Maryland head coach Bobby Ross's football camps. Maryland was about three hours away. "We both wanted to go there. I fell in love with Maryland as a teen," Ed said. "We had interest in anybody who had interest in us. We wanted to go to school for free and play pro ball."

"We were Terps," Mike Tomlin said in 2020 on Maryland's website. "We were Bobby Ross football campers. That was the first football camp I ever went to."

Mike Tomlin's oldest son, Dino, a three-star prospect at wide receiver rated as the thirty-fifth best player in Pennsylvania, signed with Maryland in 2018. He later transferred to Boston College. Three decades earlier, Dino's uncle, Ed, signed to play football at Maryland.

A *Washington Post* article prior to the start of the 1989 season said Ed Tomlin "might be the hardest hitter on the team." Tomlin made a quick adjustment from junior college linebacker to Division I safety. "Being a linebacker, my makeup mentality was to hit," he said in the article. "Now the problem is taking care of my responsibility and then coming up to lay a lick on the guy."

"I didn't play in the secondary until I got to Maryland," Tomlin said. "Me and Neil O'Donnell were co-captains in 1989. They recruited me and signed me as a linebacker. I told my recruiter I want to play in the secondary.[1] He told me we will put you on the clock and if you run fast enough, we'll start out there. I ran 4.41, 4.38. I was special teams captain my first year. I started in my second season and had three picks and was third on the team in tackles and first in the secondary in tackles. In the short time I was there, I was honored to be voted a captain my senior year." Ed Tomlin's football career ended when he suffered a broken foot entering the final two games of his senior season against Penn State and West Virginia.

Mike Tomlin graduated from Denbigh High School in Newport News in 1990. He was an outstanding student-athlete whose academic ability was considered to be greater than his athletic potential. Producing superior grades was second nature to Tomlin, who participated in a statewide scholastic competition called *Odyssey of the Mind* his final two years in high school. Tomlin and his fellow students placed second in the state championship one year.

"I just wanted to be one of the guys, hang out with the ballplayers," Tomlin told Clifton Brown of the *New York Times*. "But, eventually, word got out . . . because my mother sang about my academic achievements from the rooftops."

Tomlin received commissions to West Point and Annapolis and he could have attended several Ivy League schools. "The service academies were interested and he was naturally interested in the service academies," Ed Tomlin said. He also considered

---

1 "That don't get me no tables," added Tomlin, referring to O'Donnell's three interceptions with the Steelers against the Dallas Cowboys in Super Bowl XXX.

Hampton University, a historically black college located in his backyard, but the feeling wasn't mutual.

Mike Tomlin's future William & Mary teammate, Shawn Knight, grew up on the other side of Chesapeake Bay, in Norfolk. "Growing up on the peninsula in Hampton Roads, Mike really wanted to go to Hampton University and tried to get them to be interested," Knight said. "Sent them film. And couldn't get any interest. I had a similar experience. The HBCUs in our area (Hampton, Norfolk State) did not really recruit me. It was a different time, I think, for HBCUs. I think some of them felt like players that were being recruited at a certain level were not in their reach so they did not go after them."

The Tomlin brothers' biological father, Edward Tomlin, played running back at Hampton on a football scholarship. He was selected in the 10th round of the 1968 NFL Draft and later played football in Canada. "Our biological father starred at Hampton," Ed Tomlin said. "We have a special connection with Hampton University. They ran a summer program that bussed kids from the neighborhood and did camps in that setting. We were very familiar with Hampton. That's home."

At the end of the day, the College of William & Mary made perfect sense for Tomlin. Only twenty-two miles from Newport News on Interstate 64, it's the second-oldest institution of higher education in the United States (trailing only Harvard) and the ninth oldest in the English-speaking world. William & Mary's football team was coached by Jimmye Laycock, who was an impressive 18–6–1 in 1989 and 1990 with back-to-back NCAA Division I-AA playoff appearances.

Ironically, Tomlin and Knight made their recruiting visit to William & Mary on the same weekend. They were the only two recruits visiting the law school, young African American men from nearby Hampton Roads visiting a predominately white academic institution with a black student population of around 5 percent.

Their ethnicity, love of football, and love of the law drew them together.

"We got to talking and really took to each other right away, just really connected," Knight said. "Our personalities, our commitment, and our values aligned.

"Mike and I had a similar experience that weekend. When we visited William & Mary, we felt very good about that being the place for us. We knew we'd be challenged [academically]. It was an institution where I knew an education there would set me up for success in my life."

Within six months of graduation, the "career outcomes" rate of William & Mary's class of 2021—graduates employed or attending graduate/professional school—was 93 percent.

Often on those recruiting visits, the last thing student-athletes and their families do before departing is to have breakfast and meet with the head coach. Tomlin and Knight ate together with their families.

Both of their fathers were employed by the US Postal Service in Norfolk, which required them to work at night. Knight's father, William Smith, attended his son's entire recruiting visit. Leslie Copeland, who was a sorter at the post office, got off from work in time to join Mike in the school cafeteria on the final day.

"My dad would come home from work and tell these stories about his co-worker, this guy named Les," Knight said. "We later found out that Les was always talking about Smitty, who was my dad.

"Les walked into the cafeteria that Sunday while we were having breakfast. Our dads looked each other like, 'Hey, Les. Hey, Copeland.' It turned out they were good friends on the job. Nobody knew anything about it until Mike and I connected that weekend."

The recruiting visit clinched it for the pair from Hampton Roads. "It was nice to have someone, not only as a teammate, but somebody that really was family," Knight said. "Our families connected. Our dads already knew each other from working together.

"We had already made up our minds that we wanted to be roommates," Knight said. "All of that took place before we realized our dads knew each other. We were supposed to room together as freshmen. Somehow housing mixed that up so we didn't room together that first year. The next year we moved off campus to an apartment complex where several other athletes lived. That was our home the rest of the time we were there. It was our little corner apartment, our respite. One of the most enjoyable things after football games was having our families back at the apartment together.

"I'm about family, I'm about people. Mike is built much the same way."

Kelchner projected Tomlin, who was 6-foot-1 and a slender 160 pounds soaking wet, for what he could be in college rather than what he was in high school. "He didn't put up big numbers from the wide receiver position," Kelchner told the *Pittsburgh Post-Gazette*. Denbigh High featured a run-oriented offense and didn't pass much, but Tomlin, who also participated in the triple jump on the track team, oozed with athleticism. "When Mike was coming out of high school, he really wasn't highly recruited," Sauer said.

"He was a strider, tall, kind of gangly. It wasn't like he came in as the guy," former William & Mary offensive coordinator Zbig Kepa told the *Pittsburgh Tribune-Review.* "His learning curve, he cut it down pretty quick."

Tomlin bulked up to 6-foot-2, 205, ran the 40-yard dash at a top speed of 4.4-plus seconds, and improved his vertical jump to 40 inches.

"Mike worked his tail off in the weight room," Sauer said.

As a black quarterback who stood 5-foot-10 and weighed 175 pounds, Knight's options were limited where he could play college football. He was looking for a coach who valued his quarterback skills and accepted him for who he was.

"There were some schools who thought I was too short to play quarterback for them," Knight said. "'OK, I'll show you how I can play this position.' It always baffled me that some of the larger schools just decided I wasn't tall enough.

"Coming from my area, the kids I knew, the athletes I knew, they didn't go to a William & Mary. William & Mary never had a black quarterback to start there. That was not lost on me. I wanted to show cats you can go to a school like that and ball, too."

William & Mary head coach Jimmye Laycock tried to convince Knight he wasn't like other coaches who weren't sold on his skill set. Laycock didn't want Knight to change positions; he considered that a waste of talent.

"I can remember looking at him in high school, looking at his release point and how he threw the ball over the top," Laycock told the *Virginian-Pilot.* "Even though he wasn't tall, he had that high release point."

Like most William & Mary football players, Knight was a student first, an athlete second. There were no exceptions.

"Coach Laycock would bring in athletes and their number one goal was getting a degree," Sauer said. "To do that, with all the demands that were put on them by coaches, by me, and by professors, you had to have your stuff in order. It's not a school where if you're an athlete, they might kind of bend over to help you. There's none of that going on. None. It's not like some schools where you don't have to worry about going to class. The people they bring in are very disciplined. If they're not, they don't last."

"You have to go to class here," former William & Mary offensive coordinator Zbig Kepa told the *Pittsburgh Tribune-Review*. "You don't go to class, you have problems."

Tomlin was a perfect fit at William & Mary.

Hammons described Tomlin in two words: "closet nerd."

"He doesn't let on how intelligent he is," Hammons told ESPN. "He used to read the newspaper every morning. I didn't know anybody our age who did that."

Said Knight: "I wanted to go to an institution where two things had to be assumed if you were playing quarterback. You had to be able to handle the intellectual part of the game, in terms of understanding offenses, reading defenses and playing the position of quarterback that way because you were not going to be able to survive there at quarterback if you couldn't. That my ability to pass the football would never be questioned because coach Laycock's programs are synonymous with the passing game.

"Me being a shorter, black quarterback who could run, I didn't want to be pigeonholed into that stigma or category because I could also throw the football."

Laycock challenged his players to *think* football and not just play the game. It wasn't enough for them to memorize his offense. He wanted them to learn it inside out so they could not only talk about it but offer suggestions about what they saw in the defense and what plays in William & Mary's pro-style offense might work.

"Coach Laycock wanted to hear from his players, wanted to understand what his players were seeing," Knight said. "Some coaches just want the information flowing one way, from coach to player. That was not coach Laycock's way. We had the freedom to communicate those things, to share what we were seeing from the field and share our perspective."

When Knight became the starting quarterback in 1993, he and Tomlin found themselves spending more time in their apartment discussing the gameplan, their relationship as quarterback and receiver, and how each of their roles connected with the rest of their teammates on offense.

Knight marveled at Tomlin's sensitivity to other players and his ability to realize the importance of building chemistry. Tomlin was extremely reflective and introspective in terms of assessing his own performance and how it related to team bonding, and understanding what different players required.

As the starting quarterback and starting wide receiver who happened to be roommates, Tomlin and Knight were constantly discussing ways to improve, individually and collectively as a unit, and analyzing the pieces of the offensive puzzle and how to put everything together.

Tomlin was particularly adept at understanding his teammates and knowing who they were as individuals, where they came from, and what made them tick.

"He was definitely a guy who was diagnosing things as much as I was from under center," Knight said. "We often were seeing the same things.

"I can remember after a game my first year as a starter, we had another receiver and there appeared to be a little tension in the film room."

There may have been some feeling that Knight was trying to get the ball to Tomlin and needed to pass the ball more to fellow receiver Corey Ludwig, who was the main target of now departed quarterback Chris Hakel from the previous season.

In response, defenses shaded more coverage toward Ludwig, resulting in Tomlin becoming Knight's primary target.

"Mike and I had a conversation about that after film study," Knight said.

"It wasn't about invalidating those feelings or pushing back against that other player's feelings. Quite the opposite. It was about validating those feelings and understanding where it's coming from. And, so now, how does the team go about keeping that player engaged without increasing that tension?"

In William & Mary's 47–23 victory against Maine, Knight completed 15 of 21 passes for 322 yards and a school-record six touchdowns. Ludwig had a season-high seven receptions for 123 yards and tied a forty-four-year-old school record with four touchdown catches.

It marked the continuation of a concerted offensive shift that resulted in Ludwig scoring nine touchdowns in his last four games after going scoreless the first five games.

When Chris Hakel was the quarterback, "we'd throw thirty or forty times, but we haven't done that the last couple years because we don't have to," Ludwig told the *Newport News Daily Press*. "[W]hen you're only throwing fifteen or twenty times a game, somebody is going to get left out."

"We navigated that very well," Knight said. "That player became a pretty hot target and we had a great relationship. On game day, I was still throwing to the open receiver. That didn't change. But it was about building that relationship and affirming confidence in that player so that he understood this is not a situation where Knight is just trying to throw to his roommate."

In the same game, Tomlin had three receptions for 151 yards, including an 85-yard touchdown on the first play that spoke to the importance of film study and the synergy between Tomlin and Knight.

"Mike and I saw the same things in our preparation that we could strike early," Knight said. "Part of the gameplan was we were going to take a shot the first play if we had decent field position."

"I remember games where we started off with Mike on post routes or deep routes and it was 6–0 right off the bat," said Kepa. "He got behind people."

"Mike and I talked it over in our hotel the night before the game," Knight said. "There was no question we were going to execute the play, if I was going to deliver the football, and if he was going to catch the football. It was about the preparation, it was about the film study, it was about understanding the game plan, understanding the opponent and trusting each other. Me trusting he was going to run his route and be open. Him trusting that all he had to do was run his route and the football would be there."

Tomlin said playing wide receiver at William & Mary prepared him to think like an NFL head coach.

"Really, in pursuit of playing aspirations all along, I didn't realize that I was sharpening my sword for coaching, because I was really passionate about the game, and playing to win, and leading, and really getting into the schematics of it," Tomlin told Carl Francis and Vernon Lee of the Hampton Roads Youth Foundation. "Not only from the inside the helmet perspective, but just globally. When you're a wide receiver, a lot of people have got to do their jobs in an effort for you to do your job. I would never take anybody's word for it, so I had to gain global understanding of why I wasn't getting the ball enough. That's why to this day, I have so much patience for those that play the position, because, guilty as charged."

In Knight's first season as a starter, he set a Football Championship Subdivision (then known as Division I-AA) record for passing efficiency that still stands. He completed 125 of 177 passes (70.6 precent) for 2,055 yards, 22 touchdowns, and just four interceptions.

* * *

What makes a good head coach? There's no better place to find that out than the College of William & Mary which, truth be told, cornered the market in developing NFL head coaches.

The common denominator is Laycock, who retired in 2018 following 39 years as the school's head coach.

"Coach Laycock always had a lot of expectations for his staff," said Sauer, who was William & Mary's strength and conditioning coach for 31 years and now holds a similar position at Montana State. "My first year there in 1988 we were OK. But we started getting better and started getting other coaches in there and better players. It was an uphill battle for a long time. Our facilities were poor. If you were a coach, you went there to coach. You weren't going there for anything but that. Those coaches were part of that approach." Laycock's teams were prepared, perhaps even overly prepared to some degree. No matter how successful a coach may be, there are going to be players who have a very good opinion about him, and there may be some who don't adapt as well to the culture of the program. Laycock's level of expectation was always clear. It was always about excellence. It was always about doing the right thing, and doing things the right way. There was an expectation that players were not only going to do what the coaches were instructing them to do. Those players were also made to understand why they were doing what we were doing.

That preparation, that base and that foundation, and the ability to adapt—to personnel, to changes in the game—when you look back over coach Laycock's career, he was successful over a long period of time with very different personnel. It was his approach to the preparation that allowed for that adaptability and flexibility.

"You don't think of William & Mary, from a distance, as a football power because of the academic reputation of the school," Laycock told the *Williamsburg Yorktown Daily.* "When you combine a good, solid football program with players who come in here and [are] intelligent, and choose football as a profession and have the wherewithal, [they] go on and do pretty well."

From 1991 to 1997, five men who either played or coached under Laycock during that span advanced to become head coaches and/or coordinators currently in the NFL. No other school can match William & Mary's current total of three NFL head coaches.

It's an impressive list, featuring one Super Bowl–winning head coach and a total of three Super Bowl appearances among two head coaches.

Alan Williams (1988–91): Chicago Bears defensive coordinator (2022–present); Minnesota Vikings defensive coordinator (2012–13). During Williams's four seasons at William & Mary, he totaled 1,200 rushing yards and 15 touchdowns. He returned to William & Mary to coach running backs in 1996 and 1997 and defensive backs from 1998 to 2000. Williams has been an NFL assistant coach since 2001 when he joined the Tampa Bay Buccaneers staff along with fellow alum Mike Tomlin. Won Super Bowl XLI with Indianapolis Colts as defensive backs coach.[2]

Mike Tomlin (1991–94): Pittsburgh Steelers head coach (2007–present); Minnesota Vikings defensive coordinator (2006). Tomlin started three seasons at William & Mary. He was a co-captain his senior year. Tomlin averaged a school-record 20.2 yards per reception. When Tomlin led the Steelers to victory in Super Bowl XLIII, he became the youngest coach to win a Super Bowl. Tomlin led the Steelers to the Super Bowl twice in his first four seasons. He won Super Bowl XXXVII with Tampa Bay as defensive back coach. He did not have a losing record in his first 16 seasons as a head coach, which is the longest such streak in NFL history.

Dan Quinn (1994): Dallas Cowboys defensive coordinator (2021–present); Atlanta Falcons head coach (2015–20); Seattle Seahawks defensive coordinator (2013–14). Quinn did not play collegiately at William & Mary. He was a defensive line assistant

---

2 Williams resigned two games into the 2023 season.

there for one season. He has coached in the NFL since 2001 and led the Falcons to Super Bowl XLVIII in his fifth season. Won Super Bowl XLIII with Seattle as defensive coordinator.

Sean McDermott (1993–97): Buffalo Bills head coach (2017–present); Carolina Panthers defensive coordinator (2011–16); Philadelphia Eagles defensive coordinator (2009–10). A walk-on, McDermott played in all 46 games of his career at William & Mary. He made 322 career tackles and led his teams to a combined 32–14 record. McDermott has coached in the NFL since 1998.

Brian Daboll (1997): New York Giants head coach (2022–persent); Buffalo Bills offensive coordinator (2018–21); Kansas City Chiefs offensive coordinator (2012); Miami Dolphins offensive coordinator (2011); Cleveland Browns offensive coordinator (2009–10). Daboll did not play collegiately at William & Mary. He was a volunteer assistant for one year under Laycock where he developed a relationship with McDermott, who later made him offensive coordinator with Buffalo where he was credited with developing quarterback Josh Allen. Daboll left Buffalo to became head coach of the Giants. Won four Super Bowls with the New England Patriots as an assistant coach (XXXVIII, XXXIX, XLIX, LI).

Of the five, Tomlin has the most connections with his fellow alumni coaches. He was teammates with Williams for one season (1991) and teammates with McDermott for two seasons (1993 and 1994). Tomlin was a senior during Quinn's one year as an assistant in 1994. McDermott and Daboll were together for one season (1997). Tomlin and Williams (2001) and McDermott and Daboll (2018–21) are the only William & Mary coaches to work on the same NFL coaching staffs.

When Tomlin's Pittsburgh Steelers played host to McDermott's Buffalo Bills in 2019, it was the first NFL matchup between two former college teammates-turned-head-coaches.

What was Laycock's secret?

"Mike, certainly, and Sean, I think you see that in each of those guys," Knight said. "You see that in their ability to adapt and not necessarily just be 'systems people.' But to be 'people people.' To be 'players' people.' To be able to coach players to be able to coach people, to be able to motivate people, and to be able to relate to people. And have people be able to relate to you.

"During Mike's time in Pittsburgh, I think that's very evident. I think you're hard-pressed to find a player who's played for him who doesn't have a high opinion of who he is as a man, in addition to who he is as a coach. There was a high expectation for that at William & Mary. There were some who even took that a step further. You could see that in Mike early on."

2

MY FIRST JOB

VIRGINIA MILITARY INSTITUTE (VMI)
(WIDE RECEIVERS COACH, 1995)

"Eight pounds in a five-pound bag."

IN Mike Tomlin, NCAA football programs across the nation were about to discover a young, upward bound, supremely intelligent and confident black coaching unicorn who checked all the boxes despite having no actual experience in a profession that was anything but welcoming to coaches of color.

Tomlin's role models—i.e., coaches who looked like him— were few and far between. Tomlin faced a steep challenge in cracking the good ol' boy code.

"Not a lot of people who looked like him for the position he wanted to be in," said former Memphis head coach Rip Scherer Jr., who hired Tomlin after he left VMI.

Truth be told, Tomlin was blind to those impediments.

"Mike doesn't see color," Scherer said. "Maybe he looked at the landscape and it was like, 'Hey, this isn't something I can't overcome.'"

In 1994, Tomlin's senior season at William & Mary, there were two black head coaches in the NFL—Art Shell of the Oakland Raiders and Dennis Green of the Minnesota Vikings. The number increased to three in 1995 when the Philadelphia Eagles hired Ray Rhodes, followed by the Tampa Bay Buccaneers hiring Tony Dungy a year later. Moving over to the college ranks, there were *zero* black head coaches among the Associated Press Top 25 teams in 1994. A total of *three* black head coaches were hired to lead college programs between 1981 and 1993, and two were at the same school (Northwestern). Green was hired at two schools (Northwestern and Stanford).

Those were the negative statistics confronting Tomlin and his decision to enter the coaching profession when he penned a letter of introduction to Virginia Military Institute (VMI) head coach Bill Stewart in February 1995, three months after the conclusion of his final year of college eligibility. In the letter, Tomlin referenced Dan Quinn—who coached the previous season at William & Mary and had only recently accepted a coaching position at VMI—regarding an opening on Stewart's staff and expressed his desire to coach.

"Dear Coach Stewart . . . Through our mutual acquaintance, coach Dan Quinn, I have learned of a possible opening in your staff . . . I am extremely eager to pursue a career in coaching . . . Although I lack formal coaching experience, I consider myself a true student of the game," Tomlin said in the letter written on his mother's kitchen computer that appeared in the *Pittsburgh*

Post-Gazette. "I have worked extremely hard as a student-athlete at not only understanding my duties, but at understanding how they fit into the overall goals of the system in which I played. I have put forth effort to understand other systems and their goals. I not only view coaching as an honorable profession, but as an opportunity to stay close to the game I love and hopefully be a positive influence to other young men who share that same love."

Tomlin graduated from William & Mary with a degree in sociology three months after writing the letter to Stewart. Thumbing through his post-graduate options—continuing his football career in Canada, attending law school, or coaching—Tomlin, presented with the opportunity to tryout with a couple NFL teams, chose coaching.

"My mom wanted him to go to law school. Mike wanted to go to Canada to play football," said older brother Ed Tomlin. "Those that don't do, teach. He loved football and wasn't good enough to do it at the highest level. This is the best way to stay closest to it and stay a part of it."

"What inspires me as a coach to be blunt . . . my failures as a player I could never live with," Mike Tomlin explained on the *Pivot* podcast. "I wanted to be a great player and I wasn't. I never got over that."

While many small college athletes were still figuring out if they were talented enough to stick it out and give the pros a try—either that or call it a day—Tomlin had already weighed his options. If he couldn't *play* football, he would damn well live vicariously by doing the next best thing.

Coaching football.

"I think to some degree we both still had dreams and aspirations as players," said Shawn Knight, who ultimately decided not to attend law school and became the pastor at Baptist Liberty Church in King William County, northeast of Richmond, Virginia. Knight is also an assistant director at the Virginia High School Coaches Association. "I was realistic about my opportunities in the NFL because of my height," Knight continued. "I was also playing [minor-league] baseball, so my attention at that point as our college careers were winding down, were to baseball with a legal career on the other side."

Instead of joining the San Diego Padres' Class-A ballclub, Knight, who set two NCAA records for passing efficiency and finished his college career with 5,705 passing yards and 46 touchdown passes, signed with the CFL's Toronto Argonauts. He played in five games during the 1995 season and was released the following year.

"I'm not surprised at all by Mike coaching," Knight said. "When we first talked about it, I remember telling my mom and dad about it. They were like, 'I thought he was thinking about law school.' I said, 'Mike is doing exactly what Mike is supposed to be doing.' I firmly believe that."

Now at VMI, Quinn kept thinking about the year he spent at William & Mary, what a great experience it was, and the wide receiver who took him under his wing and simplified his transition to the coaching profession.

Tomlin had a way of making Quinn feel like a member of his family while keeping it real on the football field.

Quinn couldn't forget Tomlin and the fun times hanging out at those frat parties, even if he tried.

"I knew Mike wanted to play, obviously, but he also wanted to coach," Quinn said. "VMI had played William & Mary that season. It might have been a day or two before spring practice.

I hadn't been there that long, just hired in February, so it was probably March. The receiver coach left. Coach Stewart opens it up: 'We have a receiver job open. Does anybody have anybody?'

"I raise my hand, the new guy.

'I got a guy.'

'All right, who is it?'

'Mike Tomlin.'

'The receiver at William & Mary?'

'Yeah.'

'You think he'd be interested?'

'Yeah, he'd be interested.'

"I called Mike. He may have interviewed two days later. In the morning. He was coaching spring ball that afternoon. We're at practice and here he is with the receivers.

"It was easy for me to speak up for him at a staff meeting when I didn't really know anybody to say, 'I got a guy,'" Quinn said. "That was my way of wanting to pay it back to him to say, 'In my first year of coaching he was looking out for me.' I was going to look out for him."

When William & Mary defeated VMI 45–7 in the fourth game of the season, Tomlin "had something like six catches for 130 yards in the first half," Ed Tomlin said. "Mike and Shawn Knight both wore baseball caps on the sideline in the second half.

"Mike is a verbal guy," Ed Tomlin said. "He talked to guys. His best friend in high school played at James Madison. He'd be on the phone with those guys during the week talking trash. Coaches get a sense and feel for that type of stuff.

"When Mike finished playing," Ed continued, "one of the VMI assistants called and said Bill Stewart inquired about his interest in coaching because he needed a receivers coach. He brought

Mike down for a weekend of spring drills. He was still a *student* at William & Mary. When he got there, he thought they were going to be showing him around. Well, they didn't have a receivers coach. They gave him a script and had him go through drills with the guys and do install. The guys he was coaching, he had burned their ass in the fall. He knew those guys. He played against those guys."

Not unlike Quinn's influence in the job search, the Bill Stewart-Jimmye Laycock connection was another example of a coach putting in a good word for Tomlin in an industry that thrives on word-of-mouth recommendations. Stewart was an assistant at William & Mary for three years. He came on board one year after Laycock took over as head coach.

"My Dad knew Jimmye Laycock really well from his time at William & Mary," said Blaine Stewart, who was two years old when Tomlin joined VMI's coaching staff and would later become a Pittsburgh Steelers assistant under Tomlin. "My dad told him to come down and spend the weekend with us and see if it's something you'd be interested in. By the end of the weekend, he was coaching the wide receivers. My dad had a way of, not throwing you in the fire, but just kind of talking you into giving it a try and then—bang—it stuck."

Next came the hard part for Tomlin: Explaining to his mother why he decided to become a football coach instead of attending law school.

There were plenty of black lawyers. Not so many black football coaches, college or pro. Not then. Not now.

Julia Copeland did what a good many mothers would do. She pushed back.

"He told me he wanted to be a coach, and I just went ballistic," Copeland told the *Pittsburgh Post-Gazette*. "We sent you to

William & Mary, and you want to *coach?* What are you talking about? He said, 'Well, I got a plan. I got to start somewhere, and I'm going to start at VMI.' I was really upset. I didn't want him to coach. I wanted him to go out and get a real job. 'How much does that pay you?' 'Just a stipend? What is a *stipend?*'"

"I got into coaching my very first year," Tomlin told the *Footbahlin with Ben Roethlisberger* podcast. "My mom made me promise that if I was going to continue coaching, I would get my masters. I made $8,000 a year. I was on top of the world. They used to call it restricted earnings coach. That just means you were broke."

Tomlin wasn't considered a graduate assistant (a mere technicality) because VMI (located in Lexington, Virginia, approximately three hours from William & Mary) didn't have graduate students. He resided on the post and lived in the single men's quarters (there were no female students). He ate all his meals with the football team at the training table.

"Everything at VMI had initials," said Donnie Ross, the younger brother of NFL and college football head coach Bobby Ross. Donnie Ross was the school's running backs coach upon Tomlin's arrival and later became the primary fundraiser at the military academy. "Mike stayed at the BOQ—Bachelor Officers Quarters," Ross said. "It was an old frat house that used to be part of Washington and Lee (University) years and years ago. We called it post because it's a military school. We don't call it a campus. Mike and a lot of the people there for the very first time, that's where they lived. You slept there a couple hours a night. That was about it. We were in the football complex all the time."

Ross arrived at VMI in 1994, one year before Tomlin. "Bill Stewart had been an assistant at William & Mary, North

Carolina, and the Naval Academy," said Ross, highlighting some of the area football programs where Stewart coached previously. "He always had the Richmond area recruiting-wise. I was coaching my high school team (Benedictine College Preparatory). Bill would always come by. He wanted a VMI guy on the staff.[1] It's important because you're living on the post. Football players aren't used to that kind of lifestyle."

"Donnie Ross gave us the whole VMI history because none of us knew much about it. He kept us grounded," said Dan Hammerschmidt, who was VMI's secondary coach in his only season at the school. "I remember watching football players at the end of the Rat Line (referring to the tradition of new cadets walking at rigid attention along a prescribed route whenever they're inside barracks). They had to climb a muddy hill. As they got halfway up, a kid would kick 'em down after they ran six miles. It was a whole day of brutality. I was like, 'Oh, my God. These are our football players. What is going on?'

"The military thing was big," continued Hammerschmidt, now the safeties coach at Oklahoma State. "They make those kids get up at 6 a.m., get in line. We recruited this big-time D-lineman from Florida and he's getting yelled at by some little guy. The kids from military families, you had a better shot with them because they kind of knew that culture. It was hard to keep them from jumping on the midnight train. We did a lot of coddling."

Stewart had an eye for identifying good coaches. In '95, he combined young coaches like Quinn and Tomlin with more

---

1 Ross, who graduated in 1974, played baseball at VMI.

experienced coaches such as Hammerschmidt, Ross, Kevin Sherman, and offensive line coach Bobby Solderich and turned them loose at a school where they all had to work their butts off just to be in a game, much less win it.

"They allowed us to coach," Quinn said. "It wasn't a Power Five school. Mike London, the current head coach at William & Mary, was the defensive line coach at VMI. I was his assistant. Mike would take the D-ends and say, 'Hey, Dan, why don't you take the defensive tackles?' That just doesn't happen a lot for somebody right away.

"Mike going to VMI and getting to coach the wide receivers his first year out of college . . . you learn, you fail. You make mistakes. You fix your own problems. A lot of that goes on when you have your own room of guys. You're responsible for them. I had to figure it out on my own, you know? There's no other person who's going to help me through this, so figure it out."

"We were just having a good time," Hammerschmidt said. "We would go out to restaurants together and hang out. We'd go golfing together. It didn't matter if you golfed or not."

Stewart needed Tomlin to find out if he really wanted to be a coach.

"That was a unique environment," said Ed Tomlin, who visited his younger brother whenever he could. "Coach Stewart was a unique guy. He was a special dude. My brother was a young coach. And we were young people. That guy looked at us and knew exactly who we were. Mike would mess up and come to the bus late. He was like, 'stay out of trouble.' He would talk to us like some of the players, but in a respectful way. That guy had a lot to do with my brother's growth and maturation."

"Bill said we were going to teach Mike how to be a ball coach," Hammerschmidt said.

Some things came naturally to Tomlin. He was the youngest coach on staff and related well to his players. "We really needed that," Ross said. "Football coaches, sometimes, we can be like drill sergeants and run you into the ground. He knows how players react to certain coaches and had a calming effect. They gravitated to him. That makes a big difference, especially at a military school like VMI where they're getting hounded all the time: 'You gotta do this, do that.' Bill wouldn't ease up at all. At VMI, you want to have the true experience that all cadets have because that's what we believe. To play Division I football on top of that is a lot of pressure."

Tomlin's peers soon discovered he was no soft touch despite his age and relative inexperience.

"Mike was not afraid to discipline," Hammerschmidt said. "He wasn't going to take any junk. He was going to coach them. He was like, 'You're going to have to run this route exactly right. I want to see your thumbs in catching the ball. If you're a minute late, you're getting a three hundred on the StairMaster, buddy. I don't care what the excuse is. Go play someplace else if you don't like it.' He focused on the little things, which a lot of kids don't want to hear."

Hammerschmidt took Tomlin on his first recruiting trip. First stop? Tomlin's old stomping grounds.

"We went to Virginia Beach. Every doggone school he walked in he was like the fricken mayor," Hammerschmidt said. "I said, 'What am I doing teaching you how to recruit?'

"We couldn't talk to players. But we could talk to all the administrators, teachers and coaches. From one school to the next in Virginia Beach and Tidewater, Mike knew somebody everywhere. He was hugging them. He'd have stories. We were in those schools way too long. We're supposed to hit eight schools a day and we'd get to four or five. We'd stay there for two hours and hang out: 'Wait a minute. Bobby works here?' 'Yeah. He's coaching track.'

"Really, that's the best recruiting you can do," Hammerschmidt continued. "It was fun listening to him. I got a lot from him as far as the social part. Dang, you mean I just can't jump in here and get names and say hi to the coach for fifteen to twenty minutes? You've got to get to know these people. Mike enabled us to recruit some good receivers and defensive backs for the future. He kind of set the groundwork for that."

Tomlin's one season at VMI helped him decide he wanted to coach for a living.

"The thing I will remember about that season is when I got into it, I wasn't sure how committed I was in terms of a profession," Tomlin told *USA Today.* "I think I knew in an instant after that season that this is what I wanted to do for a living. That season left that type of impression. Working in that location with those men, those players, I knew what I wanted to do with the rest of my professional life."

VMI finished the season with a 4–7 record after going 1–10 the previous year. Tomlin (Memphis), Quinn (Hofstra), and Hammerschmidt (Colorado State) all left VMI for new jobs.

"Mike's the kind of guy that anybody who likes football would love to play for," Ross said. "I never really heard him raise his voice at anybody. And when he does it's in a positive manner: 'You can do better. I know you can. I'm counting on you my friend. I know you're going to be ready for your teammates.'

That's the kind of guy he is. It was so much fun to be around a coach who was so upbeat and positive. He was just there for a few months for the '95 season. And then he was gone."

Hammerschmidt said being around Tomlin revealed to him there are different talent levels of coaches. After that one season, he realized Tomlin could be one of the best that ever was.

"There's a lot of smart ball coaches, but then there's guys that can multitask," Hammerschmidt said. "They're a step ahead. They know what the heck's going on. I can't multitask. I coach my guys, you know? I get locked in at a meeting. I'm a DB coach. It's my deal. I know that position and I know what we're going to do that day. Mike's got that brain where he can multitask and plan and organize.

"He can carry on a conversation like anything. I'm one of those guys that talks too much football. You start talking ball, he can go there. He was a young guy and he knew offense, he knew coverage. We were at VMI. We had to make it simple, try to win games. I remember us talking a bunch of ball and what they did at William & Mary and could we handle stuff like that at VMI. You could tell that for a young guy, he loved it."

3

GRADUATING TO GRADUATE ASSISTANT

UNIVERSITY OF MEMPHIS
(GRADUATE ASSISTANT, 1996)

"We don't live in our fears. We live in our hopes."

THE hotel lobby is the place to be at the American Football Coaches Association (AFCA) convention, the largest educational gathering in the football coaching industry. Every year, more than six thousand coaches from all levels of coaching and persuasions attend meetings and seminars addressing the following subjects:

- Personal Development
- Professional Development

- X's and O's
- Program Management
- Personnel
- Administrative
- Ethics
- Character

Seminars and meetings are great, no doubt, but Mike Tomlin and many of his peers attend the convention for a different reason: finding a job.

Recently married, the newlywed planned to put his people skills to good use following the conclusion of his apprenticeship at Virginia Military Institute.

If Tomlin couldn't secure a coaching job here at the convention in New Orleans, he probably would have no choice but to unpack his sociology degree from prestigious William & Mary, prepare for law school, and get a "real job," as his mother emphatically put it when he attempted to explain why he had accepted a low-paying position at VMI the previous year.

With that in mind, Tomlin made the calculated investment—both mentally and financially—to attend his first AFCA convention in 1996, with the understanding that it's not *what* you know but *who* you know.

Running out of options for the upcoming football season, Tomlin was fortunate to connect with Memphis head coach William Bernard "Rip" Scherer Jr. Out of literally thousands of coaches attending the convention, Tomlin and Scherer—who had last seen each other during the 1994 college football season—reunited. It was almost like finding a needle in a haystack, since Tomlin didn't know they would bump into each other. And even if they did connect, what would that accomplish? There were no guarantees a job was in the offing. Tomlin was rolling the dice coming to New Orleans.

Formerly the head coach at James Madison, Scherer faced Tomlin when he was a star wide receiver at William & Mary. Scherer's James Madison teams went 3–1 against Tomlin's teams from 1991 to 1994. During Scherer's four years at James Madison, his teams set or tied over 140 school records and posted a 29–19 record. Scherer parlayed a 10–3 season in 1994 into a job upgrade at Memphis, where he went 3–8 his first year. That was the backdrop for his reunion with Tomlin prior to the 1996 season.

Scherer remembered enough about Tomlin to give the youngster valuable career advice, while also offering him the coaching position he was desperately seeking.

"Mike was at VMI and I ran into him at a coaches convention," Scherer said. "He told me he was going to law school."

Although appreciative of the time he spent at VMI, Tomlin had no plans to return to the military academy. He now had a wife who had aspirations of becoming a doctor but set her career goals aside so her husband could fulfill his dream of being a football coach. If football didn't work out, Tomlin would have to buckle down and get a *real* job.

Based on his initial conversation with Scherer, Tomlin appeared to have made up his mind about making a career change. Or did he? He was twenty-four, and law school would require at least another three years of study. And he would still have to pass the bar. On the other hand, he already had a foot in the door based on his one year of coaching experience and a pocketful of influential contacts, like Scherer and Bill Stewart.

If Tomlin felt that strongly about attending law school, why make the trip to New Orleans knowing that every college coach in America would be there?

Tomlin owed it to himself to see this thing through before swearing off coaching for good.

"I go to the coaching convention that year; it's my very first [one]," Tomlin told the *Footbahlin with Ben Roethlisberger* podcast. It's in New Orleans and I'm hunting a GA [graduate assistant] spot. Naïve. I'm thinking I'll get a GA spot not knowing how hard these things are to come by. The only one I could get was at Memphis, and it was a defensive GA spot. The only reason I got that one was . . . Rip Scherer was a William & Mary graduate. He kind of recognized me and knew who I was and just on the strength of the alma mater game I got on. It wasn't an agenda; it was a GA job."

Scherer talked, Tomlin listened.

Scherer wasn't a mind reader, but he knew enough about Tomlin's football background to realize the sport was in his blood. And that all it would take was a little understanding— and some prodding; *not to mention a job offer*—from Scherer for Tomlin to get his life, and coaching career, back on track.

Ed Tomlin knows what makes his brother tick better than anyone in the world when he says, "He's a glorified gym coach. He *loves* football."

Pouring his heart out to Scherer about what transpired at VMI—the good and the bad—Tomlin held nothing back. Spilling the beans about being torn over what to do next, Scherer convinced him to hold on a little bit longer.

Once again, Scherer talked, Tomlin listened.

"I think Mike was a little disillusioned at VMI," said Scherer. "I know he loved coach [Bill] Stewart. But I think he was like, 'Oh, my God. I've got such a mountain to climb to get to where I want to go in this business.' Stew was building it back, but I just think that Mike was like, 'I'm starting so low.' I don't think he foresaw the accelerated path he ended up on."

Scherer saw something in Tomlin that Tomlin didn't—or couldn't—see in himself.

"He just had a presence about him," said Scherer. "The way he carried himself. You could tell as a player he was smart and savvy."

Scherer envisioned a promising coaching future for Tomlin, his encouraging words convincing him to stick with it.

"When he told me he was going to law school, I made this statement," said Scherer. "I told him, 'If you come to Memphis and be a GA, you'll be in the NFL before you're thirty-five.' But I didn't mean as head coach of the Super Bowl–winning Steelers."

Scherer realized that Tomlin came from a strong coaching lineage. He learned the game from a coach who knew football inside and out, a man who was taught the same principles that were instilled in Scherer. That lineage would forever be a part of him, even if Tomlin—caught up in the moment and wanting to make the right career move—didn't know it at the time.

Scherer and William & Mary head coach Jimmye Laycock— Tomlin's college coach—both attended William & Mary and knew each other personally. In fact, Scherer replaced Laycock at quarterback the year after Laycock graduated. Heck, Laycock probably helped recruit Scherer to William & Mary.

Laycock played quarterback at William & Mary from 1966 to 1969 under coaches Marv Levy and Lou Holtz; Scherer played quarterback at William & Mary from 1970 to 1973, the first two years under Holtz.

"Jimmye was a senior when I was being recruited," said Scherer. "I've known Jimmye from my recruiting time, then through the coaching profession. I became the head coach at JMU. For four years, Jimmye never spoke to me."

William & Mary and James Madison were about three hours apart. Of the two schools, James Madison, located in Harrisonburg, Virginia, held far more social appeal for a young black man from Hampton Roads.

"We had a lot of guys from the Tidewater area on our team," said Scherer. "Mike would come up on some weekends in the offseason to hang out with those guys. Better social life for a black kid from Virginia Beach than William & Mary, and I'm a William & Mary graduate. White or black, there's not a lot to do in Williamsburg. Frat parties, and that's about it.

"I got to know Mike a little bit through competing against him, and through him coming up to JMU periodically to see some of his good high school friends. One of them passed away in October during the 2022 football season. Mike came down and delivered the eulogy."

Scherer had a special way with words with a certain segment of the coaching population. He had a reputation for advising and helping young black assistants navigate their way through the coaching ranks.

"Because of my number of years in coaching at that time [Scherer began as a graduate assistant at Penn State in 1974], I had kind of fallen into good favor, especially with younger black coaches I had on my staff," said Scherer. "I had a couple young guys at JMU that within a couple years I was able to help them move to a place like Kentucky. I remember the guy that I hired away from Delaware, I said, 'Why do you want to come here?' It was kind of like, 'Coach, you have a reputation for really helping young, black coaches move on.'

"I told Mike I've been able to help some young black coaches move on to other opportunities. That was one of my selling points. The other was, 'I just think you need to give it a shot. You have a chance to grow in this business.' He went from a program at VMI that was less than William & Mary to a program that was above William & Mary," Scherer continued. "Memphis wasn't great, but we had some good days and some big wins.

"In talking with Mike at times, he was in the middle, and then he said, 'OK, this is really what I want to do,' Scherer continued. "He became convinced, 'I can do this.'"

College coaches spend long, grueling hours watching film, putting together game plans, recruiting, directing practices, motivating as well as discipling players, not to mention trying to win football games.

Tomlin was like the fraternity pledge in the movie *Animal House* who said to his dean of pledges, "Thank you sir, may I have another?" No task was too difficult for the graduate assistant.

"He was a GA on defense," said Scherer. "I put him on defense because that's where the opening was. I told him, 'This will be good for your career.' At that time, he was an offensive guy. He was a receiver. I said, 'You'll bring an offensive approach to the DB room, and you'll get a defensive perspective down the road if you continue to be an offensive coach. He balked just a little bit early. I know he has said at a couple different functions he's glad I forced him to do that."

It's not unusual for graduate assistants—especially when they're just a year or two out of college, like Tomlin was—to be about the same age or within a year or two of the players they're coaching. Some GAs fall into the trap that they're above certain responsibilities, that they're too important to settle for scraps when what they really want is filet mignon.

Tomlin was observant and understood the value of patience. Scherer's words had a dramatic effect on him. He knew, with hard work and dedication, that his time would come.

"Mike had a way of handling himself that he didn't pretend to be too important. He'd jump in there and roll up his sleeves," said Scherer. "He was a fun guy; he had a good time, don't misunderstand me. It's a fine line as a GA to walk. You don't want to give the impression that, 'Hey, I've arrived. I'm a fulltime coach.' But you can't be one of the guys and be their teammate either. The things that really stuck out to me was his maturity and his professionalism for his age, his work ethic and the fact that no task was too small."

Scherer is the cousin of former Steelers general manager Kevin Colbert. Seeing something in the young man, Scherer became Tomlin's "Mr. Miyagi," so to speak. Tomlin considered Scherer a mentor as well. Even after Tomlin left Memphis for a full-time coaching opportunity at Arkansas State following a brief detour at Tennessee-Martin before moving on to the University of Cincinnati two years after that—and all the way up the coaching food chain to the NFL—the two discussed every career move: before, during, and after.

Should I stay? Should I go? If I do move, what should I know? Who do I need to know?

"Mike and I stayed in touch all the time," said Scherer. "He called me before he took the Cincinnati job. He called me before he took the Tampa Bay Buccaneers job. He called me before he took the Steelers job. I always stayed in touch with him. I was a guy he would lean on a little bit for advice.

"When I think back on him as a young GA to where he is now and will be an eventual Hall of Fame coach, it's like, 'Wow,'" continued Scherer. "I don't mean that I was part of the journey or had anything to do with it. It's just fun to see the journey and say I remember him when."

Things were falling into place for the Tomlin family. Mike now had the opportunity to follow his dream of working for a head coach who had his back. And though he was living in a strange city, his home life was made easier by the fact that his wife, Kiya, was also living his dream right beside him.

When Mike and Kiya relocated to Memphis, it was an unexpected move that set Kiya—now a fashion designer and founder of the Kiya Tomlin brand that has expanded to include licensed NFL apparel—on a different career path.

A psychology major who competed on William & Mary's gymnastics team, Kiya graduated a year after Mike. "I had never heard of William & Mary, but I knew I wanted to do gymnastics," Kiya said in the school's alumni magazine. "I was offered an athletic and academic scholarship."

Mike and Kiya met in the training room when they were both injured. It was a whirlwind courtship. They were engaged the Christmas of her senior year and married two weeks after her graduation.

"I remember Mike telling me about this gymnast he met. He was kind of feeling her," Shawn Knight said about his roommate. "It was wonderful to see their relationship grow and blossom into the wonderful family they have. I remember him saying he knew she was the one."

After moving to Memphis in the spring of 1996, Kiya was preparing to take the MCAT exam for prospective medical students. She changed her mind the day of the exam.

The more she thought about it, the more she realized that becoming a doctor is among the most demanding career paths to undertake. On second thought, she didn't think that she and Mike could both choose demanding careers and raise a family the way they wanted, especially knowing the volatility of a coaching career and how often they change cities—specifically on the lower rungs of the collegiate level.

"I don't think I was nervous or anxious that morning," Kiya said. "I think I had come to the realization that Mike wanted to coach. When we got married, I didn't know Mike wanted to pursue coaching as a career. I thought he would get his master's, get a regular job, and I would go to medical school and be a doctor and everything would be happily ever after."

4

THE TRANSITION FROM OFFENSE TO DEFENSE

ARKANSAS STATE (WIDE RECEIVERS/DEFENSIVE BACKS/ SPECIAL TEAMS COACH, 1997-98)

"Practice and participation will be our guide."

IN December 1996, after five years as the offensive coordinator at Ohio State under friend and longtime mentor John Cooper, and fresh off a Rose Bowl victory over Arizona State, longtime college assistant Joe Hollis Sr. was named the new head coach at Arkansas State in Jonesboro. Part of the appeal of the job—aside from putting his stamp on the football program—was being on the ground floor of the university's transition from Division I-AA Division I-A.

Hollis possessed an extensive coaching resume. Prior to his stint at Ohio State, he was the offensive line coach at Georgia for a total of six years (including Vince Dooley's final two seasons). He was also an assistant at Troy State (six years), Auburn (two years), and Tulsa (four years) also under Cooper, and the head coach at Jacksonville State for one year.

Hollis knew what he was getting into by accepting the job at Arkansas State. The transition to big-time football wouldn't be easy, necessitating an immediate upgrade in personnel and coaching staff.

And *patience*.

"Football is always going to be a challenge at Arkansas State," Hollis told ESPN after being let go in 2001. Over five seasons, he had amassed a 13–43 record. In the year prior to Hollis's arrival, the Red Wolves went 4–7 against the likes of Austin Peay, Northern Illinois, and Southeast Missouri State, and now would be facing Georgia, Miami, and Virginia Tech.

Tomlin was one of Hollis's early hires. It was a chance meeting that brought together Tomlin, Hollis, and Randy Fichtner—Arkansas State's new offensive coordinator.

Some things are simply meant to be.

"I met Mike after I had been at Arkansas State for about a month," Hollis said. "I had already hired Randy. He was coming off the staff at Purdue (where he had been the wide receivers coach for three seasons). We went to Memphis East High School to recruit. We went into the coach's office and a young man was sitting there in a UT-Martin jogging suit."

That young man was Tomlin who, after one year as a graduate assistant at Memphis, was wearing his third different school jogging suit in three years. Tomlin was representing UT-Martin, one of seven campuses in the University of Tennessee system after being hired by former Memphis assistant Joe Campbell.

"We introduced ourselves," Hollis said. "The Memphis East coach became kind of a second thought. Randy, Mike, and I visited some more in the coach's office. That's how we got acquainted."

Tomlin's reputation had preceded him; he was fast becoming a known commodity on the coaching circuit.

"That's the guy everyone's talking about," Fichtner told Steelers.com in 2018. "I finally met him."

As usual, Tomlin worked his magic. He talked, Hollis and Fichtner listened. Tomlin has an engaging delivery and personality that forces people to pay attention. The three men, *who barely knew each other*, shared their thoughts about football, recruiting, life, Memphis, UT-Martin, and Arkansas State. Thirty minutes passed before Hollis realized something: *There was no way he was about to let Tomlin get away.*

"I knew I had one more position to hire," Hollis said.

"We had gotten all the information, so it was just us visiting with each other," Hollis continued. "We knew who the guys were that should be recruited. I told Randy, 'I'll meet you at the car.'"

Hollis left Fichtner behind to continue his conversation with Tomlin. Fichtner returned to the car with a recruiting list and Tomlin's contact information.

"Randy said, 'Coach, I got his phone number and how to get in touch with him.'"

Bingo.

With one more vacancy to fill, Hollis reached out to Tomlin.

"I called Mike," Hollis said. "He had gotten a job at UT-Martin and had been there just a few weeks since the end of football season."

Hollis offered to put Tomlin in charge of Arkansas State's wide receivers. After going back and forth with his decision, Tomlin, who had been on the job less than two months at UT-Martin, finally accepted.

"He felt bad about leaving this coach after he had just gotten there," Hollis said.

Tomlin considered the possibilities . . . good and bad. The good news for Tomlin was moving up in status. UT-Martin played in the Football Championship Subdivison while Arkansas State was a member of the Football Bowl Subdivision. The bad news was the unspoken expectation of "loyalty to the job" and Tomlin leaving UT-Martin high and dry. He expressed those feelings to Rip Scherer Jr., his mentor.

Should I stay, or should I go?

"The conversation was something to the effect that the important thing is to get that first fulltime (Division I-A) job," Scherer said.

* * *

Hollis discovered what coaches at William & Mary, VMI, and Memphis witnessed daily: Tomlin's rare ability to connect and communicate with coaches and players alike . . . something that separated him from the rest of the pack. He had a way of getting his players to perform drills and make them think they came up with the workout. They also didn't want to disappoint him, showing how they fed off his positivity and caring demeanor toward them. And, most importantly, he elevated their play.

Tomlin was young, but he didn't act his age. He was quick to ask questions. What he didn't know, he studied and hit the film room and practice field until he familiarized himself with the material backward and forward. Being a teacher isn't just understanding the material, but being able to teach it and explain in a manner so that the students are able to learn and understand not only *why* they're learning it, but also how it'll help them moving forward. Hollis gave Tomlin the added responsibility of being in charge of kickoffs and kickoff returns.

"It didn't take long for me and the other coaches to know Mike had a lot of things going for him," Hollis said. "The kids liked him. He would run sprints with them and get to know them. The only thing Mike didn't have was a whole lot of experience. He was eager to learn. He was like a sponge. I hired him as a receivers coach because that was the only position open. When he wasn't in an offensive meeting, he would take his notebook and go to a defensive meeting. He was always in a meeting on either side of the ball."

In Arkansas State's first season in Division I-A in 1997, the Red Wolves finished the season with a 2–9 record and were outscored by Georgia, Virginia Tech (ranked No. 14), Miami, and Memphis, 168–26. In 1998, they finished 4–8 and shut out Hawaii 20–0 for the program's first I-A road win.

Fichtner, whom Hollis trusted implicitly, also played a role in Hollis hiring Keith Butler as his defensive coordinator in '98.

"Randy was probably more responsible for us being there than anybody," Butler told Steelers.com in 2018. "He had a big influence on Joe Hollis. Joe trusted him. When he got Mike, there was Randy."

Coaches come and coaches go. The world in which they operate is exceedingly small.

On Scherer's recommendation, Fichtner was Memphis' offensive coordinator from 2001 to 2006. When Tomlin became the Steelers' head coach in 2007, he hired Fichtner to coach wide receivers.

Butler arrived at Arkansas State from Memphis after spending eight seasons coaching linebackers, defensive ends, and special teams. Tomlin, based on the pair's previous relationship at Memphis, requested that Hollis make him a defensive coach.

Even before the request, Tomlin had been sitting in on the defensive meetings, and was already given the duties of coaching special teams.

"Mike let me know he wanted to move to defense," Hollis said. "Without saying it, I knew I was going to be very fortunate if I kept him that second year. He had a lot of things going for him. After we hired Keith, Mike said, 'I will stay if you move me to the secondary.' He wanted to coach the secondary and he wanted to coach with Keith."

The feeling was mutual.

"They told me [to find out] if Mike would move over to coach the secondary," Butler told Steelers.com. "I didn't know anybody over there. I knew him well because he was in Memphis with us."

"I was uncomfortable about the switch," Tomlin said on the *Nittany Game Week* podcast, "but I quickly realized that it gave me a three-hundred-sixty-degree perspective on the game, and the growth associated with coaching on the opposite side of the ball on which I played was one of the reasons why I think I matured and developed, particularly at the early stages of my coaching career. I was always uncomfortable, and I think to be uncomfortable is a nice platform for growth and development."

Among Tomlin's many duties, Hollis also entrusted him with recruiting. "Recruiting came so natural to him," Hollis said. "He was consistent, got to know the recruits. Everybody liked him. He just had that personality that he could be honest and be himself. There was no BS that coaches or recruits could see through."

Tomlin wasn't the recruiting coordinator, but Hollis sent him to close the deal on a recruit no one thought he could get.

Hollis credited Tomlin and Fichtner with signing running back Jonathan Abrams from Osceola, Arkansas, approximately fifty-five miles from Arkansas State's campus.

Abrams, who rushed for 2,227 yards and 38 touchdowns as a senior and led Osceola to three consecutive Class 2A state titles, was Arkansas' all-time leading rusher when he was being recruited.

The 1-2 recruiting punch of Tomlin and Fichtner was too much for Alabama, Arkansas, Ole Miss, and Memphis to contend with.

"He was one of the better recruits [in the South]," Hollis said. "And we signed him."

Abrams had a tremendous college career, amassing 3,005 career rushing yards (fourth in school history) and 17 touchdowns, averaging 4.5 yards per carry.

Tomlin's coaching accomplishments resulted in rival schools inquiring about his availability. An offer from the University of Cincinnati was one Hollis knew he had to beat.

Facing prodigious odds to keep him, Hollis made a final attempt to retain Tomlin's services for at least one more season.

"We didn't pay our assistants very well at Arkansas State," Hollis said. "Mike could go to the University of Cincinnati and basically double his salary."

To prevent Tomlin from leaving for Cincinnati, Hollis asked Ohio State's Cooper if he would consider hiring Tomlin as an assistant coach the following year. If Cooper agreed to Hollis's request, it would then be up to Hollis to convince Tomlin to remain at Arkansas State for one more season.

Cooper was intrigued by the possibility of Tomlin joining Ohio States's coaching staff if he first agreed to spend another year in Jonesboro.

"He [Cooper] said, 'Sure.'" Hollis said.

Hollis was almost certain that Tomlin would turn him down. "I knew it wasn't going to work, but I did throw it out there," Hollis said. "I said, 'Mike, you know you could skip that step along your career at Cincinnati and stay here another year.'"

After turning again to Scherer for advice, Tomlin told Hollis thanks, but no thanks.

"My advice to him was the old 'bird in the hand,'" Scherer said. "In this business, things change so radically. How real that really was . . . I know it was in conversation that was thrown out to try to keep him. I was a GA at Penn State. I started my career there. Coach [Joe] Paterno advised me to make your moves early. You build your network, build your reputation, and then you can pick and choose your moves more distinctly or discretely as you get older. I passed that on to Mike that it's a move up. There's always somebody above you on the food chain. There was somebody above us at JMU to move to and guys would leave. Same with Memphis. I told him you're going to have other opportunities. The key is to bet on the bird in the hand right now. You just never know what's going to happen in this business. If something happens to John Cooper, they have a bad year."

Tomlin's departure was the way of the world in college football. He accepted a position at UT-Martin, but made an unexpected detour to Arkansas State without ever having coached a game at the FCS school.

UT-Martin's loss, Arkansas State's gain.

For a developing mid-major program like Arkansas State, having a fast riser such as Tomlin coach its football team for two years was an unexpected bonus.

Arkansas State's loss, Cincinnati's gain.

"It was a joy to have Mike the two years we had him at Arkansas State," Hollis said. "If he stayed in college, he would have taken the same path he did to the NFL. He would have been a college head coach in a matter of time. Absolutely. That was a no-brainer."

Tomlin continued to call on Scherer for advice, and that included the next stop in his ascension through the coaching ranks: the University of Cincinnati.

5

BUILDING A REPUTATION
WITH THE BEARCATS

UNIVERSITY OF CINCINNATI
(DEFENSIVE BACKS COACH, 1999–2000)

"Routine plays routinely."

THERE was a moment at the conclusion of the 1988 college
football season when the destiny of Mike Tomlin's coaching
future hung, albeit delicately, in the balance. Presented with the
possibility of remaining at Arkansas State for one more season
under head coach Joe Hollis and perhaps joining Hollis's friend
and longtime mentor John Cooper at *The* Ohio State University
the following season, Tomlin took the road less traveled and
instead accepted an offer as the new cornerbacks coach at the
University of Cincinnati. It was a shared coaching position for a

Cincinnati team that had finished 3–8 the previous season with seven losses of 25 or more points. Yet it was also a team coached by Rick Minter, the former Notre Dame defensive coordinator whose reputation for hiring and developing assistant coaches for Power Five and NFL jobs was legendary. Not to mention that Tomlin and wife Kiya would be moving into a higher tax bracket with the salary bump.

Just as no one could have foreseen the calculated moves that delivered Mike Tomlin to college football outposts in Lexington (Virginia), Memphis (Tennessee), and Jonesboro (Arkansas), relocating to Cincinnati (Ohio) for his fourth coaching job in five years—fresh out of William & Mary—was the result of his high regard among the coaching underground.

As usual, it started with a single phone call.

"Rip Scherer, who's a good friend of mine, was the head coach at Memphis and had Mike as a GA," said Minter. "Mike might have inquired, but I think Rip followed up with a phone call. He said, 'You ought to check this guy out.' Mike came highly recommended. I reached out, got the ball rolling, and brought him in for an interview."

Where some job candidates were all spit and polish, Tomlin, one of three finalists, exuded energy. He lit up whatever room he entered with his presence. It took a lot to impress Minter, a coaching veteran who entered the profession two decades earlier, but, like previous coaches who were dazzled in the interview process, he also fell under Tomlin's spell.

"I tell people this all the time when they ask me about Mike," said Minter, who's currently a defensive analyst at Michigan. "Mike was twenty-six. He comes walking in the door to do the interview. Just as Mike can still do to this day, he just beams when he walks in a room. He's got that look about him. He's got that jaw. That smile. Of course, he was much younger. But even then, he commanded respect. I had already talked to him on the phone, but when he walked in the door I knew within five seconds, 'That's the guy I want to hire.'"

Minter knew a thing or two about defense. After two years as a graduate assistant (at Henderson State and Arkansas State, respectively), he began coaching defenses in 1979 (at Louisiana Tech). As Notre Dame's defensive coordinator in 1992, his unit allowed an average of 91 yards rushing and 277 total yards over the final nine games of the season. Notre Dame, led by the iconic head coach Lou Holtz, won the Cotton Bowl over Texas A&M (28–3) to finish 10–1–1 and ranked fourth in the final polls. During his first two seasons at Notre Dame (he would return to the school as its defensive coordinator in 2005, holding the job through the 2007 season), Minter coached twenty-one defensive players who went on to play in the NFL.

With Cincinnati, Tomlin delivered as advertised, conveying Minter's message to the back end of the defense in his own unique style. A team player, Tomlin accepted a subordinate role as cornerbacks coach with no pushback. Defensive coordinator Rick Smith—who also sat in on Tomlin's interview—coached the safeties.

Tomlin watched hours upon hours of practice tape. As was his custom, he jotted everything down in his trusty notebook and presented the coaching staff with detailed reports of the successes and failures of each of his players.

"From the outset, Mike had a way with coaching the corners," said Minter. "He had a way with coaching special teams. He had a way with recruiting. He was just a people, skill-oriented guy.

He could coach them hard, but it was always tough love. They played their butts off for him."

"He brought a level of expectation that we didn't have the year before," said DeJuan Gossett, who was a starter in both of Tomlin's seasons with the Bearcats. "He was the DB coach. Rick Smith came in as defensive coordinator. Together, they sent shockwaves through the defense with their tenacity, their approach, and their businesslike perspective. You knew you had to come in every day and give it everything you've got. There was no opportunity to slack. If you did, they were on you. It got to where we were all self-accountable."

In Tomlin's first season, Cincinnati jumped over fifty schools to improve from 111th to 61st nationally in pass defense. Though the Bearcats finished 3–8 and were winless in Conference USA, Minter found a silver lining—a 17–12 upset victory over then seventh-ranked Wisconsin (who would finish the season ranked ninth).

"We did not win a league game," said Minter. "But we took Ohio State to the wire in Columbus. And we beat Wisconsin. But we could not beat any team in our league because we could not hit a field goal (missing 14 of 21 attempts). In 2000 we turned right around and made 29 of 32 field goals with the Lou Groza Award–winner [Jonathan Ruffin], who was the same kid who couldn't hit the side of a barn as a freshman."

Cincinnati's win over Wisconsin was the biggest victory in school history at that time. "We knew [Heisman Trophy winner] Ron Dayne was going to get his yards (231 on 28 carries to become the Big Ten's all-time rushing leader)," said Minter. "We had to play a little bit of bend-but-don't-break and stiffen up inside the red zone. They had the ball inside the 10 on two occasions, and because of a turnover and a stop on downs they got three points out of those trips. Our corners made the key stops on fourth down. Mike did a great job in his schemes."

"As bad as we were in '98, we beat Wisconsin in '99," said Gossett. "The secondary was so crucial in that game. Jeff Burrow and Bobby Fuller caused fumbles on the goal line. Ivan Keels stopped Ron Dayne at the two-yard line. Those were all DBs that just had that dog mentality from Mike. He made you feel almost invincible and gave everybody the confidence to succeed. We went up to Ohio State that next week after beating Wisconsin and were up 17–3. It was just the attitude and confidence he gave you; he made you feel invincible. You think you can run through a wall with him behind you. But he also taught you everything you needed to know to be in the right place to make the play. You're thinking that you know what everyone's going to do before it happens."

In 2000, Cincinnati improved to 7–5 and 5–2 in conference play. The Bearcats would make it to only their second bowl game in school history, but fell to Marshall in the Motor City Bowl, 25–14. Tomlin's secondary ranked eighth in the nation with 21 interceptions.

According to the team party line, the Bearcats developed affection and respect for Tomlin who reciprocated in kind—so long as they played by *his* rules.

"My true freshman year before he came, I tore my ACL, PCL, and both my meniscus. They didn't think I was going to play football again," said Gossett. "I came in as a cornerback, but my redshirt freshman year I played strong safety. Then I played outside linebacker my sophomore season. When Mike came in, I was moved from outside linebacker to traditional safety.

He made that transition possible so that by the time [my college career] was done, you wouldn't know I played linebacker. He gave you that vision, what you *need* to do, what you *can* do, what your potential is. You didn't want to let him down."

Tomlin's arrival in the Queen City coincided with heightened accountability and productivity from his underrated secondary.

Once Tomlin had their attention, it was a wrap. No longer tethered to their past, Tomlin's way or the highway approach changed hearts and minds . . . as well as lowered body fat levels.

"Terrible Tuesday," said Gossett, drawing out the two words for emphasis. "We knew that Tuesday was always going to be terrible from an intensity standpoint in practice."

The best way to describe those brutal Tuesday practices?

"You would think we were a doggone track team," said Gossett.

"Every Tuesday practice, we knew we were going to hit, we knew we were going to run, and we *knew* we were going to run gassers. The level of practice was so intense. It was awful.

"He called it *Terrible Tuesday*," continued Gossett, repeating the term. "He gave it a name so that mentally you knew you were going to approach this practice that was going to be high level in intensity. We knew mentally going in it was going to be terrible, but that you were going to feel great after that. I never ran that much in my life, but we were never tired in a game."

A sociology major in college, Tomlin's designated mental strategy coaxed the very best effort from his players, though some needed more coaxing than others. Some in his secondary were self-starters, but they all needed to be pushed harder as Tomlin attempted to bring them all closer together.

As a result, the Bearcats didn't take it personally because they understood where their coach was coming from. "We had such a bad year in '98," said Gossett. "I think we really had to break some bad mental habits and we found ways to do that. Terrible Tuesday was just another way to be different, to change. But also, you've got the same players coming back. You're not going to overhaul a season with one recruiting class like you can now with the transfer portal. You had to play with what you had. They knew what everyone could potentially do, and tried to get the best out of us."

Tomlin coached and developed several Cincinnati defensive backs who were either drafted by NFL teams or signed as free agents. It was an impressive accomplishment, considering the roster was filled with players who weren't considered "good enough" for Ohio State and Michigan.

"I was a late bloomer," said Gossett. "There were thirty kids on my high school team. I didn't know if I was going to play D-I football until I went to Cincinnati's summer camp. Rick Minter saw me at the camp and offered me a scholarship. I played all four years, but didn't get drafted. I had a workout with the Dallas Cowboys and failed my physical. The Giants signed me, but I tore that same knee in training camp and I couldn't pass the physical anymore.

"Some of our defensive backs were among the best out there. Blue Adams (seventh-round pick by the Lions in 2003) thrived under coach Tomlin. Lavar Glover (seventh-round pick by the Steelers in 2002) was a little dude, but just the technique he had."

After Tomlin's first season at Cincinnati, Minter realized he probably wasn't going to be there more than a couple years. Call it a hunch. Current Texas A&M head coach Jimbo Fisher was also on the staff with Tomlin in 1999, as the team's offensive coordinator. Fisher lasted just one season at Cincinnati before leaving to become LSU's offensive coordinator/quarterbacks coach.

"I had a bunch of guys come through there," said Minter. "I had John Harbaugh. I had Rex Ryan and Don ["Wink"] Martindale and a bunch of guys all at the same time. So it wasn't unusual for me to, one, know what I'm talking about when I'm looking for a coach and, two, our job was attractive enough for a guy looking transitional. They're not going to stay forever. You come in, pay your dues, put a year or two or three in, and, generally, good things happen to you. I was at Cincinnati for 10 years and hired fifty coaches, counting my first original hire choices. I averaged about four or five coaching losses a year."

"Everyone gave coach Minter a hard time for losing so many coaches," said John Widecan, Cincinnati's associate AD for football operations. "When he hired a coach, he wanted to hire someone who was going to bring something into the program. That's why we had so many good coaches that worked under him. Everyone said, 'He can't keep coaches.' A lot of times they were guys that were between Power Five jobs or NFL jobs. Minter saw value in having them for one or two or three years, and learn from them. And if we had any young coaches, he would help bring them along."

Thanks, in part, to the upset win over Wisconsin, Tomlin received his first big job offer from Syracuse. "He was like, '[head coach] Paul Pasqualoni called me today, man,'" said big brother Ed Tomlin. "'I'm going to do this interview with Syracuse. I'm geeked about the Syracuse job. I did my research.' I'm like, 'Yeah, like this, that, and the other.' It's a good move, good next move.

"He got back from Syracuse. 'Ed, they're going to straighten me out with six or seven blazers. We're going to set the wardrobe out. They're going to let me recruit the 757 (Hampton Roads area code).' It was like a recruiting trip."

Minter knew the sand in the hour glass on Tomlin's tenure at Cincinnati was running out. He was hoping to get at least two years out of his star pupil. He also wanted to make sure Tomlin thought things through before taking another job after only one season at Cincinnati.

"I knew after his first year with us that Mike was probably going to become a hot commodity," said Minter. "He went to Syracuse and met with Paul Pasqualoni. I finally sat him down and talked to him. At that time, Syracuse was in the old Big East. We were in Conference USA. It would have been a step up. But I know he and his wife really enjoyed Cincinnati and the area and our staff.

"I told him to be diligent and patient and wise before making a decision. He didn't want to get the reputation as a guy who's going to bounce around every year for another job, seeking out higher ground."

From past experiences with staff members, Minter knew that young coaches had a tendency to live in the moment instead of planning for the future. He emphasized the importance of looking beyond the name of a school and paying more attention to the quality of the program.

Minter told Tomlin to look before he leaped at the first big job offer to come his way.

"I was talking about Syracuse," continued Minter, "and no disrespect to Paul Pasqualoni and Syracuse, but I said, 'Mike, if this is Ohio State or Notre Dame or Michigan calling you at this stage after one year, you might have to consider it. To go to some programs that are not too far off from our level, you might be better to [stay] another year.'

"Part of that was selfish. Of course, you want to keep the guy. But part of it was heartfelt for me to say I knew what I was talking about in terms of him eventually being a superstar."

In Minter's and others' educated eyes, Tomlin, despite his youth, was already a "made man." If not now, then soon . . . very soon.

"It goes back to the first time he walked in the door," said Minter. "He just has a charisma about him and a presence about him that commands respect. As long as he knew what he was doing on the field and could help the players and not be full of BS, you knew he had all the makings. He just needed time, he just needed maturity, he just needed to ripen a little bit."

As Minter predicted, job offers from other schools continued to flow Tomlin's way. By now, interested college coaches realized it wasn't enough to simply call Tomlin to determine if he was the best person for the job. Given the high volume of schools blowing up his cell phone, it might just be their only opportunity to speak with him.

"Just like Mike wasn't going to be at Arkansas State very long," said Widecan, "he wasn't going to be at Cincinnati very long, either."

In other words, don't call unless you're prepared to make an offer.

"Then it was Michigan and Notre Dame. I was like, 'This is crazy,'" said Ed Tomlin. "Looks like something's about to happen.

"Teryl Austin was the DB coach at Michigan. Mike was like, 'Yo, this dude right here, this young black DB coach at Michigan, he's going to make sure when he moves on, that I get that [job]. He's going to make that happen for me.'"

Austin joined the Seattle Seahawks coaching staff in 2003 after a dozen years coaching on the collegiate level; Mike Tomlin beat him to the NFL by three years, and later hired him on his defensive coaching staff with the Pittsburgh Steelers, promoting him to defensive coordinator in 2022.

* * *

During an offseason pickup basketball game taking place at what is now known as Fifth Third Arena, Tomlin excused himself to answer his cell phone. Those within earshot understood that Notre Dame head coach Bob Davie was offering Tomlin a job.

"We thought he was going to go to Notre Dame. He interviewed there," said Widecan, who said he always played on Tomlin's pickup team because Tomlin rarely lost. "He's on the phone with Bob Davie, and he's offering him the job."

"Bob Davie called me about Mike. His name was getting out there," said Rip Scherer Jr., who hired Tomlin as a graduate assistant at Memphis a few years earlier. "The term [being used to describe Tomlin] was *rising star*. He was on a very accelerated path. My dad [William Scherer Sr., also known as "Rip"] coached Bob at Moon Township [in suburban Pittsburgh]. I would work out with Bob in the summer."

Before Tomlin could respond, his cell phone clicked again. "Mike said to Bob Davie, 'Can I put you on hold for one second?'" said Widecan, chuckling at the memory.

Tomlin coolly put Davie on hold and switched over to his new call.

It was Tampa Bay Buccaneers defensive coordinator Monte Kiffin.

"Monte Kiffin had a conversation with coach Minter," said Widecan. "Coach Minter was trying to help Mike."

"My original mentor in coaching when I started at Arkansas [in 1978, as a graduate assistant] under Lou Holtz and Monte Kiffin, Monte was my guy," said Minter. "I was at NC State with Monte and Greg Robinson. Pete Carroll was our defensive coordinator. Monte and I stayed in touch through the years.

"Monte picked up the phone and called me," continued Minter. "They lost Herman Edwards to the Jets. He says, 'I understand you've got this rising star as a DB coach.'

"I said, 'You must be referring to Mike Tomlin.'

"'Yeah. Mike Tomlin. Tell me about him.'

"'Monte, I'll tell you this. If you were to bring him in for an interview, you will hire him.'"

Kiffin had seen it all. He was a tough coach to impress, so, given the history between the two longtime colleagues, Minter felt the need to emphasize just how highly Tomlin was valued to the hard-to-please Kiffin.

Kiffin wasn't buying it . . . at least, not at first.

"You have to know Monte a little bit," said Minter. "He said, 'Now wait a minute. You don't know everything.'

"That's a funny story between Monte and I to this day. We have laughed about that."

After speaking with Kiffin, and being invited to Tampa for his first interview with an NFL team, Tomlin had to click back to his *other* call.

Davie was still holding.

"Mike switches back to Bob Davie and he's like, 'I'm going to have to call you back," said Widecan.

"As soon as he got off the phone, we went back to playing basketball.

"I was literally standing right next to him when it went down," Widecan said, incredulously. "Everybody was like, 'Oh, shit.'"

Oh shit, indeed.

6

WELCOME TO THE NFL

TAMPA BAY BUCCANEERS
(DEFENSIVE BACKS COACH, 2001–05)

"I don't care how you cut it. We all swim in the same water."

TONY Dungy didn't yell. He quietly made his point to his players behind the scenes, away from prying media eyes and curious fans. Players never wanted to disappoint the man.

Dungy once got upset with linebacker Derrick Brooks because Brooks spoke with the local media about injuries. Dungy said during a team meeting that he was unaware Florida State (Brooks's alma mater) was giving out medical degrees to undergrads. Or that Brooks graduated with honors and received a doctorate in medicine (he didn't). Even though Dungy never raised his voice, Brooks wanted to shrivel up and hide. The main reason Dungy called out Brooks was not because he talked about his *own* injury, but rather that he shared a teammate's injury status with reporters. Brooks never mentioned injuries to the media again.

Dungy's players said he didn't have to yell and cuss or threaten to bench them. He could give you a look, or he could just talk about how they've got to do better; that they're capable of doing better. Dungy had a way of talking to his players in a normal speaking voice. And if you weren't on your game, players felt so bad, like they were letting him down—and not just him, but the entire team.

Warren Sapp spoke about the time Dungy talked to him about being overweight. Dungy brought him into his office one day and showed him a tape of the Buccaneers playing the Detroit Lions the previous season. In the video, Barry Sanders had broken a long touchdown run. Throughout the video, Sapp was in the frame trying to catch Sanders. He never caught him, but Sapp was visible every step of the way. Dungy then put on a tape from the previous week. It showed Sapp in the picture. The opposing player in the picture kept running with the football. Then it showed Sapp out of the picture. According to Sapp, via Associated Press sports reporter Fred Goodall, Dungy was telling him he was "overweight" without ever saying it. No way he was going to catch Sanders in the first video, but Sapp stayed in the picture all the way to the end zone. The second video was only about a 25-yard run; it wasn't an 80-yard run like the first one. Sapp got the message.

Dungy spoke softly, yet ruled with an iron fist. He didn't play favorites. Brooks and Sapp are both members of the Pro Football Hall of Fame.

Dungy surrounded himself with coaches who didn't necessarily remind him of himself, but who had the same sort of demeanor. You never saw coaches on Dungy's sideline out of control. First and foremost, he always emphasized the value of having good teachers on the coaching staff. He looked for coaches who could communicate with the players. That was his philosophy: You need talented players, but you also need players who are smart. Guys who are smart want to be taught; they're open to being taught. It's human nature that if you bring in a smart guy and you give him a plan, they want to please you. You don't have to yell and scream at them and try to beat them down to get their talent to shine. You get smart players who are also talented and you've got yourself a winning combination—especially when you pair that with great teachers.

"In talking to Dungy over the years, he always emphasized the value of having good teachers on the staff and having smart players," said Goodall, who has covered the Tampa Bay Buccaneers since 1983. "He was criticized for not showing emotion on the sideline. But he said it was his experience if you get the right kind of player—you get good people, you get smart players—they want to get better. In general, they want to be successful, they want to please the coach, so to speak. They're looking for a plan to maximize their potential."

And so it was that when Dungy needed a new secondary coach to replace Herman Edwards in 2001, who had been hired as the head coach of the New York Jets, the name Mike Tomlin was brought to his attention.

"If I had two words to describe him," said Dungy, "it would be *teacher* and *communicator*."

Tomlin met Dungy's top criteria: he was smart, graduating from the College of William & Mary—regarded in some corners as the "Ivy League of the South"—in four years with a degree in sociology and gave serious consideration to attending law school.

Dungy identified Tomlin as a young man mature beyond his years who, in his most recent capacity as secondary coach at the University of Cincinnati, "takes a lot of the guys that Ohio State doesn't want and turns them into NFL-caliber players."

"I called our scouting department in," said Dungy. "We had a personnel meeting, but I asked, 'Can you guys give me any names of people who are very, very good college coaches, good technicians, good communicators that might be able to handle this room of a mixture of All-Pros and young guys?' Two or three people mentioned Mike. I said, 'I need to talk to this guy.'"

Defensive coordinator Monte Kiffin was one of those people. During his successful 13-year run with the Buccaneers, he was directly involved in the hiring of six assistants who would go on to become NFL head coaches: Rod Marinelli, Lovie Smith, Raheem Morris, Gus Bradley, Herman Edwards, and Tomlin.

"We interviewed fifteen, sixteen guys for the secondary job," Kiffin told the *National Football Post* in 2013. "Then we heard about a young guy at the University of Cincinnati by the name of Mike Tomlin. Rick Minter was the head coach. I had worked with him [at the University of Arkansas and NC State]. I said, 'I heard you have a young coach who is under the radar.' He said, 'how did you hear about him?' I said, 'I've been snooping around.' So I called Mike, and I said, 'This is Coach Kiffin from the Tampa Bay Buccaneers.' He didn't believe it was me."

Dungy said, "I got in contact with him, we brought him into Tampa, and in five minutes I could tell the scouts were right."

Displaying absolutely no signs of nerves or indecisiveness, Tomlin presented his case before two of the greatest defensive minds in NFL history.

"He just came across with the idea of, 'Hey, I know what I'm doing. I'm very confident, but I'm not cocky or overbearing,'" said Dungy. "'I have some good thoughts on how you play winning football.' It was amazing. He sat for about two hours with Monte Kiffin and our defensive staff."

"He was outstanding in the interview," said Kiffin. "I took him out on the field."

Several years later, when Brad Childress was considering Tomlin for the Minnesota Vikings' defensive coordinator's job, he highlighted Tomlin's impromptu Tampa Bay interview that shifted from inside the team facility at One Buc Place to the practice field.

"He's sitting there for an interview. Then they said, 'Let's get down and get on the grass. Let's go put on a pair of shorts and a T-shirt,'" said Childress. "He thinks he's going to do X's and O's, next thing you know he's down on the grass with those guys. He's telling them and showing them and coaching them and saying how he'd say it. He's in Tampa and it's humid. He said, 'I got a flop sweat going.' They were out there for about an hour, then they said, 'OK, that's good.' Everybody kind of walked away from him. He got a shower, then they sent him on his way.

"He's like, 'How'd I do?'"

"We'll get back to you."

"Of course, they hired him."

"It's how you connect with your players," said Kiffin. "There are some really smart coaches who are great on the blackboard.

But we use the term, 'can you take it to the grass?' We would take them on the field, go through drills. I call it the 'it' factor. Some guys just have it. You can feel it."

* * *

Tomlin fit the mold of a typical Dungy hire. That is, nobody really knew anything about him. He came from the University of Cincinnati, a program not considered a football factory. He was only twenty-eight when he was hired, and turned twenty-nine on March 15. Granted, Lovie Smith was a defensive backs coach at Ohio State when he was brought in to lead the linebackers, but Dungy saw something in him that others didn't. Before coming to Tampa Bay, Dungy hired Edwards as a scout for the Kansas City Chiefs when Dungy was an assistant coach there. Jim Caldwell came from Wake Forest—a program known mostly for its basketball prowess.

"It was something I was intentional about," said Dungy. "I wanted to hire young guys that had potential, and I wanted to give them an opportunity to flourish.

"Bringing Lovie Smith into the National Football League. Hiring Herm Edwards when he was in personnel and making him a scout. Hiring Mike Tomlin for his first job in the NFL. I hired Leslie Frazier when he was in between jobs and out of work and it didn't seem like he was going to get another opportunity.

"Those guys are good," continued Dungy. "And knowing that and recognizing that, then giving them an opportunity to flourish, and, I don't want to say, promoting them, but letting the NFL landscape see those guys are good."

Dungy did what came naturally, what he learned in his four years as Minnesota Vikings defensive coordinator under head coach Dennis Green.

Green, the second African American head coach (after Art Shell) in the modern era, didn't hesitate to put coaches in positions that weren't normally in those positions. And then push them beyond that to become head coaches.

One of Green's first hires was making Dungy his defensive coordinator. When Dungy left Minnesota, he goes to Tampa Bay, brings Kiffin with him as his defensive coordinator, hires Edwards as his assistant head coach, and recruits Smith and Tomlin from the college ranks.

"Denny expected his coaches to be goal-oriented, to be determined to not only coach their positions but to also want to make an impact on the football team to the point they were developing themselves for the next step, which, in this case, would be head coach," said longtime Minneapolis sports journalist Larry Fitzgerald Sr., whose son Larry is a future Hall of Famer and who hosted Green's weekly radio show when he coached the Vikings from 1992 to 2001. "Denny knew exactly where he was in the annals of history, and he was going to take full advantage of finding a way in building a team the way he wanted to build it.

"Tony Dungy had the No. 1 defense in '93 and then suddenly the door opened in Tampa and created this rivalry between Denny and Tony," continued Fitzgerald, who considered Green a personal friend. "That opened the door for Mike Tomlin."

Dungy saw what happened when he was in Minnesota and took it to the next level when he was named head coach of the Buccaneers in 1996.

"Dennis Green got me ready to go," said Dungy. "He gave me access to things. He prepared me to be a head coach. I saw him do the same with Tyrone Willingham, with Brian Billick.

"I felt it. He had me in meetings that a normal defensive coordinator wouldn't have been in. He would call me into his office when he was making a quarterback change, for instance, and say, 'This is what I'm doing. You're going to be in this position at some point down the road. I want you to be aware of this.'"

"He let me talk to the media and he promoted me," continued Dungy. "That was how I did it in Tampa. We had good people and it was part of my DNA to try to select good people, but also to put them in positions for success. We didn't have restrictions who the media could talk to. I wanted those guys to experience that. I think that helped them get opportunities, but that just allowed them to show what they could do."

Of the sixteen black men who became fulltime head coaches after Dungy, five served as assistants under him and a sixth, Steve Wilks, was an assistant under one of his proteges, Lovie Smith. Marvin Lewis, an intern with Kansas City while Dungy was an assistant there, became the Cincinnati Bengals' head coach. Two more black future head coaches, Hue Jackson and Vance Joseph, were on Lewis's Cincinnati staffs.

* * *

On Tomlin's first official day on the job, Dungy invited him into his office. Worried about being the father of a three-month old son and the demands he would face as a rookie coach in the NFL, Tomlin said the visit changed his entire perspective on coaching.

"I'm scared to death right straight up," Tomlin said on the *Pivot* podcast. "Am I going to be able to meet the demands of the job? How am I going to balance the demands of the job with fatherhood? I just didn't know what it looked like. I didn't know what the NFL looked like and how it was going to function in it. I didn't know what fatherhood looked like because I came from a broken home and so I'm trying to figure out how to navigate that.

"My first day on the job, we had a press conference, he [Dungy] said come by the office. I walked in his office, the lights were off and his son Eric was sitting on the floor with like a PlayStation hooked up to his overhead, and the kid was playing video games in his office and he apologized for it.

"I got a three-month old and that dude called me to his office and I turned that corner and that's not what I expected to see," continued Tomlin. "He showed me an image in an instant that, like, all the things I was worried about were manageable. You know what I mean? That dude was doing his job, his little son was sitting there playing video games. I was just an hour on the job. I just explained to him the other day how significant that was for me to see that, and kind of put me at ease on a lot of things that were running through my mind."

It was Dungy's turn to learn from Tomlin when he attended the newly hired coach's first meeting with the team's defensive backs. "He's in there with John Lynch and Ronde Barber, who were All-Pros and going to the Hall of Fame," said Dungy. "We had a couple other veteran defensive backs, then we had a young group of guys and he handled that meeting so well and let them know why he was here, how he was going to help them. He had the interest of everybody in that room. After four, five, ten minutes, I walked out of that room and I never went back in the DB meeting room again."

"Every word that comes out of his mouth just resonates," said Barber, who was in the room for that first meeting.

Tomlin was Barber's position coach for all five of the coach's seasons in Tampa. The two developed a special bond.

"In any one moment that he's saying something to you, it feels like he planned to say it for weeks or months," said Barber, a recent inductee into the Pro Football Hall of Fame in August 2023. "But you know for a fact it's just coming off the top of his head. It's just the way he's wired.

"I think of it in a math sense," continued Barber, "because you're talking to a room of different personalities, different people, different backgrounds. To be able to get it to a simple denominator is a skill. Mike has a way of denominating it to the whole room."

Tomlin's youthful appearance and charismatic persona—some in the media called it "bravado"—had a dramatic effect on the entire Buccaneers organization. He was black, of course, in a league where instances of black head coaches hiring black assistants was rare. Even more rare was Tomlin's age.

"I'll never forget the day John Lynch came in like, 'I'm older than my position coach,'" said Brooks.

You couldn't help but notice that Tomlin was young—Lynch was nearly a year older than his new position coach—but that didn't seem to matter once his players got to know him.

"At that point, I didn't know anything about him. Apparently, I played against him in college," said Barber, whose Virginia Cavaliers defeated Tomlin's William & Mary Tribe, 37–3, in 1994. It was Tomlin's senior year, and the same season Barber was named ACC Rookie of the Year. "I give him [grief] all the time: 'Yeah, we played William & Mary, what number were you? I don't remember you, bruh.' He was young, but he was assured."

"We had veterans on the team, but Mike had a presence about him that was impressive," said Mark Dominik, who was the Buccaneers' director of pro personnel when Tomlin was hired, and later became the team's general manager. "The ability to control a room. The ability to know when to speak up and when to hold back. But the main part was he just kind of walked in and you felt like . . . you could sense that even the veterans, the Ronde Barbers of the world who had been around the league for a little while, were like, 'OK, this guy's going to make me better.' That's really what players want is a guy who's going to make them better, regardless if they're twenty-nine, forty-nine, or sixty-nine."

Dungy's track record for successfully hiring assistant coaches directly from the college ranks encouraged his players to be less reticent in accepting Tomlin.

"What we heard [from Dungy] was, 'Don't get fooled by the ages of some of these coaches. I know what I'm doing,'" said Brooks. "It was the same thing with Lovie Smith and Rod Marinelli. He'd already been through a wave of that, getting collegiate coaches to come in and teach. He had that success with the defensive line and linebackers. This was his first attempt doing it with the secondary. He said, 'Trust me.' Quite frankly, we did."

Tomlin's presence in Tampa was, well, different. He spoke, words came out, players listened. However, it was more than just stringing a few paragraphs together to make a point. Tomlin's gift for gab meant he could speak with emphasis to gain the attention of whoever was on the receiving end of his message.

"His voice is huge," said Oklahoma State safeties coach Dan Hammerschmidt, recalling Tomlin's first season as a college coach that the two spent together in 1995 at VMI. "I know it's a God-given thing. A lot of guys have it, but most of us don't. You can have a big voice and not know how to use it. He can control a room with his voice."

"His delivery, to me, it's the best I've ever seen among the coaches I've been around," said Barber. "Because of the assured-ness of it and the impactful way that he says his words. It's impos-sible to hide confidence. And he has it in spades. He throws it around like giving kids Skittles. He truly believes everything that he says."

If Tomlin's words didn't capture a player's attention, his pen-etrating stare delivered the message to the intended recipient.

"When you talk to coach Tomlin and he gives you those eyes, you feel like you're just drawn in," said Dominik. "He can stare at you and kind of give you that little bit of a tilt of the head and he's either going to lay into you or have something important to say. He's got those eyes that kind of dig into you."

Tomlin's first meeting with Barber was memorable. Dungy trusted Tomlin enough on incredibly short notice to recruit one of his team's best defenders, who was entering free agency.

Barber wasn't a sure thing to return to the Buccaneers. He could have left Tampa, the team that drafted him, to join another team. Yet here he was, trusting his career to a new coach-ing hire that he barely knew.

"I was a free agent the year Mike came to Tampa. I hadn't signed by the time they named him secondary coach," said Barber. "He took me and my wife out to dinner and basically convinced me I needed to be in Tampa.

"He said, 'I look at what y'all do. You're the only person that can do what we're asking that position to do.' We had a great conversation, and I re-signed. Not because of him, but, like, that was what he was telling me. And then a couple months later when he was coaching us, he goes about the small details of making you your best self. I don't know if it's a personality thing with him, but I don't think a lot of coaches can get guys to do what he makes guys do and have them feel like it's what they want to do.

"I wanted to be in Tampa," continued Barber. "There was no question I wanted to stay. They drafted me. I had just started to find success here. But, you know, contracts [the team tells you to] set the market, that messes with you. It was like, 'I'll go find it somewhere else.' But the talk we had, I was pretty certain that my best opportunity was right here where I was. And, ultimately, he was right. He was 100 percent right."

* * *

To some members of the predominately white Tampa Bay media, Tomlin was someone to be questioned, scrutinized, and analyzed.

Other coaches with backgrounds similar to Tomlin's, coming from small college programs and getting the most out of kids the big schools didn't want, were often presented differently in the media. They were identified as recruiting smart kids who were good students. A black coach? Well, he's usually portrayed as a hell of a recruiter who can go into homes and sell the program to mommys and daddys and not much else.

Tomlin's arrival was almost like an aberration. According to a league source, "[Media] will look at a young white guy getting an opportunity and spin it that sometimes it's good to take a leap of faith. Or it shows what you can do when you locate young talent and give that talent an opportunity to shine."

"Nobody knew anything about him," Goodall said of Tomlin's arrival. "That was part of the skepticism here in the media. I remember sitting around in the media room and reporters saying things like, 'Where did this guy come from? What makes him so special that they would hire him from the University of Cincinnati?'

"When Dungy brought in Lovie Smith, he had a background as a [defensive back] coach from Ohio State. With Tomlin, it was like, 'Who's this cocky guy who wears sunglasses to practice?' He was vocal. His enthusiasm was evident. He was more like a player. That made him stand out."

After missing the playoffs with a 9–7 record in 2001, the Buccaneers fired Dungy in a surprise move, replacing him with Jon Gruden after first offering the job to Marvin Lewis. Tampa Bay won Super Bowl XXVII the next season, demolishing the Oakland Raiders (Gruden's former team), 48–21. Tomlin's secondary was masterful; the Buccaneers recorded five interceptions, returning three for touchdowns. Cornerback Dexter Jackson was named Super Bowl MVP.

Tomlin would eventually win the Tampa Bay media over, too, simply because he was damn good at his job. Still, there was no denying he rubbed some people the wrong way.

"There was always something about him," said Goodall. "He had this thing with the media. If he saw something that you wrote, he had a little edge to him. He was like, 'How you like me now?'"

The best way to put it, said a person close to the Buccaneers, was that Tomlin had the type of personality that talking to him was like talking to the brother on the corner on a team dominated by brothers. But at the same time, when you got to know him, you knew he wasn't a brother who hung out on the corner. You found out that he went to William & Mary. He could talk trash with the best of them, but he talked proper trash. He could straddle the fence. He could say all the right things in front of the camera and still relate to the guys.

"Once they started having success," said Goodall, "the media was accepting."

What some in the media and others not connected to the team who couldn't get past his looks and, therefore, couldn't possibly see and would never understand, was Tomlin's undeniable teaching ability. Tomlin found ways to put men in the right position. He built up players and made them feel confident in what they were doing and motivated them to become their very best selves.

Like any team, there were different personalities in the Buccaneers defensive back room. Tomlin had a gift for knowing that good coaches understand the individual needs of each player. He realized there were guys who were going to understand it the first time he said it, and others that had to go on the field and walk through it to get it to click.

Being the defensive backs coach, it was rare," said Brooks. "I remember the first time he addressed us defensively when he was presenting the plan on our third downs and putting together that package. And how vividly everybody's role was explained. And how each one of our goals matched up to the goals that we were set to achieve that week. He was also responsible for our passing game and the offensive passing plays against us. And I always got a competitive laugh to how he was going to attack me with the scout team plays. I always looked forward to how he was going to attack me and get me ready in that preparation."

When did Tomlin's players start to buy in that he was the real deal?

"That's a hilarious question," said Barber. "I remember our first OTA practices when he got here, we started doing all these everyday drills. He calls them 'EDD (Every Day Drills).'

"John Lynch comes up to me. He goes, 'Ronde, what are we doing? This young coach doing these drills?'

"Because at that point, you feel like you're a professional. You're in the NFL. I know how to get myself ready to play. I'm like, 'John, dude, I don't know. You're the veteran in the room. Why don't you say something to him?' I was just following the crowd.

"But, literally, within a month, every single player in the room knew that they were better because of doing those drills."

The players eventually saw for themselves that the EDD drills helped them in Cover 2 by opening their hips when defending a comeback route. Practicing it every day only increased their skills in such situations.

"He had a tape of sixty-three plays from the year before, and detailed notes on each one," Lynch said to the *Pittsburgh Post-Gazette* in 2007. That technique I used, the technique I could've used, my thoughts—he had paragraphs on each play."

"Tony hired me at twenty-eight," Tomlin explained on the *Pivot* podcast. "I had John Lynch, Ronde Barber, Brian Kelly, Dexter Jackson in my meeting room. I was the same age as those guys. Lynch was nine months older than me. I did not want to let those guys down. The whole nature of our relationship was my ability to help those dudes prepare and bring that daily. I understood that. I had no resume that they could appreciate. I came in there every day with kind of an edge of, 'How am I going to deliver these dudes to a stadium, and how are they going to play great?' I just did that so long it became habit."

When Edwards left to become head coach of the Jets, Tampa Bay's defensive backs learned to adjust to Tomlin's coaching style.

Edwards played cornerback for nine seasons for the Philadelphia Eagles and studied under Dungy and Dick Vermeil. Tomlin played wide receiver at William & Mary and coached at four different mid-major programs in six years.

"Totally different," said Barber in comparing the two coaches.

"Herm was a great theorist. He can give you why you are this. But he never really gave you the how. He never gave you the nuts and bolts.

"Herm would give you the shell of a sports car," continued Barber. "Mike T would give you the fucking engine of that same sports car."

Tomlin was the icing on the cake for Barber, who was picked in the third round of the 1997 draft—one year after Dungy's arrival. Barber got burned a few times as a rookie. He gave Dungy a lot of credit for never losing faith in him. He understood he gave Dungy no choice but to bench him at times, but appreciated that Dungy stuck with him.

One of Tomlin's favorite getting-to-know-you introductions with his players is establishing goals that extend beyond the player's own imagination. By getting players to "reach for the stars," he empowers them to seek their own form of individual greatness.

By the time Tomlin arrived in Tampa, Barber had recorded six interceptions and nine and a half sacks in his first four seasons with no Pro Bowl appearances.

"I remember him sitting down with me and telling me what he expected of me," said Barber. "It was just a simple conversation about what I could be. He's like, "'Bro, have you ever considered the impact that you're having on the position that you're playing? You could be a 20-plus sack guy.' I'm like, 'What?' I had never thought about that. I'm a cornerback.

"He said, 'The way you play the game, the way that we have you playing, you're going to be the first corner to ever have 20 sacks.' I'm like, 'Oh, shit! OK. All right.'

"It was probably like eight years before I got my twentieth sack."

Barber amassed 28 career sacks, recording at least one sack in all but two of his 16 NFL seasons, including a total of 10 1/2 in his five seasons under Tomlin.

"He set this expectation for me that set me on a path to chase that," said Barber. "In my mind, I'm chasing my own greatness. He seeded that expectation."

Barber also finished with 47 career interceptions, leaving him as the only player in NFL history with at least 45 interceptions and 28 sacks, and is the all-time sack leader for cornerbacks, according to his Pro Football Hall of Fame bio.

"The mental capacity of Barber as a nickel, it challenged me to coach different," Tomlin said as a guest on Ben Roethlisberger's podcast. "He'd be like, 'Hey, man, when they run that counter away, you want me to chase that guard?' You're like, 'Yeah.' Now I'm coaching a SAM [strongside] linebacker.

"Whenever you have unique players," continued Tomlin, "whenever you have great players, you're learning from them and applying the things they do naturally that they can't articulate . . . I think the benefit I had was I was so young in coaching. I just wasn't resistant. I wasn't like, 'Oh, no, no, no. This is not how to do it.' I was so young in coaching that when Lynch would do something freaky, I'm like, 'What were you thinking there? How can we make that a new rule?'"

Tomlin's willingness to always put his players' needs ahead of his own ego followed him throughout his rise in the coaching ranks. It didn't matter if he was speaking to a college freshman or a two-time NFL All-Pro. The message was always the same: *How can we make you a better player?*

And when it came to coaching the best of the best, Tomlin turned that knowledge into a teaching tool—for him, as well as for the player.

"I was around these unique dudes at an early age," he said. "That created this give-and-take and openness in me that I've carried with me forever. I don't know what my perspective would be like if I hadn't been exposed to them. They were special. Lynch was special. Barber was special. Brooks was special. Sapp was special. . . . That's what being around great players gives you as a coach. You know what special looks like."

In his first season under Tomlin, Barber led the league with a career-best 10 interceptions, with one returned for a touchdown. He recorded 59 solo tackles with six tackles for losses, one sack, two fumble recoveries, and one forced fumble. He was voted First-Team AP All-Pro for the first time, and made his first of five career Pro Bowl appearances.

The following season, Barber's 92-yard interception return for a touchdown with four minutes remaining in the fourth quarter clinched Tampa Bay's 27–10 win over Philadelphia in the NFC Championship Game. The Buccaneers advanced to defeat Oakland in Super Bowl XXXVII.

"I don't think there's any coincidence that the year Mike came to Tampa was the year I led the league in interceptions," said Barber. "He tightened up my technique. Gave me the little things to work on to further perfect my craft. The little things that you always think you're working on but you might not be working on the right way. I was literally the best version of myself that year."

Barber didn't make the Pro Bowl his second season under Tomlin. Caught on a sideline camera following his pick-six interception against the Eagles, Barber shouted, "Fuck the Pro Bowl, I'm going to San Diego [site of the Super Bowl]."

"That was easily the best game of my life," said Barber. "And it wasn't because of that interception. I had a sack, fumble recovery, tackle for loss, couple pass breakups. I recorded a stat in almost every category. I set a screen that is like a teaching tape on how to set a screen. If you're talking to a casual fan, it's like, 'What are you talking about?' If you're talking to a football coach, they bring up that play and it's like, 'Look how he sets this screen between pulling offensive linemen and makes the tackle.' I was overprepared and overhyped to have the game that I had."

On Friday, August 4, 2023, Barber was presented his Hall of Fame jacket by Hall of Fame teammate John Lynch and coach

Tomlin, the latter Barber chose to put his gold jacket on him at the Canton (Ohio) Memorial Civic Center.

In an interview with Rich Stroud of the *Tampa Bay Times*, Barber explained the importance of having Tomlin place the gold jacket on him, saying, "I told Mike when I was with him on vacation, 'You're going to give me my gold jacket,'" Barber said. "They called me two weeks ago and said a gold jacket [player must present the jacket].

"John knows the deal. He said, 'I'll stand there with Mike, but Mike is putting the jacket on you.'"

The following day during Barber's Hall of Fame speech, he acknowledged his unique relationship with Tomlin.

"Early in my career, I was just an ordinary guy. And by the time I finished my fourth year, I was a middle-of-the-road free agent with little to no interest, and only one place to go: stay put and get a new DB coach. And that was Mike Tomlin. Mike's not here, but he gave me my jacket yesterday. And before he ran me through his first EDD drill—and if you don't know what that means it's 'Every Day Drill'—he told me, 'Ronde, you're different.' That what he had seen me do, no one else was doing. He told me, 'You're gonna be a 20-20 guy.' OK. So we set our sights on that. And it would be 12 more years, and a 45-25 career that sent me here. Football is always changing, and Mike T, you helped me change one little corner of the game that would define me. I think he imagined this for me well before I could. And he gave me the air to breathe it into existence. Thanks for the empowerment, dude. Thank you."

Upon his return to the Steelers training camp, Tomlin, who missed his team's practice the previous night to attend Barber's Golden Jacket ceremony, spoke with reporters: "I had the unbelievable honor of putting the gold jacket on Ronde Barber," said Tomlin. "He's a former player and a really close friend of mine."

* * *

From the Buccaneers' perspective, the worst thing about winning Super Bowl XXXVI was that Dungy wasn't around to celebrate with them. Gruden was the winning coach.

Dungy endured only one losing season in his six years with Tampa Bay, advancing to the playoffs four times. Prior to his arrival in 1996, the Bucs hadn't produced a winning record since the strike-shortened 1982 season.

"People can get upset about, 'Hey, I got fired after four playoff appearances,'" said Dungy, who was the fourth African American head coach hired in the modern era, one year after Ray Rhodes with the Philadelphia Eagles and four years after Green in Minnesota. "People can look at that in a negative way, but my thing is, no, they reached out to me. They did something that other people weren't doing at that time. I got hired there, and I'm always going to be thankful for that."

After 15 years as an assistant coach at the NFL level, nine of which were as defensive coordinator (five with the Steelers and four with the Vikings), Dungy appreciated the second chance and was determined to be himself instead of what he thought Tampa Bay ownership wanted him to say. "I had a week to get ready for the interview. It didn't go great, but they did a second interview with me the following week. They wanted to know my philosophy and what I was. They had heard some good things about me. The rap on me was I wasn't going to be somebody who inspired people, I wasn't going to be this super motivator, I wasn't loud, and I didn't have a commanding personality.

"We talked about how to get guys to play well," continued Dungy. "I said, 'Look at my defense. If you don't think we play fast and hard and smart, I'm with you. But if you see guys out there playing fast and hard and smart, and you see us lead the league in defense, that's what I plan to bring to you.'"

Dungy didn't last long on the free agent market, as Indianapolis Colts owner Jim Irsay hired Dungy eight days after Tampa Bay let him go.

Dungy requested to bring most of his defensive staff with him to Indy, including Tomlin, whom Dungy wanted to promote to defensive coordinator. However, wanting to keep the coaching core intact (sans their head coach), Buccaneers ownership refused.

Tomlin wanted to join Dungy and didn't appreciate being contractually forced to remain with the Bucs, who by then had hired Gruden to replace Dungy.

How did Tomlin feel?

"Uncomfortable," he said on Roethlisberger's podcast. "I didn't want to be there. As much as I love Lynch and Barber and them, Tony Dungy gave me my break in the NFL. . . . When he got fired, the prospect of me not being able to go with him, to be contractually held here, never even crossed my mind. But that's what happened.

"They knew they had special players there," continued Tomlin. "They weren't going to disrupt that. And they had our rights contractually. All the defensive coaches—Monte Kiffin, Rod Marinelli, Joe Barry, myself—were held under contract. We came with the job like furniture. I don't even know if coach

Gruden was really interested in retaining us. We kind of motley crew came together and had instant success."

"The reality is, when Jon [Gruden] came we were two different teams," said Barber. "We were a defensive team and an offensive team. Monte was head coach of the defense; Jon was head coach of the offense. If Monte had left, the whole staff would have been fired. But they weren't firing Monte. He's one of those guys that you just don't fire. Like Jim Johnson in Philadelphia. He survives head coaches. He's too good at what he does. Monte was that same guy."

Barber said the secondary was never the same after Tomlin left in 2006 to become the Minnesota Vikings' defensive coordinator.

"He was too good of a coach to stay," said Barber. "He left, and Raheem Morris, his assistant, left the same year to be the defensive coordinator at Kansas State. The next year was a little less of a year for everybody just because of that. There was a drop-off. It wasn't the same. To me, personally, I just appreciated what he did for me in the five years I was with him. It changed the trajectory of my career."

Before deciding on Gruden, the league's youngest coach at thirty-eight who cost Tampa Bay two first-round draft picks and a pair of second-round picks, the Buccaneers also considered Marvin Lewis—who was recommended by general manager Rich McKay—as well as Steve Mariucci after being rebuffed by their first choice, Bill Parcells.

The Buccaneers' selection of Gruden and serious consideration of Mariucci (Tampa Bay offered first-, second-, and third-round choices to pry him away from the San Francisco 49ers, but Mariucci turned them down) indicated an organizational shift from a defensive-minded head coach to an offensive specialist.

Gruden did what Dungy couldn't do: win the Super Bowl. Yet the very next year he accomplished that feat . . . with Dungy's players and coaches.

Tampa Bay made only two more postseason appearances under Gruden and didn't win another playoff game. He was fired after the 2008 season, despite signing a contract extension the year before. Gruden was replaced by Morris, a thirty-two-year-old Tomlin clone who had returned to Tampa after one year in the college ranks and had been promoted to defensive coordinator. He was also receiving interest from the Denver Broncos about their head coaching vacancy when agreeing to the Bucs job.

In succeeding years, Tampa Bay's favorable history of hiring black head coaches took some of the sting away from the team's awkward firing of Dungy, who built a Super Bowl team but wasn't allowed to finish the job.

"If you think about from where they started with Bo Jackson telling owner Hugh Culverhouse not to draft him in 1986—and they drafted him anyway," said Rick Brown, former Buccaneers beat reporter for the *Lakeland Ledger*.[1] "And then the Doug Williams fiasco, which went on for years until they changed ownership groups. From where they came from to where they are now is pretty amazing."

Following Gruden's departure, two of the Bucs' next three head coaches—and three of the next six—have been black.

---

1 Jackson, who said to Culverhouse, "You draft me if you want. You're going to waste a draft pick. I can promise you that," would turn down the Bucs contract in favor of playing for baseball's Kansas City Royals. He was then drafted by the Los Angeles Raiders in the following years' draft.

"The Glazer family has always been like, 'I don't really care. Just who's the best and why?'" said Dominik, who was promoted to general manager when Morris was promoted to head coach. "Diversity's a big thing for them. They're trying to find the right people. When we went through the hiring process for head coach, there was carte blanche: 'Who do we need to talk to? Who do we need to bring in?' It was never, 'Let's think about our demographics.'"

Take the Buccaneers' hiring of Bruce Arians in 2019. At the time, Arians was the only head coach in the league to select a black offensive coordinator and a black defensive coordinator in the same season. Such a move would be unlikely without the full support of ownership.

"I'm sure the Glazers said, 'Sure, Bruce, you can hire anyone you want. Go ahead,'" said Brown, who wondered how many NFL owners were as progressive as the Glazer family. "But when he said, 'I want Todd Bowles as my defensive coordinator . . . 'Well . . . *OK* . . . and . . . I want Byron Leftwich as my offensive coordinator . . . oh . . . oh . . . You're pushing it, Bruce. Well . . . he was with you in Arizona . . . OK, we'll let you go there.'"

By now, Tomlin was two years removed from Tampa. Following a successful one-year stint in Minnesota, he was named head coach of the Pittsburgh Steelers.

Tampa Bay envisioned Morris becoming Tomlin 2.0 and taking over a revamped roster with young players. Both men were young, black, spoke their mind, connected with their players, and were excellent teachers.

"Raheem can relate to today's NFL player," said Tampa Bay co-chairman Joel Glazer after making Morris the second black head coach in team history. "The game has changed a lot. It's always changing . . . if you don't adapt to those changes, you can't compete."

"The way the Glazers operate, they don't look at the black and white issue," said Williams, who spent five seasons as personnel executive with the Buccaneers before being named director of pro personnel in 2009. "It's about green dollars. They do what's best for their organization. If you leave it up to the ownership, I think it's a lot easier to go to Tampa and get a job."

Tomlin and Morris were, and have remained close. Raheem has a lot of Mike Tomlin in him," said Williams. "Raheem can talk to anybody. And the fact that he was in Tampa helped a lot. Raheem was there. They had a chance to sit down with Raheem. They probably thought they could transfer into Raheem and get it done. Mike Tomlin gave Raheem a lot of confidence. And the fact that Raheem was able to see Mike go and get a job, quite naturally he felt like he can too because that's his protégé."

After only three seasons—including taking a 3–13 team in 2009 to an impressive 10–6 campaign in 2010—Tampa Bay fired Morris and replaced him with former Rutgers head coach Greg Schiano, who lasted only two seasons before the Bucs went to the wayback machine and welcomed former linebackers coach Lovie Smith . . . only to fire him after two seasons. Smith's replacement, Dirk Koetter, was fired after three seasons.

"Raheem Morris is the best coach I know and ever been around that doesn't have a head coaching job," Tomlin said during his interview on the *Pivot* podcast. "I don't have a problem saying it. I've never had a problem saying it. I've been saying it."

Following a run of twelve consecutive seasons without making the playoffs, Tampa Bay hit the jackpot when Arians won the franchise's second Super Bowl in his second season with the club in 2020 (with the help of future HOF quarterback Tom Brady). Arians resigned the following year after losing in the NFC Championship Game, and handpicked Bowles as his successor. Bowles became the fourth black coach in franchise history.

"I think Lovie was part of Tony," said Williams. "That's one of the reasons why he got the job. Raheem was there already, that made it easier for him. Todd was there because Arians recommended him. You look at it from that standpoint, you've got a couple guys who actually got the job because they were recommended. Not because they sat down for an interview."

7

MINNESOTA'S NEW DC

MINNESOTA VIKINGS
(DEFENSIVE COORDINATOR, 2006)

"Don't get caught in the minutiae."

FOR a few days in January 2006, it was all coming apart for Brad Childress. Four days earlier, Minnesota Vikings owner Zygmunt "Zygi" Wilf introduced Childress as the team's new head coach, just days after deciding not to renew the contract of Mike Tice. An offensive specialist who trained his final six years under Andy Reid with the Philadelphia Eagles, Childress was already plotting his first major hire, who he believed was the best defensive coordinator on the market.

"I'm an offensive guy, [so I had the mindset to] get somebody to take care of the defense and I don't have to worry about it," said Childress. "You hire somebody you know and trust.

I modeled myself after Andy Reid, who brought Jim Johnson in to be his defensive coordinator. [With the hiring of Johnson], he didn't have to worry about the other side of the ball."

Childress had the perfect candidate in mind. Steve Spagnuolo was not only an excellent defensive coach, but Childress knew him personally and was a man he trusted. They had both joined the Eagles' coaching staff in 1999, coming from college programs in the Midwest. Starting with John Wooten, the Eagles popularized the trend among NFL teams in hiring assistant coaches from the collegiate ranks. Childress ran the offense and tutored quarterbacks at Wisconsin; Spagnuolo coached defensive backs at Bowling Green. From there he went over to NFL Europe, where he was the defensive coordinator/linebackers coach for the Frankfurt Galaxy in 1998.

Quite naturally, Spagnuolo was the first person Childress thought of when he accepted the Minnesota job.

"We were close enough to where we used to jog at lunchtime," said Childress. "I'd go out and have a beer with him after work. We were good friends.

"He was more than capable and it would have been a great comfort level for me as well. He had Jim Johnson's fire zone system, which he could teach forward and backward. I wanted to model it the same way as Andy."

Childress made his first call to "Spags," hoping to bring his coaching partner and buddy in to spearhead the Vikings defense.

Many of the coaching hires made in the NFL are based on trust, familiarity, friendship, and, yes, nepotism. According to *USA Today* sports data research, twelve of the thirty-four NFL head coaches (including two interim coaches) during the 2022 season were related by family to current or former coaches in the league. Seventy-six of the ninety-three coaches (81.7 percent) with a father, son, or brother who was a current or former NFL coach were white, compromising nearly one-fifth of the league's white coaches. By comparison, 5.4 percent of coaches of color had family connections.

Having built a relationship of trust and familiarity, Childress made his first call to Spagnuolo. It was also the same mentality applied by Reid when he hired Childress to be his quarterbacks coach in Philadelphia, as the two had coached the offense together at Northern Arizona in 1986.

Childress's choice for offensive coordinator was Darrell Bevell, who was the starting quarterback at Wisconsin from 1992 to 1995 under Childress. Bevell had previously been with the Green Bay Packers from 2002 to 2005, with the previous three years as their quarterbacks coach.

"When you interview for a job, you had to fill in a roster of coaching candidates," said Childress. "I had a listing of potential staff members: 'Here's my offensive line coach. Here's the first defensive coordinator I'd like to hire. Here's who I want as my running back coach, who I want as my offensive coordinator, Darrell Bevell.'

"I'm talking to Spags because I'm buddies with him. Spags is on Andy's staff. He's a linebacker coach. He can't move [up] because Jim Johnson's there; they're not getting rid of Jim Johnson. Back then, if a coach didn't want to let you leave, he didn't have to let you go from a linebacker job to a coordinator job. Andy didn't want to let Spags go.

"I remember Andy calling me after I took the Minnesota job," continued Childress. "He said, 'Hey, Brad. This is Andy. Let me tell you something. I know you talked to Spags. It's wrong. Leave his ass out on this, understand? Bye.'"

Childress quickly met with Wilf, his new boss, and called an audible in his coaching search.

Mike Tomlin was a name that Childress had stored away in the back of his mind. As much as he wanted to hire Spagnuolo to be his defensive coordinator, he also knew how unpredictable the NFL could be. It was no different in his role as offensive coordinator with the Eagles. If the defense took the pass away from quarterback Donovan McNabb, that opened the door for running back Brian Westbrook to have a big game. You had to think one step ahead to survive.

Every head coach needed a backup plan. Childress was no exception. Tomlin was Childress's "break glass in case of emergency" contingency.

Even before getting the Vikings' job, Childress did his due diligence; like, for instance, being aware of other coordinators who were on the fast track to becoming a head coach. That meant scouring the league for potential assistant coaching hires among people he knew, as well as those he *didn't* know. Childress was going places at the end of the season. He needed to be ready for anything thrown in his direction.

"Assistant coaches back then worked on one-year contracts. I was talking to [Tomlin] during the season," said Childress. "You could say that's tampering. Andy [Reid] was a big 'get your work done' guy. There were days that I was sleeping in the office, just like he was down the hallway. You got your scripts done.

"At 10:30 at night, I could call an offensive line coach [from another team]. Or I could call Mike Tomlin and talk to him and debrief him a little bit: 'How do you teach this? What do you think about that?' Just so you could have some back-and-forth conversation before you get way down the road with somebody. There were a lot of those phone calls going on.

"People can say it doesn't happen," continued Childress, known as "Chilly" on the coaching circuit. "But you know what? When you've got to have your ducks in a row with somebody [an owner] that expects you to bring them a list of people you're going to hire . . . that was real."

In 2003, San Francisco 49ers general manager Terry Donahue requested permission to interview Childress, Jim Johnson, and Romeo Crennel, along with 49ers defensive coordinator Jim Mora Jr., for the team's vacant head coaching position. Childress's familiarity with the West Coast offense made him an attractive candidate to the 49ers, who ultimately hired Dennis Erickson.

"I remember interviewing with Donahue. He was scribbling through legal pads so fast," said Childress. "'How much would you pay your assistants? How about your coordinators? How many of your contracts did *you* do?'"

By now, Childress had identified the solution to the problem— his first problem—in his early stages as head coach to one person: Tomlin. He was everything Childress wanted and needed in a defensive coordinator, especially, now, with Spagnuolo off the market.

Childress was slightly familiar with Tomlin, but he didn't *know* Tomlin the way he *knew* Spagnuolo.

Still, Childress couldn't help but be impressed by what he *did* know.

Tomlin came highly recommended. Three years earlier, his Tampa Bay Buccaneers routed the Oakland Raiders in Super Bowl XXXVII. The Bucs intercepted a Super Bowl–record five passes and returned three for touchdowns. During that Super Bowl run, Tampa Bay stifled Childress's offense in the NFC Championship Game. Tomlin was a young, black coach in a league desperate to improve its diversity numbers across the board with the introduction of the Rooney Rule.

Childress pressed Wilf to make his private plane available—immediately—so he could fly to Tampa as soon as possible in an attempt to convince Tomlin to return with him to Minneapolis. Childress knew that Tomlin, who had already interviewed with the Miami Dolphins for their defensive coordinator vacancy, was a hot property at the end of his contract—the ideal coaching free agent.

"I tell Zygi, 'Look, I need to go down there and get Mike Tomlin. I'm going to get him and his wife. I'm going to bring him up here, and I'm planning on hiring him as my defensive coordinator.'"

During the interview process, Tomlin presented his case to Childress.

"Just a great communicator and a great teacher," said Childress. "I wanted that Tampa 2 style he coached. [Former Bucs linebackers coach] Lovie Smith had taken it to St. Louis, and they got better on defense. [Rams head coach] Mike Martz was scoring a lot of points. I could identify that and knew what I was looking for. It was more Tampa Bay's system than anything else. Tampa Bay had a lot of good players, they were well coached, and it was damned tough to move the football against them."

Childress recalled from personal experience just how good Tampa Bay was on defense. The Bucs played Philadelphia five times between 2001 and 2003, when Childress was the offensive coordinator and Tomlin coached Tampa Bay's secondary.

The Eagles won three of the matchups, but their high-octane offense averaged only 15.6 points per game.[1]

"We played Tampa Bay as much as anybody during that time [outside the division]," said Childress.

Even when the teams didn't play each other, Childress couldn't help but notice Tomlin.

"The big thing was I knew him from [the NFL] combines, and attended workouts where he was running the drills," continued Childress. "He was the coach taking the guys through the paces. He was the coach communicating with the players to get them to do what he wanted to see. His background, having coached with Tony Dungy and having coached all the guys that he coached—all the All-Pros on the back end—that's not an easy thing."

The more Tomlin discussed his defensive philosophy and how he would implement his system in Minnesota, the more Childress knew he was perfect for the job.

"Somewhere, you've got to know. There's got to be a connection on some level," said Childress. "Usually, in the first five minutes, you've either got the job or you don't.

"I wanted somebody who could teach that forward, backward, backward, forward. He could talk the talk, whether he was talking to Kevin Williams, Pat Williams, or Jared Allen. It didn't make any difference whether he was talking to the linebackers or all the guys on the back end."

Even when Childress decided he wanted to hire Tomlin, nothing was certain until he looked into the coach's contract status with

---

1 To put into perspective, the Eagles averaged 21.3 (2001), 25.9 (2002), and 23.4 points per game over those three seasons.

Tampa Bay. A few years earlier, when the Buccaneers fired Dungy and Dungy wanted to bring Tomlin along as his new defensive coordinator with the Indianapolis Colts, Tampa Bay's ownership refused to let him out of his contract, even though his job offer from the Colts was a promotion in both title and salary.

"I had to find out what peoples' contract situation was," said Childress. "If Mike was on an off-year contract, that would have been virtually impossible [to hire him] because teams don't like to let good people go. But because they kept going on one-year [deals] . . .

"After I showed [Wilf] who I wanted to hire, he let me run with it. He let me hire everybody I wanted—except a linebacker coach who stayed at the University of Nebraska. Joe Woods was on that staff by Mike's recommendation to coach the secondary [Tomlin and Woods coached together for two years at Tampa Bay]."

Tomlin had the good sense to recommend that Childress hire Karl Dunbar as defensive line coach. Although Tomlin and Dunbar had not previously coached together, Dunbar had tutored defensive tackle Kevin Williams for two years at LSU. Minnesota selected Williams in the first round (ninth overall) of the 2003 draft, and he quickly developed into a Pro Bowl and All-Pro defender. Tomlin's Tampa 2 accentuated Williams's strength as a three-technique tackle.

"You want guys to be comfortable with who is working for them as well," said Childress. "They've got to be comfortable with me. I've got to be comfortable with them. If you've got somebody that can teach what you're looking for, then you've got a chance."

* * *

Childress loved Tomlin's story: Coaching at the lowest levels of college football to become an NFL assistant in only six years. Tomlin didn't play in the NFL and he wasn't related to anyone in the league who could have expedited his journey to the pros. Nepotism was a foreign word to Tomlin. Smart as a whip, he graduated from one of the finest academic institutions in America.

Among black coaches, Tomlin was an anomaly; climbing the ladder rung by rung in similar fashion to many of his white counterparts who never played in the NFL, yet accumulated a wealth of coaching experience—college and pro—before reaching the age of thirty.

Childress had played quarterback and wide receiver at Illinois. He graduated from Eastern Illinois in 1978, and took an assistant coaching job at Illinois right after graduation. Tomlin followed a similar career path, joining the coaching staff at VMI a few months after graduating from William & Mary, where he was a record-setting wide receiver.

Childress caught his big break when Reid hired him in Philadelphia. It was his sixth job in eighteen years.

The Eagles set a team record with 415 points in 2002, despite starting three different quarterbacks. As the quarterbacks coach from 1999 to 2001, Childress was credited with the development of Donovan McNabb, who learned the intricacies of the West Coast offense as a rookie and made the Pro Bowl in five consecutive seasons under the coach, including finishing second for the MVP in 2000.

Following the 2005 season, head coaching job offers began pouring in for Childress, who learned a harsh lesson about NFL hiring practices a few years earlier.

In an attempt to introduce more head coaching candidates from diverse backgrounds to owners, in 1998 the league—four years before the inception of the Rooney Rule—partnered with an independent consulting company, a search firm which helps corporations identify candidates, to videotape interviews of selected assistant coaches recommended by teams, with the potential to become head coaches and coordinators.

Although the league's emphasis was on increasing minority hiring, black and white coaches participated. Former NFL coaches and current college coaches were excluded. Each interview focused on background, experience, and general philosophy. Tapes and accompanying resumes were made available to all thirty-two teams as a way of introducing owners and team executives to names and faces they might otherwise be unfamiliar with. Russell Reynolds Associates conducted the hour-long interviews.

Over the last several years prior to the introduction of the videotape interviews, of the more than two dozen head coaching vacancies, none were filled by African Americans.

According to a *New York Times* article, "To prepare for the pilot project, the NFL spent months speaking to teams about potential candidates and recorded hundreds of names. The league office then whittled down the group to twenty to thirty coaches."

The idea was approved by owners, general managers, and coaches of the league's competition committee, as the Rooney Rule had yet to be created.

Childress attended the first Rooney Rule meeting in 2003, held by the Rooney Rule committee, owners, head coaches, coordinators, and other designated coaches. Childress, who submitted a videotape, interviewed with San Francisco in 2003 but did not receive an offer. He asked one owner attending the meeting if he watched his videotape.

"I was at the first meeting in Philadelphia when the Rooney Rule came out," said Childress. "It was a breakfast with owners and coordinators or whoever the head coach designated. Everybody was talking about why we should tape these interviews if they're just token interviews. A GM stood up and talked about what an interview is like. One owner stood up and said what he was looking for.

"We did videotapes at the combine so that when somebody was looking for a head coach, they could say, 'What do we know about Brad Childress?' The owner typically would go, 'I don't know that name. Who is he?' So, here, let me pop in his tape. They asked you fifteen questions. The questions are so generic: 'Where did you come from? Where did you coach? What do you believe in? How many kids do you have?' You also made sure to dress for the job, recording the video in a shirt and tie.

"I'm at the meeting sitting next to an owner. I finished my eggs, he finished his. This was after he hired his new coach. I asked if he happened to see my videotape that the NFL did.

"'Yes, I did see it.'

"I figure I've got an owner sitting next to me, so I said, 'Well, what did you think? Tell me what I need to work on.'

"'Do you want me to be honest with you?'

"Please.

"'I couldn't get by the mustache.'"

Childress was one of the few NFL coaches wearing a full mustache. The majority of coaches were clean shaven.

"I don't think I had a Fu Manchu or anything like that," said Childress. "I had an Andy Reid mustache. He had one, I had one. I'd worn one since I was nineteen years old.

"I'm thinking to myself, *If this owner can't get by my mustache, how could he ever get by skin color?*

"I'm sitting there thinking, *Holy shit.*"

Several years later, when Wilf interviewed Childress for the Vikings head coaching job, the subject of his mustache never came up (nor did he shave it off).

"Maybe because Zygi had a mustache," Childress said with a laugh. "You're thinking, 'They're accepting me as me. You've seen my picture. You've seen my tape. You've researched my age. Now you've got to meet me.'"

* * *

Childress's phone rang less than twenty-four hours after the Eagles concluded their season, with a 31–20 home loss to Washington.

It was Monday, January 2, 2006. Four days later, Childress's five-year deal with the Vikings was signed, sealed, and delivered.

Eight teams were looking to hire head coaches, and the Vikings wanted to hire Childress before someone else did.

"You always struggle with how fast the season comes to a halt," said Childress. "Everything gets quiet. Nobody's in the building. They're gone until April. I had just finished talking to the last rookie wide receiver. The phone rang and it was Kevin Warren and Rob Brzezinski from the Vikings.

"Zygi was on the phone: 'Coach, we want to talk to you about our job. What's tomorrow look like for you, or the next day? We've got a plane in Philadelphia waiting on you right now.'

"Guys, I just had the last guy walk out of my office here five minutes ago," Childress replied, a bit rattled.

"It was a bittersweet year. It was a year after our Super Bowl year. We didn't make the playoffs after going to four NFC Championship Games in a row.

"As I'm home taking a shower getting ready to fly to Minnesota, I get a call from Charley Casserly with the Texans."

Houston also had a coaching vacancy after firing Dom Capers, the first head coach for the franchise, which joined the league as an expansion team in 2002. Owner Bob McNair wanted to switch to a head coach with an offensive background after having a defensive head coach in charge for the organization's first four years.

The offensive creativity that Childress displayed with the Eagles was just what McNair felt his team was missing—especially when the franchise was expected to select USC running back and Heisman Trophy winner Reggie Bush with the first overall pick in the upcoming draft.

The NFL rumor mill was buzzing about how Childress wouldn't last long before some team made him its new head coach. Casserly, Houston's general manager since the team's inception, didn't mince words.

"'Brad, we want you to come down here and talk about the job.'"

"Charley, I'm headed to the Vikings tonight," Childress replied.

"'That's OK,'" said Casserly. "'We'll get you in here. We're gonna draft Reggie Bush. You just need to be prepared to speak to Mr. McNair about the things you're going to do with Reggie.'"

"Charley, that ain't gonna be hard," said Childress. "We just put [Eagles running back] Brian Westbrook all over the formations here. I'll bring a tape of all the stuff we do with Westbrook. Reggie Bush can do the same thing."

"'Well, good,'" answered Casserly.

"Lo and behold, who do they draft?" said Childress. "[NC State defensive end] Mario Williams. They don't even take Reggie Bush!"

The Texans never got the chance to make good on Casserly's promise. Childress blew the Vikings away during his interview. He didn't waste a lot of time with X's and O's. Primarily, he wowed Wilf—who had purchased the team from Red McCombs the previous year, and other members of the ownership group—by planting images in their mind about how grand things could be in Minneapolis with him as the new head coach. Childress spoke teasingly about leaving a winning organization in Philadelphia and working under a great coach like Reid and what it would take for the Vikings to join that exclusive club.

Childress had dinner with the ownership group Monday night. The next day, he met with legendary Vikings coach Bud Grant. He was asked to stay over for a second interview, which often means that ownership is serious about the candidate (especially with an expected contract in the millions of dollars).

It was Childress's job to read the room. He read it right.

"The whole West Coast offense thing is not only what our offense is, but how you practice, how you ramp up, how you peak at the right time," said Childress. "Whether it's Mike

Shanahan, Mike Holmgren, or Andy Reid, they put a little different spin on it—as Andy had done throughout his career, and he's grown a lot doing it. He wasn't afraid to grow. He looks like a dinosaur, but he's not a dinosaur. He's always taking new thoughts and things that people are doing in college and, if it fits, imitation is the greatest form of flattery. If it works, 'Yeah, I'll try it, that fits us.'

"It's funny how fast you get questions. When they interviewed me [the first day], I got there at 9:30 at night. We were still rolling at two o'clock in the morning. One question leads to another: 'I asked you about that. What about this?' My thing was always a handout, a sheet of philosophies that I had, a list of staff members who I was considering. It shows you put thought into it."

Wilf and Company wouldn't let Childress leave the building until they signed him to a five-year contract. Meanwhile, in Houston, Casserly, after angering Texans fans with the team's controversial selection of Williams over Bush, helped McNair hire Gary Kubiak—the fourth offensive coordinator considered for the job—as Capers's replacement before resigning with one year left on his contract.

* * *

After striking out with Spagnuolo, Childress put a full-court press on Mike and Kiya Tomlin.

Childress signed his contract on Friday and got Tomlin's name on the dotted line the following Tuesday.

"I took a plane down to Tampa. Zygi was good enough to let us use his jet," said Childress. "Brought them back to Minnesota, and we quickly did the deal. Signed a contract. Probably sent them to a relator."

As offensive coordinator, Childress was responsible for one specific side of the ball. He soon discovered that taking on the role of head coach came with an entirely new set of challenges.

In this instance, a painful and personal one.

In a league where there are no secrets, Tomlin's hiring had yet to reach Spagnuolo. He called Childress with a news flash of his own: Reid had relented and gave him permission to speak with Childress about the Vikings gig (that just went to Tomlin).

"'Brad, Andy's gonna let me go,' said Spagnuolo.

"What?

"'Andy's gonna let me go.'

"Spags, listen. I hired Mike."

Silence.

"I know Spags was crushed," said Childress. "I couldn't pick up the phone and call Mike and say, 'I can't hire you. It's Steve.' I went down that road already. This is what I want. This is who I'm going to get. This was my most important hire. I don't even need to think twice.

"It's funny because the year I was out of work [2011], I wanted to go to St. Louis to be the offensive coordinator. Spags was head coach. He hired Josh McDaniels instead of me when Pat Shurmur left."

* * *

When Childress said he was giving Tomlin full autonomy to run the defense the way he saw fit, he meant every word of it. Childress had his hands full installing Reid's offense in Minnesota and developing a rapport with starting quarterback Brad Johnson, who won a Super Bowl with Tomlin in Tampa Bay. For the first time in his coaching career—college or pro—Tomlin was in charge, no questions asked.

"The beautiful thing about the experience for me was the relationship I had with coach Brad Childress," Tomlin said in a ESPN article. "He was a first-time head coach, and he really allowed me behind the curtain and did a great job of really kind of educating me in terms of some of the things that he was having to deal with as a first-time head coach. He even shared some of the responsibilities with me to help him as he was highly involved in the offense."

In Tampa, defensive coordinator Monte Kiffin introduced defenders to something called "loafs." During film study, Kiffin and other coaches would identify players not going full speed by flashing a beam of light on the offending player and play. Tomlin introduced the concept in Minnesota, and in Pittsburgh a year later.

The intended goal of loafs is to motivate defenders into going hard on every play—even when the play doesn't involve them—by putting them on full display in front of the entire team. Sometimes, coaches emphasized, by playing at full speed from whistle to whistle, players could run themselves into plays in which they weren't initially involved. Emphasizing loafs contributed to the Buccaneers' defensive unit being regarded among the fastest in the NFL.

"Not having loafs is an expectation you put on your defense," said Ronde Barber, the Hall of Fame cornerback who said the Buccaneers didn't take the criticism personally. "People used to put on our Bucs film and some coaches would say, 'Y'all speed your film up, don't you?' No, we don't speed our film up. We don't accept loafs."

Tomlin introduced it to the Vikings as "The News." He picked out offending plays and put them on an overhead projector for everyone to see.

Tomlin made it clear that, if a player wasn't up to the standard, he was going to be on the news. He told his players what was coming. They would then hold their collective breath.

"Some of it is lighthearted and some is not," Tomlin said to ESPN in 2007. "It's just things that need to be said and a big part of us moving forward, getting the kind of football team we want. Sometimes it's pats on the back. Sometimes it's corrections."

In his defense, Tomlin always told his players: "I'm just reporting the news."

"That was something new to me," said Childress. "Those are fighting words when you do that in front of a group of men in a defensive setting, all class A individuals. It's disconcerting to those people. But then if they accept it and it becomes successful and they can see it's successful, they go with it."

"In some ways, it sucked," linebacker Ben Leber, who played for Tomlin in 2006, told ESPN in 2017. "But on a positive side, if your name was up on the board and he was correcting you . . . he presented it in such a way where he's laid out expectations and if they aren't met, we're going to make comments about it."

Childress said that pointing out loafs was a difference maker for the Vikings, who became only the second defense in NFL history to allow fewer than 1,000 rushing yards (985) in a

16-game season (behind the 2000 Baltimore Ravens, winners of Super Bowl XXXV, with 970).[2]

"It's a different level watching big, old [defensive tackle] Pat Williams going backside and running the line of scrimmage and smack somebody where something got strung out," said Childress. "[In 2005] we would have seen him step on the backside of the play and watch the ball run around the corner and say, 'I've got no chance to get it.'"

Tomlin never wavered. As was the case in Tampa, the Vikings eventually realized the benefits after seeing positive results.

"Guys would have their heads down," Williams told the *Pittsburgh Post-Gazette*. "But he held everybody accountable. He was smooth and serious. That's why all the guys loved him. He would always tell you the truth about how you were playing."

When a loaf went up on the overhead screen, it didn't matter if it was early in the week or the Wednesday before a big game. Nobody wanted to be accused of loafing. Not working hard. Not doing their part.

"It's empowering as well," said Childress, "particularly when you can get guys to go back and say,' 'Ooh, coach. Run that back. What about this right here? Did that guy get a loaf on this play?'"

Childress loved the psychology behind giving Vikings players loafs. "Is there some sell that goes on? Hell, yeah," he said. "Nobody wants to get light penned and called out. We had signage up there that told you what a loaf was: 'Somebody passing you on the way to the ball. A cut in speed when you think somebody else is going to get there before you.' You're choking your

---

2 The 2010 Steelers are third on this list, with 1,004 rushing yards allowed.

motor down to save five extra grinding steps. You need a blow, come to the sideline. When you're in there, you're one hundred miles-per-hour from this point rushing the passer all the way back to where the tackle's being made."

To help him emphasize certain points to his players, Tomlin's offensive coordinator at William & Mary sent a tape of him going one-on-one against then-teammate Darren Sharper, who was now one of the Vikings' starting safeties and a three-time Pro Bowler.

"When Mike got the job with Minnesota, he had to coach Darren Sharper," Zbig Kepa told the *Pittsburgh Tribune-Review.* "I had in my archives individual one-on-one route tapes. Mike was running routes against Sharper. He used to call him out all the time: 'Sharper, get to the front of the line. I'm up next.' On the tape there's actually a couple shots of Mike going one-on-one against Sharper. I said, 'This is a little bit of credibility when you coach those guys.'"

The Vikings won their first two games of the 2006 season. Tomlin's defense got off to a great start, limiting Washington and Carolina to a total of 29 points (19–16 and 16–13, respectively). The Vikings lost their next two games against Chicago (19–16) and Buffalo (17–12). The defense responded by sparking another two-game winning streak, holding Detroit and Seattle to 15 points per game (26–17 and 31–13, respectively).

At 4–2, the Vikings hosted Tom Brady and the New England Patriots at the Metrodome for *Monday Night Football.* It was a game that could keep the Vikings in legitimate playoff contention around the halfway point, or it could detonate their entire season.

Childress was worried. He expressed his concern to Tomlin, whose unit had yet to allow twenty points in a game.

"I said 'these guys are the best in the business at stealing signs. They have advance scouts,'" said Childress. "There was no coach to linebacker [helmet communication] then where people were radioing it in. You had to signal it in.

"That wasn't illegal. It's kind of like sign stealing in baseball. Andy Reid used to teach [backup quarterbacks] Tim Hasselbeck and Doug Pederson [in Green Bay] when Brett Favre was playing. He'd say, 'Watch the guy who's signaling over there. Tell me if you can tell when it's a zero blitz.'

"I told Mike, 'If you're using a wristband, I want you to use another wristband for the second half. If you're signaling, you need to change it.'

"They tried to run the ball on us the first play of the game," continued Childress. "Then they empty out the backfield. Brady's standing there. We send in a signal. They were good at it. Somebody's talking to their quarterback: 'You're throwing against Cover 2 here.' That's like shooting fish in a barrel. You're telling a quarterback what coverage he's got, he knows where he's going with the ball."

Brady threw the ball 43 times against the Vikings that evening, completing 29 passes for 372 yards with four touchdowns. He was sacked only once in New England's 31–7 victory.

"I remember us talking afterwards," Childress said about his postgame conversation with Tomlin.

"He said, 'Coach, I didn't know.'

"'I tried to tell you.'

It was the first time in Tomlin's new role as defensive coordinator in the NFL that his unit felt like it was overmatched against one of the best teams in the league. Individually, the New England game would serve Tomlin well for future battles against the Patriots. As a team, following their fast getaway, the Vikings won only two more games and missed the playoffs with a 6–10 record.

Childress only had Tomlin for one season. Childress took the Vikings to the playoffs twice and led them to within one game of Super Bowl XLIV. In 2009, with Brett Favre and Adrian Peterson powering Childress's high-octane offense, and with Leslie Frazier in charge of the defense, the Vikings lost to New Orleans in overtime of the NFC Championship Game, 31–28. Childress was dismissed 10 games into the final year of his contract, replaced by Frazier.

"Everybody had respect for Mike," said Childress. "He was leading half the team. There may have been some grumblings as we went 6–10 that maybe this guy should have been the head coach instead of Brad Childress. My wife tells me that got said. Whether it's fact or fiction, I don't know."

8

A BRIEF HISTORY OF
THE ROONEY RULE

"Smile in the face of adversity."

EVERY summer, John Wooten traveled to New Orleans to attend the Essence Fest, an annual music festival that evolved from being a one-time event, celebrating the twenty-fifth anniversary of *Essence* magazine, into the self-described largest African American culture and music event in the country. "New Orleans is an excellent place to vacation," said Wooten. "Good food. Good music. Walking Bourbon Street. It's a great atmosphere."

Another event on the Essence Fest docket caught Wooten's eye: famed civil rights attorney Johnnie Cochran, best known for his defense of O. J. Simpson in what some consider to be the "Trial of the Century," spoke regularly at a panel discussion called "Brother to Brother."

"I knew Johnnie Cochran from the Essence Fest," Wooten said. "Johnnie's a Louisiana guy (from Shreveport). I went there every year for the workshop."

In late September 2002, Wooten watched Cochran and fellow civil rights attorney Cyrus Mehri conduct a fascinating news conference on television.

Due to those Essence Fest workshops, Wooten was familiar with Cochran. He didn't know much about Mehri, however, who served as a co-lead class counsel in some of the largest and most significant race and gender cases in US history, including Roberts v. Texaco, Inc.; Ingram v. the Coca-Cola Co.; Robinson v. Ford Motor Company; and August-Johnson v. Morgan Stanley & Co.

Cochran and Mehri strategically presented their plan to bring more attention to coaching disparities in the NFL along racial lines and facilitate change in those hiring practices as they affected coaches of color.

Wooten was mesmerized by the dialogue.

"I'm sitting there watching TV, and here's Johnnie Cochran and Cyrus Mehri having a press conference in Baltimore," said Wooten. "They're talking about Janet Madden's study ["Black Coaches in the National Football League: Superior Performance, Inferior Opportunities"] showing that minorities weren't getting the opportunities to be head coaches."

Cochran, who in some circles was regarded as the top attorney in America, grabbed the spotlight. His reputation demanded that he push the envelope to precipitate action regarding a dormant and troubling NFL problem.

"We can litigate this. We can bring a lawsuit," said Cochran, issuing a veiled threat to America's most popular professional sports league that both loathed and feared lawsuits. "I think the NFL is reasonable. They understand that this can end up in the courts, and they'd rather not see that happen. But let's see if we can have a dialogue. You only litigate after you've done everything you can to negotiate."

"Black coaches are being held to a higher standard," continued Cochran. "Now is the time for the NFL to stand up and make a change."

Mic drop.

"When that study came out that said minorities were not getting a chance to be head coaches, that's all Johnnie needed," said Wooten. "Even though [the NFL] knew they could probably win in court because they had money and we didn't, the fact that it came from Johnnie Cochran, these people knew there was somebody willing to fight them."

Later, in a private meeting, Wooten said Cochran told Roger Goodell, who was then chief operating officer under commissioner Paul Tagliabue, "Make sure the commissioner understands that if there's any backlash to coaches or people joining the Fritz Pollard Alliance [which promotes diversity in the NFL] to push this forward, being threatened with their jobs, any kind of intimidation, make sure the commissioner knows this will be the biggest lawsuit this country has ever seen."

Wooten loved what he was hearing. Here were nationally known, highly regarded attorneys—operating independently from the NFL—speaking his language. Two powerful men who were unapologetic in their beliefs and unafraid to challenge the system.

"I called Cyrus's office in Washington, DC, and asked to speak with his administrative person," said Wooten. "Lo and behold, they put her on the phone. I said, 'My name is John Wooten. I just saw Cyrus Mehri and Johnnie Cochran speaking at a press conference on TV. Tell Cyrus if they're really committed to what they're talking about, call me because I want them to go with me to the NFL Combine. I want them to speak to minorities and Blacks in this league about how we should put together an organization.'

"Cyrus called me back. Being the lawyer that he is, and Johnnie Cochran being the tough, beat-you-up lawyer that he was, we were able to put this together and push forward."

Two months after the inaugural press conference, NFL owners announced a "comprehensive program to promote diversity that included a commitment to interview one or more candidates for the position" of head coach.

Though often people with similar goals are unable to come to a collective agreement as to their individual vision of an "end goal," this quartet of minds not only achieved said goal, but did so in a manner where egos were set aside for the greater good.

Wooten described the Mehri-Cochran-Wooten-Rooney partnership in biblical terms:

"It was God's way of putting us together," said Wooten.

* * *

Mehri and Cochran were an interesting pairing: one attorney of Iranian descent, the other an iconic African American attorney from the Deep South. They were drawn together by their passion for civil rights and seeking equal justice for all citizens.

Mehri described his relationship with Cochran, who died from a brain tumor in March 2005, as one of mutual and professional respect. Their common ground was the law, but their relationship evolved into something far greater.

"When I did the Coca-Cola [discrimination] case [in 1999], Johnnie got tangentially involved," said Mehri, who co-founded with Cochran the Fritz Pollard Alliance (FPA), which made Wooten the FPA's first chairman. "But what happened was that we became the best of friends. He and I worked on numerous cases. Literally every Monday morning, I could count on Johnnie calling me. We were always doing stuff together. For someone outside of his firm, I was probably one of the two or three lawyers that he felt closest to. I told Johnnie I had this idea to do this report. He's like, 'I'm all in.'"

Cochran was diagnosed with a brain tumor in December 2003—fifteen months after the introduction of the Rooney Rule. He underwent surgery a few months later and was seen less and less in public prior to his death.

Over time, Mehri developed a greater understanding and appreciation for Wooten, a former NFL player, player-agent, scout, and front-office executive. As for Rooney and Wooten, the foundation of their relationship was built on solid ground—more than a half-century of mutual and professional respect.

"John worked three hundred sixty-five days a year fighting for minorities getting a fair shot in the NFL," said Mehri. "He literally watched and critiqued every pro football game. He's scouting everything. He would call minority head coaches and give them feedback. He worked the phones. He was like a minister checking out his flock. He had a window into all thirty-two franchises."

"We didn't have NFL Sunday Ticket then," said Wooten, who will turn eighty-seven in December 2023. "I taped all the games and then I'd go back and look at them so that I could see what's going on in relation to black coaches."

Said Mehri, "I'd talk to John and he'd say, 'Hold on a second, I got Lovie Smith on the line. I told Lovie that his offensive linemen are not talking to each other.' And I'm thinking, 'So, John, you're sitting there in Dallas and you can tell when the offensive line isn't talking to each other? Or not talking to each other? And then tell that to Lovie?' Or I'll be hanging out at John's house and Coach [Mike] Singletary called when he was head coach of the 49ers. He's on the bus back from the game and he'll be like, 'John, give me your critique.' He was the coach of the coaches. And there's still so many things he's doing now in his eighties.

"There are so many people every single year who have a job in the NFL," continued Mehri, "because John picked up the phone and told the decision maker, 'Make this guy A, B, C. Make this guy your defensive coordinator. Make this guy your assistant head coach. Make this guy your wide receiver coach.' He does that all the time. He's the Godfather."

* * *

The Rooney Rule, named for Dan Rooney, is an example of a "soft" affirmative action policy designed to change the composition of the candidate pool, rather than changing the criteria used in the hiring process.

Mehri said the impetus for the Rooney Rule was the firings in 2002 of Tony Dungy and Dennis Green. It was Green's only season with a losing record in his 10 years coaching the Minnesota Vikings. Dungy, who took over the Tampa Bay Buccaneers after the franchise posted 13 consecutive losing seasons, went 6–10 in his first year but turned things around to go 48–32 (.600) over the next five years with four playoff appearances until his surprising dismissal. In a study released later that year, Mehri and Cochran demonstrated that even though black head coaches won a higher percentage of games, they were less likely to be hired and more likely to be fired than their white counterparts.

Representing plaintiffs in Ingram v. the Coca-Cola Co., in which black executives claimed discrimination in promotions, compensation and performance which required negotiating an injunction relief legal process requiring a party to abide by certain rules or parameters, Mehri came across an article from Clifford Alexander, the first black secretary of the Army.

Alexander rejected a list of proposed general officer candidates because there were no black colonel candidates (candidates for general are evaluated by already appointed generals). Alexander's staff looked into any colonels whose records may have been affected by "racial predisposition" by white superiors. The result was a new list of candidates for general which included a candidate left off the original list: Colin Powell, who became the first black secretary of state.

Mehri and Cochran proposed the same concept to the NFL.

"Dan Rooney in October 2002 writes a letter to commissioner Paul Tagliabue that says, 'Hey, this is serious business, but it's not the commissioner's office that has to solve it, it's us the owners," said Mehri. "And then Tagliabue appoints Dan Rooney to chair the Diversity Committee (created in December 2002 to interview one or more minority candidates for the position of "head coach") that had never existed before. On the committee was [NFL owners] Arthur Blank, Stan Kroenke, Pat Bowlen, Jeffrey Lurie. And then there was a work group: Bill Polian, Ray Anderson, Ozzie Newsome. And they met every week in the middle of the season to talk about our proposal."

In the eighty years between Fritz Pollard, the league's first black head coach, and the Rooney Rule's implementation in 2003, there were a total of seven minority head coaches. With the Rooney Rule in place, there were 13 minority head coaches hired from 2003 to 2014.

The first hiring cycle featured Marvin Lewis being selected by the Cincinnati Bengals in 2003 and the Chicago Bears hiring Lovie Smith in 2004. Romeo Crennel was hired by the Cleveland Browns in 2005, and the Pittsburgh Steelers hired Mike Tomlin in 2007. Tomlin is the only remaining head coach from that group.

Entering the 2023 season, there are three black head coaches—Todd Bowles of the Tampa Bay Buccaneers, DeMeco Ryans of the Houston Texans, and Tomlin.[1]

"Mike Tomlin is one of the relatively early breakthroughs," said Mehri, "and probably the face of the success of the Rooney Rule."

Of the most recent hiring cycles involving black head coaches, Mehri asked, "What black coaches would have actually been hired without the Rooney Rule? How about just to get an

---

1 There are a total of six current minority head coaches. Those not listed above include Robert Saleh (Lebanese) of the Jets, Ron Rivera (Puerto Rican and Mexican) of the Commanders, and Mike McDaniel (biracial) of the Dolphins.

interview? If we were back in the old system, where the owners were like, 'I've got my guy, I've got these blinders on,' who would have gotten an interview? The only one I can think of might have been DeMeco Ryans—maybe. So maybe one guy the last three hiring cycles. If you can't get an interview, how do you get hired?

"When everyone trashes the Rooney Rule, I'm like, 'OK, let's go back to the old system.' The old system, they can't even get an interview."

The number of black NFL general managers increased from one in 2019 (Chris Grier of the Miami Dolphins) to the current total of eight, with the addition of Ryan Poles of the Chicago Bears and Kwesi Adofo-Mensah of the Minnesota Vikings in 2022, and Ran Carthon of the Tennessee Titans (who was hired in January 2023). The significant bump over the last four years translates to minority GMs currently representing a quarter of the league's total.

Between 2003 and 2007, the Fritz Pollard Alliance pushed to extend the Rooney Rule to general managers. "We were told they're not enough black general manager candidates," said Mehri. "John kept bringing up all those great lists of candidates and, lo and behold, in 2007 commissioner Roger Goodell extended the Rooney Rule to general managers. And [teams hired] people like Rod Graves (Arizona Cardinals) and Shack Harris (Detroit Lions). Ozzie Newsome only became GM by title after Johnnie Cochran and I put out the report. And I wrote a letter to the league saying, 'What the heck? You don't have any black GMs. Here's a guy who's clearly a superstar in this role. He's functioning as GM but doesn't have the title.' And then they (Baltimore Ravens) bumped him up."

Mehri will debate anyone that the way the Rooney Rule was put together, like a thousand pieces in a jigsaw puzzle, was extremely fortuitous. "This stuff is really hard when you think about it. Look at how fragile this thing was," said Mehri. "If you didn't have John Wooten. If you didn't have Dan Rooney. If you didn't have Johnnie Cochran. None of this stuff would have happened. People didn't know all the stuff we were doing behind the scenes. They didn't know the Fritz Pollard Alliance was doing it on a shoestring budget; no one ever got a dime for what we did. It was all volunteer work. Thousands of hours I put into this, pro bono. But if you don't have these independent people, you don't make any progress. But it shouldn't be that darn hard."

Exploring ways to change the culture, Mehri first needed to understand the thought process of NFL owners. Dan Rooney was invaluable in that regard. "The leadership that Dan provided at that time, as the most influential owner, was a soft form of accountability," said Mehri. "So when Dan goes to Ireland [as United States Ambassador to Ireland from 2009 to 2012] and passes away [in 2017], we lost some of the juice that we had: the most influential owner behind this whole movement. No one's really picked up the mantle."

Not that Rooney was on board with every request. "He didn't always say 'yes' to what I suggested," said Wooten. "There were times he said, 'John, I can't do that. And the reason why is because I'm not comfortable with it. I don't ever want someone to think that I'm pushing them.'"

Said Mehri, "I remember talking to Dan, just him and me, about the hiring process. "What he said that stood out was, 'I don't understand my other owners. They rush to hire a head coach. This is the most important decision we make as owners. They're worried about the public response, winning the press conference. I'm trying to pick the future leader of our club for a long, long time. I need a long time to make that long-term decision. I need to cast the net wide."

That's precisely what Rooney did when he hired Tomlin. The Steelers interviewed two minority candidates before interviewing Tomlin. "The obligation of the Rooney Rule had already been met before they called me. He knew he met the obligations before he picked up the phone to call me," said Tomlin. "That's all you want—an opportunity to present yourself and compete. That, in essence, goes beyond what's on paper."

"That's essentially what we were trying to say with our report," Mehri continued. "Don't just have a laser beam focus on one candidate because that's only going to keep getting you the same white candidates over and over, whether they succeed or not. You wouldn't go into the NFL draft saying we're only going to draft players from the Pac-12. We're going to look at the SEC, we're going to look at the ACC, we're going to look everywhere."

* * *

Wooten and Mehri both agree: the Rooney Rule is constantly evolving. What worked in 2003 no longer works in 2023.

"In 2016, *Harvard Business Journal* came out with a study that says it makes a monumental difference if you have multiple minority candidates versus one," said Mehri. "Not by a difference of five times more likely or ten times more likely to get hired. *One hundred ninety times* more likely to get hired if you go from one to two candidates. In other words, having one black coach in the interview process has no impact about the likelihood of a person of color getting hired. But if you have two, it goes up one hundred ninety times more.

"I went to the league office and said we need to change the Rooney Rule to go from one minority coach to two," continued Mehri. "It took them *four years* to agree to that. But Dan Rooney was already doing that in 2007."

Following the 2022 season, Wooten believed the new policy would result in multiple minority coaching hires. When he was proven wrong, resulting in Ryans being the only black coach hired. Wooten took the slights personally.

"My whole thought this past hiring cycle was that we would get three of the five openings," said Wooten. "I thought Steve Wilks would get the Carolina job. That didn't happen. They hired Jim Caldwell and Duce Staley as assistant coaches.

"There are things that make you almost go crazy. People that you believe in, who you feel are standup people, and when they get behind closed doors. . .

"Where we are [now], as it relates to black coaches, or minority coaches, or coaches of color, it becomes very simple," continued Wooten. "The owners are going to have to take the same procedure of interviewing minority and black coaches as they do the process of bringing players to their team.

"You see the combine. You see the pro days. You see the workouts. You see the game scouting. Practice scouting. They have to take that same thought and openness as it relates to coaches. That's where the league has to go if it's true to the commitment of diversity and inclusion. In other words: 'no more good ol' boy network.'

"The interview process is still the answer. But, then, you've got to be open and real to the point that says, even though you voted 32–0 to do the interview process, you have circumvented it."

Throughout the history of professional sports, the narrative of questioning if blacks could actually coach has been a long-standing "debate." One specific example is that of Hall of Fame basketball player and coach, Lenny Wilkens, as noted in David Halberstam's iconic book, *The Breaks of the Game* (published in 1981).

"Wilkens was one of the pioneer blacks in professional basketball, a man who spanned several generations in terms of the sport's racial history. All his life he had contested the racial stereotypes of American life. One of the main reasons he had decided to coach was to show, by his own personal example and conduct, the difference between stereotype and reality, what a black was and what he could do."

As a player-coach for three seasons with the Seattle SuperSonics, Wilkens took the helm of the Portland Trail Blazers for the 1974–75 season. Even with his immense success, Wilkens's struggles to break the stereotype of black athletes not having the "skills" to coach were still at the forefront and mindset of the powers-that-be.

"In basketball another version of the myth survived. Could blacks coach? Could they handle players, including black players? They could, everyone now admitted, play with intelligence, but wasn't that really a natural gift? Didn't that instinct just come to them? Could they really sit down like a white coach and draw on a blackboard the X's and O's that defined the analytical game and distinguished it from the free-flow game that was native to the black?"

(Continued on next page)

After only two seasons with Portland, Wilkens was fired, furthering the perception and continued hesitancy of owners hiring African Americans to coach their teams.

"It was in that particular context, and Lenny Wilkens's own career-long personal campaign against stereotyping, that his firing in Portland had to be weighed. He was an early black coach, in a profession which had become black at the bottom but remained white in its hierarchy. By being fired he had been told that something larger had failed. He had deeply resented it."

Wilkens was inducted into the National Basketball Hall of Fame twice—as a player in 1989 and as a coach in 1998. He is third all-time in wins, with 1332.

* * *

To get the full scope of Wooten's six decades of influence in the NFL, you must first understand that he was respected in league circles long before the Rooney Rule existed. You could argue that there wouldn't be a Rooney Rule without Wooten, though there certainly wouldn't have been a Dallas Cowboys dynasty during the 1990s if not for Wooten's underrated contributions as a player personnel whiz. His influence is everywhere.

Wooten learned the league from the ground up. A fifth-round draft pick out of Colorado, the offensive lineman was taken by the Cleveland Browns in 1959. As a rookie, he played in all 12 regular season games. He replaced future Pittsburgh Steelers head coach Chuck Noll at messenger guard and would go on to open holes for running backs Jim Brown and Leroy Kelly. Wooten was a member of the last Cleveland team to win an NFL championship, when the Browns defeated Baltimore 27–0 to capture the 1964 title.

Wooten translated his people skills and sharp mind into becoming a player agent in 1973. While it's commonplace in 2023 to see Nicole Lynn negotiate a $255 million contract for quarterback Jalen Hurts, it was almost unheard of for a black agent to make a living during Wooten's era. And for a black agent during that time to represent black players, he had to be the luckiest person in the world. Well, in 1973—fifty years earlier—Wooten must have had a pocket full of four-leaf clovers and horseshoes when he signed not one, not two, not three, not four, not five, not six, but *seven* first-round draft picks— all of them black: Wally Chambers (eighth overall, Chicago Bears), Otis Armstrong (ninth overall, Denver Broncos), Chuck Foreman (12th overall, Minnesota Vikings), Burgess Owens (13th overall, New York Jets), Ernie Price (17th overall, Detroit Lions) Darryl Stingley (19th overall, New England Patriots), and Billy Joe Dupree (20th overall, Dallas Cowboys).

In representing the Dallas Cowboys' top pick DuPree and signing future Hall of Famer Drew Pearson to a free-agent contract with the team in '73, Wooten believes his actions convinced president and general manager Tex Schramm, as well as vice president of player personnel Gil Brandt, that a black man could evaluate player talent and negotiate contracts . . . not just play football.

"That's where Gil Brandt and Tex Schramm were probably ahead of the times," said Wooten. "Gil saw my ability to evaluate players as a [former] player, No. 1. But I also knew how to do contracts. That opened his eyes. I think he went to Tex and said,

'We're talking about bringing in black guys to work and scout, let's bring in this guy.'

"When Tex called me, I said, 'I'm not interested in coaching.'

"Tex told me, 'When you come down here, you can sit in any meeting. Anything that's going on here, you can listen in, take notes, ask questions. Every door in this office will be open to you. We will teach you how to run a football team.'"

"And that's what they did," said Wooten, who became the Cowboys' director of professional scouting in 1975. "I had the draft picks through the second round. Gil did the first round."

Wooten said his big break occurred when he assisted in the signing of star defensive lineman Jethro Pugh.

"They were having trouble getting him signed," said Wooten, "so they told me to see what I could do.

"Me and Jethro got along great. I asked him, 'What do you really want?' He told me how far apart they were and what he wanted. I told him I just bought my seven-year old son a scholarship fund so that when he's ready for college, it will already be paid for. I said, 'We're apart approximately the same amount of money as that fund. If the Cowboys were willing to buy your son that same fund, how would you feel?'

"I went back to Tex and Gil and said, 'Here's what I'm proposing.' They bought it," said Wooten. "We got the deal done."

In Dallas, Wooten worked to make higher level coaching and staffing opportunities more accessible and equitable for African Americans. He introduced what could be considered the "unofficial" Rooney Rule decades before its origin when he pushed the Cowboys to hire Al Lavan as the franchise's first black assistant coach in 1980. "When Dan Reeves left to go to Denver, Al Lavan became our running backs coach," said Wooten.

Wooten adopted Schramm's philosophy about what to look for when hiring college assistants for the NFL, which is how he became aware of Lavan, then an assistant at Stanford. When Wooten joined the Philadelphia Eagles as vice president of player personnel a decade later, he continued the trend.

"Tex Schramm told us when you're at a school looking at a player, watch the coaches—who's teaching them the right technique?" said Wooten. "You'll see the coaches we brought from college and put with Ray Rhodes in Philadelphia: Sean Payton, Bill Callahan, Juan Castillo. We brought Mike Trgovac from San Francisco. Ray had been at San Francisco with those two kids they drafted from Notre Dame [Bryant Young and Anthony Peterson]. He coached them at San Francisco and loved their technique. He said, 'Who's the defensive line coach at Notre Dame?' We went out and got Trgovac.

"I brought Sean [Payton] in this league (in 1997). Sean was on Ray Rhodes's staff. I brought him in because Al Davis was courting Jon Gruden. Ray brought Jon Gruden with him from Green Bay as an offensive coordinator.

"Knowing that Al Davis was recruiting Gruden, we knew we were going to lose him eventually. I told Gruden the only way we'd let him go to the Raiders is as a head coach. That's why we got Sean Payton, who had been at Miami of Ohio and San Diego State, and brought him to Philadelphia."

* * *

Lesser known is Wooten's reputation as a dealmaker. His run of draft picks and trades with the Cowboys, from 1989 to 1991, is as good as there's ever been in the NFL.

In the spring of 1989, Arkansas businessman Jerry Jones purchased the Cowboys and hired University of Miami coach and former University of Arkansas teammate Jimmy Johnson to replace coaching icon Tom Landry. Jones cleaned house, firing Brandt, the last original member of the staff that created the team and led the franchise to 20 consecutive winning seasons. Schramm also departed when the new regime took over. Bob Ackles, hired by Schramm to handle some of Brandt's scouting and drafting responsibilities, was retained by Jones, along with Wooten.

"[Jones] didn't have a choice,'" said Wooten. "He had nobody there. Tex was gone. Gil was gone. Coach Landry was gone. Jimmy and those guys are in. He had nobody there that knew how to run the club from the personnel [side]."

When Jones became owner, "They gave me the authority to make trades," said Wooten. "He kept me on until I got his club back up on their feet again. Then he threw me out just like the others."

Empowered by ownership to initiate trades, Wooten approached the 1989 campaign full of ideas about upgrading personnel and bettering the Cowboys' 3–13 record from the previous season. Dangling running back Herschel Walker, the team's most marketable commodity as bait, Wooten set the stage for what is regarded as the biggest trade in NFL history: nine draft picks (three first-round picks, three second-round picks, and three third-round picks) for Walker.

One day, on a hunch, "I called the Minnesota Vikings," said Wooten. "I was trying to see if they were interested in trading a kid named [David] Howard, a linebacker from Long Beach State, to us. Frank Gilliam and Jerry Reichow were the Vikings' personnel guys. While I was talking to them, Mike Lynn, their general manager, comes in the room. I could hear him saying, 'Who are you talking to?' And they said, 'John Wooten from the Cowboys.'

"Mike Lynn immediately takes the phone and says, 'What do you want for Herschel?'

"I said, 'Mike, those guys [Jones and Johnson] just got here. I really don't know them. If you're not serious, let's not get involved.'

"Mike Lynn asks me, 'What do you want for Herschel?' Of course, I'm going to tell him exactly what I want. I want three ones, three twos, and three threes. And put down what you propose to offset that.

"I told him, 'If you're serious, have whoever is working there fax your trade proposal to Jimmy's secretary, Marge Anderson. I'll let you set the proposal as long it has three ones, three twos, and three threes.'"

Wooten relayed the proposed trade details to Johnson.

I knew Jimmy when he was with Johnny Majors at Pittsburgh," said Wooten. "Consequently, when he came to Dallas in '89, we had a great relationship."

Dallas converted the draft picks into key starters for their three Super Bowl championship teams: NFL all-time rushing leader Emmitt Smith; defensive tackle Russell Maryland; Pro Bowl offensive tackle Erik Williams, and Pro Bowl safety Darren Woodson.

Dallas finished 1–15 in Jones's first year as owner, but the Cowboys now had Minnesota's 21st pick in the 1990 draft, courtesy of the Walker trade.

They targeted Smith to pair in the backfield with quarterback Troy Aikman, the number one overall draft pick in '89.

"Give Walt Yaworsky credit for us drafting Emmitt. He told me when Emmitt was a sophomore at Florida that he was the guy we want," said Wooten. "'I've got our guy, Woots,' he told me. 'When he gets ready to come out, that's who we're gonna get.'"

"Walt was the best scout that I've ever known. He played high school football in Cleveland. He knew me from my time with the Browns. He was a Cleveland guy and because of his love for the Browns as a kid growing up on the West Side, we had a great relationship."

To get Smith, the Cowboys needed to move up in the draft. Wooten leaned heavily on his relationship with Dan Rooney and the Steelers to pull off his second major trade in less than a year.

Pittsburgh had the 17th overall selection. The Steelers, who drafted running back Tim Worley a year earlier, targeted Liberty tight end Eric Green.

Based on his history with the Steelers, Wooten believed that director of football operations Tom Donohoe would agree to his proposal: that the teams exchange their first-round picks. The Cowboys would sweeten the pot by adding a third-round pick.

"I knew Donohoe," said Wooten. "The fact that I hung out with the Steelers scouts on the East Coast . . . those guys knew me. I'm working the area they're working. We hung out together. It got to the point where you ask, 'Where are you going next week? I'll be at such-and-such. Where are you staying? See you there.' Same hotels and everything. That was my relationship with them.

"When I told Donohoe I had the Steelers taking Eric Green and he could get Green with our pick at twenty-one, that was intriguing to him. He went to Chuck Noll and Chuck agreed with the deal. But Chuck wanted to wait until we got on the clock, which was almost two weeks away. The deal hadn't gone through to New York, so you really don't have a deal.

"They could have hung me out to dry," continued Wooten. "That's why I didn't say anything to Jimmy or anybody about it because that's the way Chuck wanted it."

In the meantime, Atlanta Falcons general manager Ken Herock reached out to Wooten about a potential trade. Herock offered Atlanta's 19th pick and a second-round selection for the Cowboys' 21st pick after already making the same offer to Pittsburgh.

"Ken Herock talked to Donohoe and Donohoe told him he had a deal with me," said Wooten. "Herock says to me, 'I'll give you the same deal if you let me move up to 17. I'll give you a two. That will put you at 19.' I told him we're sitting on the same guy. I'm not going to make that deal. I'm going to stay at 17.

"If Pittsburgh had come back and said, 'Atlanta's offering us a two, will you give us a two or I have to take the Atlanta deal,'" said Wooten, "they had every right because all we had was a handshake. That's trust."

On the day of the draft, Wooten finally got the go-ahead from Donohoe.

"He called me and said, 'Chuck's ready to talk,'" said Wooten.

"I said, 'Let Chuck talk to Jimmy.' I hand the phone to Jimmy and tell him, 'Jimmy, this is Chuck Noll. We've got a deal.'

"It went down just that way," said Wooten.

Smith finished his career as the NFL's career rushing leader with 18,355 yards and a league-record 164 rushing touchdowns. He's the only running back to win a Super Bowl, NFL MVP, league rushing title, and Super Bowl MVP—all in the same season.

"I told Emmitt we knew he wasn't going to go high in the first round, as good of a player as he was, because he wasn't Tony Dorsett with 4.4 speed," said Wooten. "But we knew he could play. Therefore, we felt if we could get to 17 we had a great chance to get him. He wouldn't have made it to 21 because Ken Herock would have taken him at 19."

Drafting Smith to carry the football was the next step in the Cowboys' offensive transformation, with Aikman and wide receiver Michael Irvin—the team's first-round pick in 1988—already in place. Smith, though, no matter how talented, couldn't do it by himself—nor could Aikman and Irvin. The soon-to-be-named "Triplets" required a strong foundation to operate from; namely, a good, dependable offensive line. Thanks to Wooten, there were already two players in place who would become key pieces to arguably the greatest offensive line in NFL history: Nate Newton and Mark Stepnoski.

Five years before drafting Smith and three years before Jones purchased the team from Bum Bright, Wooten had a hand in the Cowboys signing Newton, who attended Florida A&M, was cut by Washington in his first shot at the NFL, and played two years in the USFL before joining the Cowboys. Teams weren't lining up to sign Newton, who struggled with weight issues throughout his pro career. Newton became a starter at left guard one year after joining the team, and made six Pro Bowls during the 1990s.

In 1989, one month after Jones purchased the team, the Cowboys drafted Stepnoski from the University of Pittsburgh in the third round. Wooten came away impressed after observing Stepnoski during scouting trips to his designated area in the northeast. A *Parade* All-American, Stepnoski was a four-year starter at Pitt and a finalist for the Outland Trophy who blocked for future NFL runners Craig "Ironhead" Heyward and Curvin Richards, the latter whom the Cowboys selected in the fourth round of the 1991 draft.

Stepnoski played guard in college, but the Cowboys moved him to center, where he started 162 games, made five Pro Bowl appearances, and was a two-time All-Pro.

"When I was scouting that area, we just thought that he was a tough guy, great leadership," said Wooten. "We pushed hard for him in the draft to take this kind of a guy. Smart as all heck."

Stepnoski fell in the draft because he was considered undersized at 6-foot-2, 270 pounds. "Good centers are hard to come by," said Wooten. "Guys that can handle three hundred pounders by themselves in pass protection and really be able to what we call reach block or choke block if you block them for a trap or reach them if you're running on the side. If you run a play to the right, if you've got a center that can reach that two or three man gap guy and be able to cut him out of the play, that allows your guard to go to the linebacker."

Wooten located a third offensive line starter from a mostly overlooked talent source: historically black colleges and universities (HBCUs).

Wooten discovered that players from HBCU programs were good value picks. Often selected in the lower rounds of the draft, it was easier for teams to look the other way when those players failed to make it in the league. However, HBCU players that did make it were more than worth the gamble, and their successes encouraged teams to continue to dig in search of other gems from similar programs.

Offensive tackle Erik Williams from Central State, a land grant university in Wilberforce, Ohio, was one of those uncut gems who Wooten saw play for the first time in 1989.

To hear Wooten tell it, "I first saw Erik Williams against Tennessee State. I went to that game to see Anthony Pleasant."

A third-round draft pick of the Cleveland Browns in 1990, Pleasant played 14 seasons in the NFL and recorded 58 career sacks. The Tennessee State-Central State game was played at Cleveland Municipal Stadium during Pleasant's final college season, one year before Williams entered the draft.

After watching Williams dominate the line of scrimmage, Wooten all but forget he was there to scout Pleasant (who was an excellent player starring for an HBCU).

"Erik Williams just totally demolished him," said Wooten. "Knocked him up, knocked him down, jumped on him. That's the way Erik Williams played. He did them all like that when he got to the NFL, including Reggie White.

"I didn't know it at the time, but he boxed in Philadelphia where he grew up and he had that boxer mentality. You could see that he had some boxer in him."

Williams's development was nurtured by Central State head coach Billy Joe, who was the American Football League (AFL) Rookie of the Year with the Buffalo Bills in 1963. The first African American coach in the Atlantic Coast Conference as a Maryland assistant in 1971, Joe led Central State to five consecutive NAIA national championships, from 1986 to 1990. Central

State advanced to the NAIA semifinals in 1991 and won the national title in '92. Joe's 245 career wins rank second all-time to Grambling's Eddie Robinson among coaches at HBCUs.

Central State won 41 of 47 games with Williams in the starting lineup.

"Give Billy Joe credit for recruiting Erik Williams," said Wooten. "Me knowing Billy, we've got a relationship. Like most HBCUs, you get to the game and you may not find who you're looking for. There's no programs and jersey numbers could be anything.

I asked Billy after the game, 'Who's this kid?'

"'Erik Williams, he's a Philadelphia kid.'

"'Don't tell anybody about him. I'll be back.'"

"That's exactly what I said to him," said Wooten, who credited Joe with switching Williams to right tackle after he recruited him as a defensive lineman out of high school. "The guy was knocking people down. It was almost like a fist fight. He'd grab them and throw them down. When you saw him play for the Cowboys, that's the way he played in college."

When the third round of the 1991 draft rolled around, the Cowboys selected Florida linebacker Godfrey Myles and California guard James Richards with their first two selections in the round.

"Jimmy wanted to draft guys he knew because he wasn't that far removed from college, picking up guys he played against," said Wooten. "One of the guys he took in the third round was a defensive end from Florida [Myles]. When he did that, that's when I stood up in the draft room. I knew this guy wasn't better than Erik Williams. That's when I made my speech. I said, 'Jimmy, it's time for us to take Erik Williams.'

"'Well, John. These small black colleges don't play anybody.'

"'Jimmy, he can play in this league. If we don't take him, get ready to play against him on the Raiders.'

"Every game I saw Erik Williams play, the Raiders had a scout there," said Wooten. "He was from Philadelphia. I knew he was sitting on Erik Williams just like I was, but he didn't have three third-round draft picks. ' We took Erik Williams with our third third-round pick."

In Williams's rookie season, he backed up Newton and Mark Tuinei at right and left tackle. He made his first NFL start that year when Tuinei was injured. After giving up three first-half sacks to Ken Harvey of the Arizona Cardinals, Johnson switched Williams from left tackle to right tackle. During training camp the following season, Williams's dominant play pushed Newton back to his natural position at guard, which made Williams the permanent starter at right tackle.

In 1992, Williams was named NFC Offensive Player of the Week for his play against White, the Philadelphia Eagles All-Pro defensive end, in the Cowboys' 20–10 win. Williams held White without a sack. It was the only time that a Dallas offensive lineman had received the award.

In Dallas' NFC divisional playoff matchup against Philadelphia that year, Williams again dominated White to the point that in their thirty-two head-to-head matchups, White never touched the ballcarrier. The Cowboys won, 34–10, going on to capture their first of back-to-back Super Bowl championships fueled by the NFL's best running game two years in a row. Williams was named to his first Pro Bowl in 1993.

He was limited to seven games in 1994 season after a near-fatal car accident resulted in a damaged right knee, broken rib, torn ligaments in his left thumb and facial lacerations that required plastic surgery. With Williams sidelined, the Cowboys moved guard Larry Allen to fill Williams's right tackle spot. The offensive line struggled in his absence, yielding four sacks. Dallas rushed for only 99 yards in a 38–28 loss to the San Francisco 49ers in the NFC Championship Game.

Williams returned to the lineup in 1995. Although clearly not the same player after the accident, he was named to three more Pro Bowls and helped the Cowboys win another Super Bowl. Following a 10-year career in Dallas, Williams played one year with the Baltimore Ravens and retired after the 2001 season.

"If Erik Williams doesn't have that car accident, he's in the Hall of Fame five years after he retires," Irvin said about his former teammate during an NFL Network feature honoring the Cowboys' offensive line during the Super Bowl years. "He was the greatest lineman I'd ever seen when he was healthy."

Following the 1991 season in which he was the motivating force behind two of the most impactful trades in NFL history and also credited with scouting and recommending the Cowboys draft one of the league's all-time great offensive linemen, Wooten departed Dallas after seventeen years to accept a front-office position with the division rival Philadelphia Eagles as vice president of player personnel.

"They fired me on Mother's Day," said Wooten. "Jerry said they were going in another direction."

Gaining the trust and support of owner Jeffrey Lurie, Wooten convinced Lurie in 1975 to hire Ray Rhodes as the fourth African American coach in NFL history (behind Fritz Pollard, Art Shell, and Dennis Green).

Lurie said the job was offered to only two people—Dick Vermeil, who led the Eagles to their first Super Bowl appearance in 1981; and Rhodes, who also interviewed for the Rams' head coaching job.

"I told Jeff Lurie when he fired Richie Kotite—they were putting together their list of candidates—I don't have but one guy: Ray Rhodes. If it's not Ray Rhodes, I don't need to be in this meeting," said Wooten. "He hired Ray Rhodes strictly because of me."

"How many guys have the guts to tell an owner that?" said Mehri. "John didn't care. He was fearless."

* * *

Almost three decades later, Wooten tells the story of former NFL head coach and longtime defensive coordinator Leslie Frazier's plans to sit out the 2023 season with the Buffalo Bills. Frazier's reasoning made it clear that little has changed for aspiring black head coaches.

Frazier didn't interview for any of the five openings following the 2022 season. His story is one of frustration and helplessness.

The official word from the Bills is that Frazier intends to sit out the 2023 season. He plans to return to coaching in 2024.

"His heart was broken," said Wooten. "You work as hard as this man works because he wants to be a head coach again."

I asked Wooten if he wanted me to write about Frazier's situation on such a personal level and he responded, yes, it's a story that needs to be told.

Frazier replaced Brad Childress, who was let go by the Minnesota Vikings with six games left in the 2010 season. Childress hired Frazier as defensive coordinator in 2007, when Mike Tomlin left to become head coach of the Pittsburgh Steelers. Frazier went 21–32–1 in three and a half seasons, with quarterback Christian Ponder throwing 38 touchdown passes and 34 interceptions.

"I called Leslie and said, 'Physically, are you OK? Did something happen?'" said Wooten. "He said, 'No. My health and everything is fine. I just need to take a break.'

"That's what this stuff will do to you," said Wooten. "When you look at guys that you know you have done a better job than these guys, and they're getting and you don't. That's what hurts the most. He didn't get one single interview.

"The head coaching aspect is at a critical point in this league. When a coach with the ability, heart, and mind of a Leslie Frazier . . . when he takes a leave of absence, that's hurtful. When you see that, what are you going to do? Are you going to turn your back and say, 'That's life?' Change the system and let the world know that we've changed it."

Wooten emphasized the importance of the interview process. Not only to provide black candidates with the opportunity to introduce themselves to white billionaire owners who, in many instances, don't know much about them, but to also open the lines of communication.

"The interview process allows you, the individual, to sit down and tell them directly what you bring to their club that is going to make them a winning football team. That's what the process is all about," said Wooten. "That's why the interview process

is so important because you're not only in front of the owners and general managers and people who make the decision,
you're showing them where you see this team going. No other
way can you do that other than the interview process. It is *the*
opening, the opportunity, for you to tell them how you would
run their ballclub. That's so key to what we're doing because if
you're not prepared to do that, they're going to say you didn't
interview well."

Frazier obtained permission from Buffalo to observe spring
practices with Green Bay, Washington, and the New York
Giants. Frazier interviewed with the Giants before they hired
Brian Daboll in 2022.

"He's visiting with teams because we want teams looking
at him," said Wooten. "You can't just go somewhere and lay
down; they'll forget about you. He has the right to visit teams.
I just don't want him to lose who he is by disappearing. You're
going to have four or five [head coaching] jobs [available]
next year. If you disappear, you're going to be lost. That's what
I told him. Take advantage of going to various teams. Looking
at them and observing them. That was my recommendation."

* * *

Cyrus Mehri was grocery shopping with his two-and-a-half-
year-old daughter when his phone rang. "I had my daughter in
the shopping cart. I'm buying vegetables.

"John calls me: 'Cyrus, we have just won.'

"'What happened?'

"'Dan Rooney is the chair of the diversity committee and you
can't get someone better than that.'

"There was a longstanding respect between John and Dan, but mostly from afar," said Mehri. "But then, when Dan got selected as the chair of the diversity committee . . . Imagine if there was a ledge where you could watch all thirty-two clubs in action, both on the field and off the field. John's like an old warrior looking down. He'd call up Dan Rooney and say, 'This isn't right what's happening over here. We've got to fix it.' Dan would be like, 'Well, let's call the owner.' Or John would say, 'There are two finalists. One is a minority head coach.' He'd say to Dan, 'They're saying this and this about the minority coach.' Dan would be like, 'OK, let me call the owner and talk it through.'

"A lot of the hires happened when we went from one to two to three to five to eight minority head coaches because these two guys were on the phone, strategizing, figuring it out," continued Mehri. "What I'm saying is there's no owner doing that now."

Lurie is one possibility, considering his liberal views on social justice issues. Lurie was extremely vocal about the police killing of George Floyd, describing himself as "heartbroken and repulsed" by injustices suffered by African Americans. "There are no words strong enough to describe the horrific deaths and injustices that the black community continues to endure," Lurie said in a statement issued by the Eagles. Lurie added that having the empathy to relate to the struggles of people from different races and ethnic groups "is what makes us fully human."

"Jeffrey Lurie absolutely believes in these causes. Not just in football, but in society," said longtime NFL journalist and author Michael Silver. "[But] there's another level that the Rooneys went to. It'd be one thing if Dan just got the Rooney Rule through. What makes Dan Rooney, Dan Rooney, he didn't just believe it, he was willing to put his self-interests maybe not aside, but not the only thing."

Wooten remains stubbornly optimistic. He believes history will repeat itself because he saw it happen once before with Rooney, a white man who grew up in conservative Western Pennsylvania.

"I want what we had with Dan Rooney," said Wooten. "We just had that kind of knowing relationship. I want somebody to stand up and say we're going to be the moral compass of what the league is supposed to be.

"This is what we lost," continued Wooten. "And we never regained it. I remember getting on the plane with him and he said we need to put general managers in there. We need to put directors in there. He did all of that. He was in charge as chairman of the diversity and inclusion committee. He accepted that because the owners trusted him and believed in him."

* * *

Dan Rooney was a different breed of NFL owner. His ability to relate to anyone—regardless of their race—helps explain what separated him from many of his peers, who rarely ventured outside of their comfort zone. Those stark differences became apparent in how some owners approached the interview process with candidates from differing backgrounds.

Rooney ate his lunch in the team cafeteria. He was rich, but an approachable owner who didn't consider himself too important to make small talk with the workers who prepared his food. He was secure enough within himself to drive a comfortable sedan instead of a fancy luxury vehicle. He was a licensed pilot who owned a single-engine plane and would often fly to Steelers practices during training camp.

As a pilot, Rooney "was always very careful and very well prepared," former Steelers director of communications Joe Gordon told the *Tribune-Review* in 2002.

A year after his death, Duquesne University honored Rooney with a day-long symposium: "Slainte! Celebrating The Life and Legacy of Dan Rooney." The symposium featured panel discussions of Rooney's impact on Pittsburgh, Ireland, the Catholic Church, and the NFL.

Tomlin was one of the keynote speakers. He related a story about Rooney and his wife, Patricia, taking Tomlin and his wife, Kiya, to dinner after Tomlin's news conference introducing him as the Steelers' new head coach.

"He told me he would pick me up at the hotel at 6:30," said Tomlin. "I didn't know if I heard him right, an owner coming to pick me up for dinner. At 6:30, we're there in the lobby, and he and Mrs. Rooney are there to pick us up. Outside, there is a red, two-door sedan. It was his car. That's what we were riding in. It was a two-door. I was going to get in the back, but Mrs. Rooney said, 'The ladies will get in the back.'"

Rooney's world changed forever in 1962 when a Roman Catholic priest named Mark Glasgow was assigned to Rooney's church. In his 2019 book about his father, *A Different Way to Win*, Jim Rooney said Glasgow often spoke about civil rights.

> Dan, now in his early 30s, was already involved in the Urban League and the NAACP chapters in Pittsburgh. But Father Glasgow's homilies and private conversations persuaded him that he could be doing more. In 1965,

after civil rights workers and advocates were beaten and, in several cases, murdered, he and a couple other priests went to Selma (site of a series of three marches that took place in 1965 from Selma to Montgomery, Ala.). Father Glasgow invited Dan to join. In a decision that my father would regularly refer to as the biggest mistake of his life, he did not go.

Dan Rooney followed the cue of his father, Art Rooney Sr., often referred to as "the Chief," who purchased the Pittsburgh Professional Football Club in 1933 (later known as the Steelers).

Art Rooney Sr. was a relationship builder who crossed racial lines and connected with prominent black businessmen in Pittsburgh, such as Gus Greenlee and Cumberland Posey.

"Posey was Art's mentor at Holy Ghost Academy (founded as a junior seminary in 1897) where Posey was playing ball while Art was a high school student," said University of Pittsburgh professor, author, and historian Rob Ruck. "Art modeled his game as a leadoff hitter and center fielder after him. Art learned a lot about promoting sport from Posey."

In later years, Rooney provided money to Posey to start training for his Homestead Grays baseball team to make a profit. In 1931, the Grays fielded arguably the best Negro League baseball team in history. The team consisted of National Baseball Hall of Fame players Oscar Charleston, Satchel Paige, and Josh Gibson. Rather than commit to the league, Posey believed he and his team could generate more revenue playing teams on the road, consisting of white professional players instead of playing in organized leagues.

No stranger to Pittsburgh's black community, Rooney frequented Greenlee's Crawford Grill, home to jazz legends Duke Ellington, Louis Armstrong, and Miles Davis, who often performed there.

Rooney encouraged Greenlee to purchase the Pittsburgh Crawfords baseball team. Greenlee created the East-West All-Star game held in Chicago's Comiskey Park, which became the centerpiece of the new Negro Leagues. In return, Greenlee allowed Rooney's football team to play exhibition games at Greenlee's own Greenlee Field, which cost $100,000 to build and was one of the first black-built, black-owned baseball fields in the US.

"Art was close to the black community," said Ruck. "When the North Side changed, he never left. During the riots following the assassination of [Dr. Martin Luther] King [in 1968], he walked around the neighborhood. Reverend Jack O'Malley [considered a champion of civil rights who referred to so-called acts of disobedience as "divine intervention"], a radical priest in the neighborhood, said nobody would touch [Rooney]. Everybody respected and appreciated him. Dan grew up in that world.

"Art and Dan are probably as progressive a couple of white guys as you're going to find in that day and age," continued Ruck. "Dan Rooney and Art Rooney were both Republicans. But that was when the Republican Party was often to the left of the Democrats."

Therefore, it was not surprising that Dan Rooney viewed people of color differently from his fellow owners. He hired former sports editor Bill Nunn from the famed *Pittsburgh Courier* to scout and sign players from black colleges and universities, becoming the first NFL team to do so. Nunn, who is most noted for scouting players such as Mel Blount, John Stallworth, Donnie Shell, L. C. Greenwood, and Sam Davis, who played integral roles in the Steelers' four Super Bowl championships during the 1970s, became the first black scout inducted into the Pro Football Hall of Fame (as a contributor) in 2021. Rooney also gave Joe Gilliam from HBCU-member Tennessee State a chance to start at quarterback over Terry Bradshaw. He made Tony Dungy the first black defensive coordinator in the NFL.

In 2021, former Steelers receivers coach Lionel Taylor, among the league's first black assistant coaches, revealed he was given the authority to call the play that became known as the "Immaculate Reception," Franco Harris's miraculous last-minute touchdown to beat the Oakland Raiders in a 1972 playoff game. Taylor told the *Logan Banner* (West Virginia), "I called the play. It was supposed to be a simple hook to Barry Pearson for a quick first down, but Bradshaw had to scramble and didn't get enough on the ball."

When the Rooney Rule was introduced, Rooney told reporters, "We want to do the right thing. We want to have diversity in the league. Whatever that takes is what we're going to do."

Whether endorsing the Rooney Rule, hiring a head coach, or voting for the President of the United States, Rooney did things his way.

In 2008, Rooney, a lifelong Republican, endorsed Barack Obama over Hillary Clinton to secure the Democratic nomination. Clinton won the Pennsylvania primary, but Rooney campaigned for Obama on a "Steel Blitz for Barack" bus tour to win over white, working-class voters in the part of the state known as "Steeler Nation."

Less than two weeks after Obama was inaugurated, Rooney's Steelers won the Super Bowl led by second-year black head coach Mike Tomlin.

"Dan Rooney brought in Bill Nunn and Chuck Noll at the same time. It was history repeating itself years later when he hired Mike Tomlin and endorsed Barack Obama," said Reverend Dr. Aubrey Bruce, a sports columnist for the *New Pittsburgh Courier*, who has covered the Steelers since 1978 and considered Nunn a mentor both privately and professionally.

"Rooney was comfortable going against the demographics in Western Pennsylvania by endorsing Obama which is something nobody could have imagined. He did the same thing when he hired Tomlin."

When Rooney passed away on April 18, 2017, Steelers cornerback Ike Taylor, a member of three Super Bowl teams who spent his entire 12-year career in Pittsburgh, was one of eight pallbearers. The other seven pallbearers were Rooney's grandchildren.

In a 2013 video, Rooney and Taylor shared a story about Taylor taking a nap in Rooney's office one day after practice.

"One day I was tired, real tired," said Taylor. "I asked Mr. Rooney if I could take a nap on [his] couch. That tells you what kind of guy Mr. Rooney is. He goes in his son's office [Art II], closes the door."

"You were there for at least an hour, hour and a half," said Rooney. "He was sleeping so I closed the door so nobody would disturb him."

Soon after Tomlin became Steelers head coach, Rooney invited Kiya and the couple's two young sons to his office.

"My sons are five and four at the time, and Mr. Rooney invites them into his office, and I'm like, 'How can I quickly get them out of there?'" said Mike Tomlin. "I get pulled away down the hall, and when I come back the boys are playing with cars on his desk and my wife has her feet up on the couch. He had orchestrated it all."

"That lets you know what kind of guy Mr. Rooney is," said Taylor. "Down to earth. Humble. Regardless of his stature, people respected him."

And vice versa.

9

THE STEELERS LOOK FOR
A NEW COACH

"It's not what you're capable of, it's what you're willing to do."

ONLY three months into my job covering the Steelers as a sports columnist for the *Pittsburgh Tribune-Review*, I, along with everyone else in the football-crazed city of Pittsburgh, was caught up in the moment. Everybody was jockeying to get inside information on who was going to be the team's next head coach, and which paper was going to break the story.

Pittsburgh was a unique market because it was truly a two-newspaper town, which was unheard of for a city of that size (314,674 in 2007, according to the US Census Bureau). You had two families—the Scaifes and the Blocks—that were basically willing to lose millions of dollars to support local journalism, but a lot of it was also driven by ego. Who was going to sell the most papers, who was going to get the bigger scoops, and who was going to tell the more incredible stories.

From a reporter's perspective, it was fantastic. They were giving you resources that, when you looked around the country, a lot of other newspapers were going through layoffs and buyouts and downsizing. Pittsburgh was still having its heyday, as these two families were literally pouring obscene amounts of money into supporting news organizations that were unprofitable.

The *Tribune-Review* (or *Trib*, as it became known in and around Pittsburgh) and the *Post-Gazette* (also known as the *P-G*) were two of the last vestiges of family-owned newspapers in America, compared with the huge media conglomerates now controlling newspaper chains in 2023.

In 1992, billionaire Richard Scaife, a principal heir to the Mellon banking, oil, and aluminum fortune, founded the *Pittsburgh Tribune-Review* after the Scripps-Howard chain rejected his bid to buy the *Pittsburgh Press* at the end of a strike. Scaife wanted to open a Pittsburgh newspaper, and moved into the city to compete with the *Post-Gazette*, the first newspaper west of the Allegheny Mountains. Paul Block published the first-ever *Pittsburgh Post-Gazette* in 1927. It was the *P-G*'s purchase of the now-defunct *Pittsburgh Press* that led to Scaife creating the *Trib*; hence, the rivalry between the two competing newspapers.

"Within the *Trib* newsroom, there was always an attitude that the *Trib* had a chip on its shoulder," said former *Trib* staffer Andrew Conte, who now directs the Center for Media Innovation at Point Park University in downtown Pittsburgh. "The *Post-Gazette* was a bigger newspaper than the *Trib*. It says right on the *P-G*'s masthead, it tells you it's one of America's great newspapers. People were like, 'Oh, the *Trib* is just some start-up' or 'the *Trib* doesn't have the history the other paper has.'

"Reporters at the *Trib* always had this attitude like, 'Nobody respects us. We've got to work harder than everybody else to get stories,'" Conte continued. "In some cases, that could also translate to, 'We need to take some bigger risks to be noticed and to tell stories in a way that maybe another newsroom wouldn't.'"

This was especially true about the *Trib*'s sports department. The Steelers were—and still are—the biggest story in Pittsburgh. I recall editor Frank Craig, who ran the show at the time, telling me that Monday editions of the paper the day after Steelers games were huge money makers. Craig was always looking for ways to cut into the *Post-Gazette*'s circulation numbers. He even created a *Trib PM* afternoon edition, presented in a tabloid format, that teased to Steelers stories on the front cover.

Frank and I go way back. He had hired me at the *Toledo Blade* in Northwest Ohio back in 1998, where I was that paper's sports columnist. He later created the "Steelers columnist" position for me at the *Trib*. I heard whispers around the newsroom that, in spite of my credentials, the only reason I was hired was because of my skin color (even though I had received national sportswriting awards working in several major markets prior to coming to Pittsburgh, including Philadelphia, Detroit, Dallas-Fort Worth, and Tampa Bay). But let's face it, my hiring in October 2006 made me the *only* black reporter in the *Trib*'s sports department. The majority of players on the Steelers roster when I joined the paper were black, so you can do the math.

My first big story after joining the *Trib* was a long-form feature about Pro Bowl linebacker Joey Porter, who would become a free agent at the end of the 2006 season. We met in the team cafeteria one day after practice. Despite us barely knowing each other, Porter, who sparked the Steelers' playoff run on their way to winning Super Bowl XL, was surprisingly candid and revealed that although he wanted to remain with the Steelers, money would probably dictate him leaving Pittsburgh. That's exactly what happened. When Porter signed with the Miami Dolphins, he arranged it so that I broke the story. Other players on the Steelers told me the article I wrote about Porter—and another feature I later wrote about cornerback Ike Taylor—made it easier for them to trust me and tell me things they wouldn't tell other reporters covering the team.

As persistent rumors rose to a crescendo about head coach Bill Cowher likely retiring at the end of the 2006 season, the *Trib*'s sports department was as ready as it ever was going to be. During that time, the relationship between beat reporter Scott Brown and myself was becoming more comfortable, as were our surroundings in the first season (for each of us) covering the Steelers. *Trib* management did its part, sparing no expense in sending at least three reporters and two photographers to every road game.

When the Steelers defeated the Cincinnati Bengals in the season finale, 23–17, to finish 8–8, the race was on between the *Trib* and the *P-G* to be the first newspaper in Pittsburgh to report Cowher's next move.

The message from our editors was straight to the point: *Whatever you do, don't get beat.*

* * *

Cowher operated on a timeline he established during a meeting with chairman Dan Rooney and president Art Rooney II, two days after the Steelers' season finale. Cowher originally planned to return to Pittsburgh the following Monday after driving to Raleigh, North Carolina, to join his wife and the couple's youngest daughter at the family's new home. Instead, Cowher informed Dan Rooney Thursday afternoon he had made up his mind and saw no reason to wait. The Steelers scheduled a news conference for Friday.

Before a packed house at the team's South Side facility, Cowher, then forty-nine, made it official: he was resigning as the team's head coach, but left the door open for a possible return to coaching in the future.

"There is no timetable," Cowher, who had a 149–90–1 (62 percent) record over 15 years at the helm, said in Brown's article about his coaching future: "The only sideline I'll be sitting on is up in the stands and watching my kids play basketball in the next couple of years."

Trib sports columnist Mike Prisuta took a different tact, after noticing that Cowher failed to shake hands with Art Rooney II at the press conference. As he wrote:

> Cowher . . . did not reveal specifics when pressed on the role of compensation issues as they related to why a coach who keeps insisting he isn't burned out would walk away from a team that's a year removed from the Super Bowl. . . . As for quitting the Steelers, Cowher needs to apologize to no one. If he feels he has the juice to take a year off and then break the bank as a coaching free agent—and he does—more power to him. But the transition could have been more respectful.

With this vacancy, it was the first time the Steelers had to look for a new head coach in fifteen years, setting the stage for the team to hire only its third coach in thirty-nine years. The previous two coaches hired by the Steelers (Chuck Noll and Cowher) were both in their thirties, and had defensive backgrounds.

Cowher's resignation enabled the Steelers to quickly arrange their first interview. When a team begins looking for a head coach in the midst of the playoffs, it's often expected that they're waiting to talk to someone whose team is still in contention. One of those coaches was Chicago Bears defensive coordinator Ron Rivera, who turned forty-five when the Rooneys and director of football operations Kevin Colbert interviewed him on January 7—his birthday, in Chicago—a week prior to the Bears' opening playoff game against the Seattle Seahawks. Rivera, a starting linebacker on Chicago's 1985 Super Bowl championship team, and the Bears defensive coordinator since 2004, was the first person to officially interview with the Steelers for a head coaching position since 1992. It was also the last time the Steelers would be allowed to interview him until his team was officially out of the playoffs.

With Rivera's interview completed, the Steelers brass returned to Pittsburgh and filled their calendar with four more interviews over the next six days, including in-house candidates Ken Whisenhunt and Russ Grimm (the team's offensive coordinator and assistant head coach/offensive line coach, respectively), who had both served under Cowher since 2001; a thirty-four-year-old African American defensive coordinator named Mike Tomlin; plus another surprise candidate, current Georgia Tech head coach Chan Gailey, a former assistant under Cowher, from 1994 to 1997, and offensive coordinator for the last two of those seasons.

Grimm, a Pittsburgh-area native who starred collegiately at Pitt before embarking on a Hall of Fame playing career, interviewed for the job on January 8. This wasn't Grimm's first rodeo on the interview circuit. A coach in the NFL since 1992, he was a finalist for the Chicago Bears' opening in 2004 when Lovie Smith was hired. The following year, he interviewed with the Cleveland Browns before Romeo Crennel was hired. Then, in 2006, he was considered a frontrunner to become head coach of the Detroit Lions, with Rod Marinelli ending up getting the nod. During the current hiring cycle, Grimm interviewed with the Arizona Cardinals one day after meeting with the Steelers.

Grimm was endorsed by some of the current Steeler players.

"I wanted Russ to get the job," said Pro Bowl guard Alan Faneca. "It's a guy we know, and a guy I'm experienced with."

Tackle Willie Colon, who started two games as a rookie with Grimm as his position coach, said, "Me being a guy who spent a year with Russ, I just felt like that was going to be my shoo-in to finally crack the lineup."

Midway through his interview with the Cardinals, Grimm told reporters in Arizona, "Part of the interview process is myself interviewing them to see how an organization is run from top to bottom, to see how things are handled. I'm a little different than some of the assistant coaches looking for head coaching jobs. I don't make myself available to certain situations. I'm not going to get excited about a job or take a job where I don't feel comfortable about things."

Next up in Pittsburgh was Whisenhunt, the Steelers' OC since 2004—the season in which quarterback Ben Roethlisberger was named AP Offensive Rookie of the Year. After winning Super Bowl XL, he turned down an opportunity to coach the Oakland

Raiders in order to wait for better offers. Whisenhunt's patience was rewarded one year later. In addition to interviewing with the Steelers on January 9, he also interviewed with the Atlanta Falcons and Miami Dolphins, as well as the team that would hire him for their head coaching vacancy, the Arizona Cardinals.

The Cardinals were busy, interviewing eight candidates in search of a replacement for Dennis Green, with Rivera being among them.

On paper, Gailey, fifty-five, didn't fit the Steelers narrative since their previous three head coaches were hired in their thirties. "I feel young," Gailey told the *Trib*. "Looks may be deceiving, but I feel young." Nor did his background as offensive coordinator considering the Steelers' track record for hiring defensive-minded head coaches. There was a rumor floating around that Gailey received an endorsement from Cowher but Gailey said it was just that—rumor—when he interviewed on January 13.

"I talk to Bill a lot," said Gailey, "but what he said [to the Rooneys] I do not know."

* * *

Tomlin was the fourth coach to officially interview, meeting with the Steelers January 10—one day after Whisenhunt, two days after Grimm, and three days before Gailey. Based on the resume of the other top candidates, Tomlin was the obvious wild card.

Dan Rooney wasn't made aware of Tomlin until being brought to his attention while attending a Fritz Pollard Alliance meeting in December 2006 in New York City to discuss the effectiveness of the Rooney Rule. The meeting was attended by, among others, NFL Commissioner Roger Goodell; NFL general counsel Jeff Pash; NFL executive vice president of football operations Ray Anderson; Fritz Pollard Alliance and civil rights attorney Cyrus Mehri; Hall of Fame linebacker Harry Carson; Fritz Pollard Alliance counsel N. Jeremi Duru; and former NFL front office executive John Wooten, who had replaced Carson as the Alliance's executive director.

The timing of the meeting coincided with the upcoming off-season, when teams hire new head coaches, general managers, and front-office staff. During the meeting, a ready list of potential minority head coaching candidates was presented to Goodell and Rooney, who represented NFL owners at the meeting and for whom the Rooney Rule is named.

Tomlin's name was on the list.

"Every December, we meet at the league office with the commissioner and top NFL brass where John Wooten would present what we call the ready list," said Mehri. "Leading up to that meeting, John talked to coach Dungy. Coach Dungy said, 'Look, John. This is a rising star.' It was in that meeting that we had Mike Tomlin on our ready list for head coach, even though he'd only been a coordinator for a year.

"Dan Rooney is sitting in the meeting and on that list is 'Mike Tomlin, defensive coordinator.' John is pushing Mike Tomlin. Dan Rooney *did not know* Mike Tomlin.

"If John and Dan aren't talking to each other, you don't even get Mike on the ready list," continued Mehri. "And you have an owner sitting at that meeting where we go over the ready list. And here's this unknown guy. Until [Rooney] heard about him, he wasn't on the radar, really. We also had Ron Rivera [a minority head coaching candidate] on the list. We had other great people on the list. Dan got a competitive advantage by coming to our meetings. The other owners should have been there, because then they could hear about all the emerging talent.

"What people don't know is the ready list," continued Mehri. "They don't know about John Wooten and Dan Rooney talking that frequently. No one reported that. Everyone is so focused on the commissioner and the office on Park Avenue. They don't realize there's so much other action happening. There's a lot more richness to this story than has probably been reported."

Tomlin was trending upward, and it was only a matter of time before teams looked past his age and requested to interview him. If not this year, certainly in the future. The ready list helped the Steelers learn more about Tomlin, but they still weren't sure. Wooten took a leap of faith, leaning on decades of built-in equity between him and Dan Rooney to ask his old friend a favor.

"We all thought that Ken Whisenhunt or Russ Grimm was going to get that job," Wooten admitted. "Mr. Rooney had already interviewed two minority candidates [Rivera and one unnamed candidate who's currently still in the league], so he more than satisfied the Rooney Rule requirement.

"He didn't have to interview Mike Tomlin, but the relationship we had allowed me to say to him, 'Mr. Rooney, I know that you have already interviewed two minority coaches. There's a youngster up in Minnesota that I just want you to go take a look at as a favor to me.' Mr. Rooney said, 'I'll do that. I'll fly up there tomorrow.'

"You know, he's a pilot. He flew his own plane up there.

"The next evening, around 9:30, 10, Mr. Rooney calls. He said, 'Johnny, is it too late to talk?' I said, 'No, sir. Not at all.' He said, 'That kid is something special. I've got to bring him down here and take a look at him in Pittsburgh.'

"And he brought him down! He and his wife picked him up at the hotel to take him to dinner. First of all, they didn't send a car for him. Mrs. Rooney got in the back seat so they could talk up front."

In Minneapolis, Brad Childress had just completed his first season as Vikings head coach, compiling a 6–10 record. Regarded as an offensive guru from his days with the Philadelphia Eagles under head coach Andy Reid, Childress relied greatly on Tomlin, who was the youngest defensive coordinator in the league and whose unit led the NFL in run defense.

Aware that Tomlin was on the fast track in the coaching profession, Childress tried to prepare his young protégé for the inevitable.

"I called him the next day after the exit meetings with all of our players," said Childress. "I said, 'Mike, I've got to talk to you. Understand this, you're a hot commodity right now. People are going to want to interview you for head coaching jobs.'

"He looks at me and goes, 'Coach, I just got here.'

"'Mike, I'm just telling you my experience with it and what I've heard.'

"'Coach, I don't know if I want to do that. I just want to get this defense better. We've got good guys on this team. We'll be another year further along. I just want to coach these guys.'

"'Let me just tell you something. You need to go home and talk to Kiya. If you want to put an [interview] book together, I'll help you do that.'"

"The next day he comes back and says, 'Yeah, if that happens, I think I'd like to take a swing at it.'

"I gave him my book. I told him: 'Take what you want.'"

The Miami Dolphins were the first team to contact Tomlin about their head coaching vacancy. Owner Wayne Huizenga flew the team jet up from South Florida and met with Tomlin in Minneapolis.

"Wayne put a Dolphins mat on the tarmac," said Childress. "Mike and Wayne talked. They had dinner on the plane.

"Later in the week, Mike went to the Steelers and interviewed with them."

Miami didn't offer Tomlin the job. Years later, a *Miami Herald* article detailed what may have occurred during the interview process.

"Dolphins interviewed but did not hire coach Mike Tomlin after the 2006 season," wrote *Herald* columnist Greg Cote, "opting instead for failure-in-waiting Cam Cameron (1–15 record in his only season with Miami), after then-CEO Joe Bailey was overheard referring to Tomlin as 'too hip-hop.'"

"In their mind, they had a vision of what they wanted their head coach to be, which basically equates to white," said former Miami Dolphins beat reporter Omar Kelly, who covered the team for the *South Florida Sun-Sentinel*, from 2007 to 2022. "It's somebody more relatable and makes them feel comfortable. What's interesting about that process is Cam Cameron didn't impress them in their first round of interviews and they still brought him back. They waited until he finished his playoff run [with San Diego] and they brought him back for a second interview to hire him. Because they had this offensive [guru] in mind, that's who they wanted to hire."

Pro Football Hall of Fame cornerback Ronde Barber, who made the Pro Bowl three times when Tomlin was the Tampa Bay Buccaneers' secondary coach, said Tomlin connected with everyone—from ownership on down.

"As relatable as Mike is—call it hip-hop, call it whatever you want—the reality is you could throw on a Journey song and Mike would know that, too," said Barber. "It's not a cultural thing. It's a relatable thing: 'How do I relate to the people I'm having to lead?' If he was going to IBM to be hyperbolic and lead a bunch of white guys, he could probably do that damn good, too. He has that ability. I've seen him in different situations and different scenarios that aren't related to football, and he's just as good. He's got a lot of superpowers."

Miami had two bites of the apple to hire Tomlin. One year earlier, Tomlin interviewed for the Dolphins' defensive coordinator position on head coach Nick Saban's staff, based on the recommendation from then defensive line coach Dan Quinn, currently the defensive coordinator of the Dallas Cowboys.

It was not to be. Seeking coordinators with previous NFL head coaching experience, Saban hired Mike Mularkey to lead the offense and Dom Capers to run the defense with the title of special assistant. At fifty-five, Capers was twenty-two years older than Tomlin. He was also the highest-paid assistant coach in the NFL, with an annual salary of $2.6 million.

"Mike was a DB coach with Tampa Bay at the time," said Quinn, whose relationship with Tomlin went back to their days at William & Mary and VMI. "After the interview, our coaches were asked, 'Who do you think did the best job?' It was clear: Mike Tomlin."

Dan Rooney didn't know what to expect when the Steelers interviewed Tomlin the first time in Pittsburgh.

"To be honest with you, before the interview he was just another guy who was an assistant coach," Rooney told Greg Garber of ESPN.

Going directly to the source, Art Rooney II tried to pick Childress's brain about Tomlin's coaching intangibles.

"He said, 'Talk to me about Mike Tomlin,' said Childress. "I said, 'You want me to tell you the truth, or you want me to lie to you?' He goes, 'Well, I'd prefer the truth.' I said, 'I don't ever cast another eye on the defensive room. I go in there and sit from time to time and listen and watch guys learning and watch him teaching.'

"He said, 'Give me an example about his leadership.' I said, 'Listen, he's got [safety] Darren Sharper in that room. He and Darren Sharper went to school together at William & Mary, one playing defense, one playing wide receiver. And he's got to dress him down the same way as everybody else.' Sharper [would] freelance if he thought he could make the play. In his own inimitable way, Mike was able to communicate with him."

Never mind his age, Rooney was still focused on Tomlin's leadership. The Steelers were a veteran team one year removed from winning a Super Bowl. It would take a confident, strong-minded coach to command Pittsburgh's locker room overflowing with strong personalities.

"He asked me how he's going to be standing in front of a team?" said Childress. "Well, you know what? He's going to look a lot like a lot of that team, but the biggest thing is he's going to be able to communicate to them and if he's got something he's going to correct you on, he's not going to pick and choose. He's going to treat everybody the same and communicate with you and tell you the truth—either you want to hear it, or you don't."

Rooney's line of questioning convinced Childress that Tomlin was a serious candidate for the Steelers head coaching job.

"I felt it was legitimate interest and legitimate questioning," said Childress. "Just who he was. How he acted. How he talked. What did he do off the field? What kind of worker was he? But, you know, that position is all about leadership. And with these guys only having had three coaches in the last however many years, he wasn't looking for it as a stopgap. And he wasn't looking at it in a black-white sense, saying let me fulfill the Rooney Rule that my dad propped up there.

"Mike's got a great presence. He's going to make some statements in a way nobody's left trying to understand where he's coming from. He's going to tell you I'm firmly on this side.

"The Sharper thing was the biggest deal. Here's a guy that's his peer, and he has to ride herd on him."

Both Wooten and Tony Dungy, who gave Tomlin his first NFL coaching job, prepped Tomlin for the interview.

In his 2019 book about his father, *A Different Way to Win*, Jim Rooney describes how Tomlin was briefed every step of the way:

> One of the most meaningful moments in that process, Tomlin says now, came at the very beginning, before he even had an interview. Dungy, for whom Tomlin has worked in Tampa, and Wooten both called him to let him know of the Steelers' interest. And they each told Tomlin that the Rooney Rule requirement had already been met.

"Dan Rooney had a blueprint his whole time being in charge in Pittsburgh of what he was looking for in a head coach," said Dungy. "He wanted young, good communicators. He wanted defensive coaches because he felt the blue-collar nature, the weather come playoff time if you had a strong defense, that would carry the day. And that's what he was looking for in that coaching search. He didn't know Mike, but Mike fit the design and the blueprint."

* * *

Julia Copeland didn't hold out much hope that the Steelers would hire her son.

"When he was interviewing for the Steelers job, I was trying to prepare him because I really didn't think he was going to get it—you don't go from being a coordinator in one year to head coach," Copeland told Chuck Finder of the *Pittsburgh Post-Gazette* in 2007.

Following Tomlin's interview, the *Trib*'s Mike Prisuta, attributing the story to a source in Pittsburgh, wrote, "The Steelers are expected to conduct one or more follow-up interviews once their initial round of meetings are completed."

Whisenhunt, apparently still in the equation for the Steelers job, met with Arizona a second time, on January 12. The interview led to the two sides beginning contract negotiations the following day. Whisenhunt was named the Cardinals' head coach on January 14.

Arizona was desperate for a culture change. The Cardinals featured future Hall of Famer Larry Fitzgerald and Hall of Famers Kurt Warner and Edgerrin James on offense (as well as Pro Bowl wide receiver Anquan Boldin), and tackle Darnell Dockett and hard-hitting safety Adrian Wilson on defense. But they lacked direction, focus and discipline.

Whisenhunt, a product of Pittsburgh's winning organization, beat out Houston Texans assistant head coach Mike Sherman.

"I really think it's a great opportunity," Whisenhunt told ESPN's Len Pasquarelli. "It's a team with a lot of young talent on both sides of the ball. The more I studied the situation, the better it looked, and the more I wanted that job."

Back east, the Steelers narrowed their scope to three finalists: Tomlin, Grimm, and Rivera. The lede paragraph in a presumptuous January 15 Associated Press article, based on Art Rooney II's statement issued by the team, described Grimm as the "frontrunner." It was the start of a pattern of media misinformation regarding the coaching search. Rooney II's statement did not match the AP's opening paragraph: "We now will move into the second interview phase," said Rooney, "and we are confident that each of the candidates on our short list will be excellent head coaches in the NFL. It is our task to determine which one is the best candidate for the Pittsburgh Steelers. The team's statement did not identify Grimm as the "frontrunner."

On January 14—one week after Rivera interviewed with the Steelers—Chicago defeated Seattle in overtime in its first playoff game to advance to the NFC Championship Game against New Orleans, which meant the Steelers wouldn't be able to interview Rivera again until the Bears were eliminated from the playoffs. Rooney II's statement released the next day implied the Steelers were still interested in Rivera.

Mehri revealed that the Steelers had more than a passing interest in Rivera.

As shown, the media—especially the *Trib* and *P-G*—saw this as a two-man race between Grimm and Tomlin. However, in speaking with Mehri, he revealed to me that, "In the end, it was Ron Rivera and Mike Tomlin, and Dan didn't know what to do. It was such a close call. Dan told John Wooten, and John told me.

"Put yourself in Steelers headquarters," continued Mehri. "Dan in his office. Pacing. Agonizing. Rivera or Tomlin?

"The only people who know are Dan Rooney—who's passed away—John Wooten, and me. John was a listening ear to Dan. Dan, in confidence, was asking John and sharing with John what he was agonizing over. By then, Grimm was gone. Whisenhunt's gone. They weren't even in the final decision.

"At the end of the day, Dan loved both of those guys [Tomlin and Rivera]. He thought they would both be amazing coaches. You've got two coaches who have been Super Bowl coaches as his two finalists."

The Steelers interviewed Tomlin at the team's facility for the second time in six days. Speaking with reporters following the interview, Tomlin said he does not so much subscribe to a particular scheme as much as he does the philosophy that stopping the run and running the ball are two of the biggest keys to winning.

"Once we interviewed him the first time, he just came through and we thought it was great," Dan Rooney told Garber of ESPN. "And we brought him back [for a second interview] and talked to him on the phone and went through the process that we do."

"It's an honor to be invited back," Tomlin said in an article I wrote for the *Tribune-Review*. "It's been a positive experience in every way."

Minter, who hired Tomlin at the University of Cincinnati and offered sage advice over the years, said Tomlin radiated positive energy during the Steelers' coaching search.

"Mike had been gone from me now about six years when he calls out of the blue and says, 'Coach, I think I'm going to get some opportunities to look around the league a little bit,'" said Minter. "'Maybe it's due to the Rooney Rule but, whatever it is, I want to take advantage of this and get practice with some of those interviews. I really believe I can be a head coach in this league. I said, 'Go for it.'

"He went down to Miami. It went good. Then he went to Pittsburgh. I said, 'Just go in and give it your best shot. There's a lot of rumors they're gonna stay in-house with Whisenhunt or Grimm. Just go for it.' He did.

"He comes back, we touch base and he says, 'Coach, I'm gonna get a second interview with the Steelers.' I said, 'Dude, they are wanting you or they wouldn't be back for a second one. Just put it all together, Mike, and go in there and knock it over.'"

Tomlin had a similar conversation with Rip Scherer Jr. during the interview process.

"Cleveland wanted to interview me for the offensive coordinator's job," said Scherer, who was the Browns' quarterbacks coach. "I called Kevin Colbert for some background on what to expect. Kevin flipped the switch on me and said, "It's ironic that you called." He wanted to ask about Mike. I said, 'Oh, is this a Rooney Rule deal with the Steelers?' He goes, 'No. It's the real deal.' We got off the phone and I immediately called Mike and said, 'This thing with the Steelers, just so you know, it's legit."

With Tomlin's interview fresh in their minds, the Steelers interviewed Grimm twenty-four hours later. After meeting with the search committee for six hours, Grimm was quoted in the *P-G*: 'I'm excited about this opportunity. I think it's a point in time in my career where I'm ready to make that next move." Grimm added, "It's flattering to have the chance to get [the job], and it's kind of exciting once you go through the process and see all that's involved."

While Tomlin and Grimm were interviewing in Pittsburgh, Rivera was in Chicago preparing for the NFC Championship Game. He granted Brown an exclusive interview that was published in the *Trib* two days before the title game at Soldier Field. Rivera discussed his January 7 interview with the Steelers and also assessed his chances of winning the job.

"The Rooneys have a specific idea of what they're looking for, and my first interview I thought was very positive," Rivera said. "I got a feel for what they were looking for, and I really loved what I heard from them in terms of the direction they believe they're headed, the support they're going to give the coach."

Brown asked Rivera if he thought the Steelers were seriously considering him despite the NFL's no contact rule until the Bears' season ended.

"I would like to think so," Rivera said, "because they haven't made a decision yet, and everything I've read in the papers has been very positive in terms of looking for the right person."

Rivera added: "Coach Cowher was there for fifteen years and probably could have been another fifteen if he wanted. Chuck Noll was there forever, and I think that speaks very well for whoever the next head coach is because you know you're going to have the opportunity to be there awhile and win awhile."

* * *

Tomlin, Grimm, or Rivera?

Who? When? Why?

Both the *Trib and P-G* wanted to be the first to write the definitive article about who the Steelers new head coach would be. With no more interviews scheduled for the January 20–21 weekend, it seemed certain the Steelers were nearing a decision—unless the team liked Rivera enough to wait to interview him again.

At the *Trib*, the pressure was rising to break the city's sports story of the year.

Brown was in Chicago, where he interviewed Rivera and stuck around to cover the NFC title game. Of the sports writers at the *Trib* covering the Steelers, Brown was assigned to cover Rivera.

I was assigned to cover Tomlin, and spoke with his agent, Brian Levy, whenever possible. For that reason, I wasn't thrilled about being sent to Indianapolis to cover the Colts-Patriots AFC title game. To me, covering that game wasn't as important as identifying the Steelers' new coach.

Prisuta, whose primary focus was Grimm and Whisenhunt— because they were both represented by Pittsburgh-based agent Eric Metz—remained at home.

All three of us understood the urgency of the moment: Pittsburgh was an incredibly competitive, super intense, newspaper market. If you got scooped by the competition, especially on the Steelers beat, and especially on a story like this one, you were embarrassed to show your face in the newsroom that day. Your editor wanted to know, *How did you get beat? Why did you get beat?* Not only do you have to find out what the other paper had—*not only do you have to find something new to write about*—it needs to be even better.

On January 20, our worst fears at the *Trib* were realized. What saved us—at least at that point in time—was that the *P-G* didn't write the story.

Michael Silver reported for *Sports Illustrated* that the Steelers had settled on Tomlin to be the team's new head coach. Silver wrote: "Tomlin, thirty-four, impressed the Steelers during the interview process with his organizational skills, intelligence and grasp of the game, according to a source familiar with the coaching search."

I can't begin to tell you the shockwaves that story created, as it didn't come from either of the two Pittsburgh newspapers, but instead from an outside source.

Tomlin raised the temperature when he denied the report to ESPN: "It is untrue," Tomlin said. "I have no idea where it's coming from. I haven't talked to the Rooneys today."

Later, in a brief *P-G* article, Dan Rooney said, "There's nothing to that story on the wire."

Silver, who wrote the article from Indianapolis where he was covering the AFC title game, explained his state of mind following Tomlin's denial.

"I was at the Ram Brewery in Indy having lunch the day before the game. I was talking to a very high-level person in the restaurant. I got a call back from this person, and I stepped over to a quiet area. I was like, 'Do you know what's up with Pittsburgh?' And I go, 'Whisenhunt or Grimm?' There's a pause. And he goes, 'No, Tomlin.' I almost had chills," said Silver, currently a columnist with the *San Francisco Chronicle* who has covered the NFL for more than thirty years, including thirteen with *SI*, six with Yahoo! and eight with NFL Network. "I was like, 'Really? Wow.'

"And then Tomlin was at some football camp that same day and when they caught up to him, he said, 'I don't know anything.' Even when Tomlin had the quote, I'm like he might know and been told not to say anything. He might not know. I circled back with my original source and my source held firm. I'm like, 'OK, man, I'm going to trust it.'"

Several hours later on Saturday after *SI* had reported the Steelers decided on Tomlin as their next head coach—with both Tomlin and the Steelers denying he had the job—the *P-G* reported its own version of the *SI* article via the newspaper's website. The three-paragraph article read:

> The Steelers have informed Mike Tomlin, the Minnesota Vikings defensive coordinator, that he will be their next head coach. The team plans a news conference to announce his hiring.
>
> The sides were negotiating a contract tonight for four years and an option year.
>
> The Steelers made their decision today between Russ Grimm, their assistant head coach and offensive line coach, and Tomlin. They informed Grimm today that they had chosen Tomlin.

This had now become more than two newspapers fighting a local turf war. Now it was personal with three different media outlets in the fight. Full disclosure: The *P-G* article bothered us more than the *SI* article.

We understood the *P-G* was the top newspaper in the city—and still is. We, on the other hand, were considered the *P-G*'s little brother. For that reason, the *Trib* had to work harder for stories. We had to be more credible. For a lot of us working there, you not only had to work harder, but you had to have more sources, and you had to *make sure* things were locked down before you hit the *send* button.

I was tapped out. Levy wasn't returning my calls. Brown was tapped out. Prisuta, though, had a breakthrough.

One of Prisuta's sources told him the Steelers made Grimm a contract offer to become head coach. And Grimm accepted.

On the one hand, *SI* reported that Tomlin is the Steelers' new head coach, followed by the *P-G* reaching the same conclusion later that day.

On the other hand, an article appearing in the *Trib* the next day reports that it's Grimm.

Who's right? Who's wrong?

Please, God, let the *Trib* be right.

Before he pressed the *send* button, Mike and I discussed the article over the phone, as he, Scott, and I did with every story we wrote during the coaching search. Mike was in Pittsburgh. I was pacing in my hotel room in Indianapolis.

Right or wrong, the article would impact the three of us, along with everyone associated with the *Trib*. I thought it was a great story and told him so. But I had some concerns, as the biggest sports story of the year in Pittsburgh story hinged on a single, unnamed source.

I remember during our call telling Mike, "Yeah, write the article and say that an offer was made, but maybe don't say it's a done deal. Don't say he's taken the job. Just say he was *offered* the job.

That gave the *Trib* an out. If Grimm gets the job, we get the scoop. If he doesn't get the job, we can argue the Steelers pulled the offer.

Dated Sunday, January 21, Prisuta's article appeared in the *Trib* and on the newspaper's website, under the headline: "Steelers Pick Grimm, Source Says."

Russ Grimm has been offered and has accepted the Steelers' head coaching position, a source in Pittsburgh confirmed late Saturday.

Grimm, 47, succeeds Bill Cowher, who coached the Steelers for 15 seasons before resigning January 5. The hiring of Grimm will be announced Monday at a news conference.

ESPN and *SI* reported yesterday that Minnesota Vikings defensive coordinator Mike Tomlin had been chosen to replace Cowher.

An NFL source confirmed yesterday that Tomlin had not heard from the Steelers and no contact negotiations had taken place.

Grimm, a native of Scottsdale, Westmoreland County, and a Pitt product, has been the Steelers' offensive line coach since 2001 and the team's assistant head coach since 2004. He played 11 seasons as a guard and center for the Washington Redskins from 1981 to 1991 and is among 17 finalists for the Pro Football Hall of Fame's class of 2007.

Grimm was one of three finalists to replace Cowher, along with Tomlin and Chicago Bears defensive coordinator Ron Rivera. Tomlin and Grimm had second interviews with the Steelers last week.

The Steelers would have had to wait until the Bears' season is completed to interview Rivera a second time. Chicago hosts New Orleans today in the NFL Championship Game.

Ken Whisenhunt, the Steelers' offensive coordinator last season, and Georgia Tech coach Chan Gailey, a former Steelers assistant, also interviewed for the position.

Whisenhunt has since become head coach of the Arizona Cardinals.

The elevation of Grimm to his first head-coaching job figures to be welcomed by the Steelers' players.

Even before Cowher officially stepped down, a consensus had formed among players that they preferred the Steelers stay in-house when the team hired its next head coach.

Wide receivers coach Bruce Arians has said he believes his chances of becoming Steelers offensive coordinator were very good in the event Grimm became the head coach.

The *Trib* story caused Silver to question his own article.

"I felt confident the whole time because my sources were so good, but, you know, it's jarring when there's a published report saying the opposite," said Silver. I was like, 'This guy is plugged in. How could he have someone telling him that Russ is taking it?'"

The Steelers released a statement on Sunday addressing the coaching search: "At this point in time, the Steelers have not concluded a contract agreement with a new head coach, nor do we expect to do so today. There will be no other announcement from this office today." The statement did not deny the Steelers had settled on a new head coach, only that a contract agreement had not been reached. The team's response left both coaching possibilities—Tomlin or Grimm—open.

Late Sunday afternoon, on January 21, the Chicago Bears defeated the New Orleans Saints to advance to Super Bowl XLI. The Bears' win effectively eliminated Rivera from the coaching search when the Steelers announced that Tomlin would be their next head coach.

I was sitting in the press box at the RCA Dome watching the Colts rally from 18 points down to defeat the Patriots and advance to face Chicago in the Super Bowl. The phone call I had been waiting for finally lit up my cell. It was Levy, confirming Tomlin's hire.

Like many people in Pittsburgh, I was surprised that Tomlin was the Steelers' choice. I'm not going to lie and say otherwise.

Tomlin himself was surprised by the hire.

"I was shocked they bought it," Tomlin revealed on the *Pivot* podcast. "I'm glad they bought it. But I was shocked they bought it."

As for me personally, it wasn't that I thought he was under-qualified. He was just so young, and the NFL wasn't particularly fond of hiring young head coaches at that time —particularly young, black coaches, or black coaches of any age, for that matter.

Despite Silver's *SI* article, I was totally in the dark until Levy called me with the news. Tomlin and his agent kept a lid on the entire process, a trait he carries to this day.

According to Levy, he didn't begin negotiations until the job had been offered and accepted. The two sides agreed to a contract in principle shortly after 8 p.m. that night.

* * *

Like everyone else at the *Trib*, I wanted our story to be right. When the story initially broke, people in the newsroom didn't know what to make of the misfire by the sports department.

"We were all shocked when it happened," said Conte. "To have a single-source story like that. Especially with a headline saying it's Grimm or it could be Grimm. It was like, 'This is it. It's definite. We've got it.' The fact that it wasn't locked down, it was difficult for a lot of people in the newsroom to see."

Going to the *Trib* office for the first time since we got the story wrong, I remember having a sinking feeling in the pit of my stomach. As one of the reporters whose job it was to write about the Steelers, we rarely went into the office. We were either at the Steelers' facility on the South Side watching practice, attending a game, or traveling to a game.

The *Trib*'s main newsroom was located on the third floor of the D. L. Clark Building, located at 503 Martindale Street near downtown Pittsburgh (but has since moved to Tarentum, approximately twenty-five minutes away).

I was almost hoping that the elevator wouldn't move from the ground floor. The message from our editors delivered early in the season was still ringing in my ears:

Whatever you do, don't get beat.

The three of us—Brown, Prisuta, and myself—met in executive sports editor Kevin Smith's office with other editors.

They all wanted to know how we got the story wrong. We all voiced our opinions . . . I'll leave it at that.

It didn't matter that we believed the Grimm story was right when it was first written—Tomlin was now the head coach, not Grimm. The bottom line was that all of us realized the Grimm article would hurt our daily coverage of the Steelers—not to mention trying to build a relationship with their brand-new head coach—and what we could possibly do to patch things up with the team.

All I know is that it took a long time before things felt normal again.

For too long, the narrative has been cloaked in sources and rumors and wrapped in innuendo and he-said, she-said gobbledygook.

We have heard the same narrative about how Tomlin became head coach of the Steelers. More than one reporter in Pittsburgh has claimed that their cousin's best friend's uncle heard from someone close to the Steelers that the *real* reason why the Rooneys hired Tomlin is because the family felt pressure to live up to the NFL rule named after them. And *that's* why they told Grimm he had the job only to take it away from him at the last minute and give it to Tomlin.

That's an unfair characterization of the Rooneys, as well as an insult to Tomlin.

It's time to set the record straight.

Cyrus Mehri, who along with the late Johnnie Cochran created the Rooney Rule twenty-one years ago, finally broke the code of silence when I asked him what role the Rooney Rule played in the Steelers hiring Tomlin, as stated in the previous chapter on the Rooney Rule.

The key, according to Mehri, was understanding the relationship between Dan Rooney and John Wooten.

"Before the emergence of the Rooney Rule, Dan and John knew each other and had mutual respect," said Mehri. "Don't forget the Cowboys-Steelers Super Bowl rivalry. Don't forget they were the two premier franchises of the '70s. Dan was the architect behind the Steelers. John was a major force behind both the '70s and '90s dynasties for the Cowboys.

"John had so much respect for Dan because Dan was the guy making sure there were black players on the Steelers. John saw how Bill Nunn was brought in. Bill brought in the HBCU players. John was doing something similar with the Cowboys that Bill Nunn was doing with the Steelers."

Wooten was Noll's teammate on the Cleveland Browns. "I think what Dan Rooney saw in Mike Tomlin is what he had seen in Chuck Noll," said Wooten. "Great teachers. Very calm in the storm. We both knew what Chuck Noll brought to that team because we know who Chuck Noll was and we felt like Mike Tomlin brought that same thing."

Wooten operated as a voice of reason in Tomlin's decision to accept the Steelers' offer.

When Tomlin expressed concern that Dick LeBeau, who spoke with the team about Cowher's vacancy, was ownership's choice to remain as defensive coordinator, Wooten told him to see the big picture.

"Mr. Rooney wanted him to keep LeBeau as defensive coordinator. Mike was a little uncomfortable. You're talking about the defensive coordinator. He had wanted to be the head coach; rightfully so," said Wooten.

"When Mike talked it over with me, this is what I told him to do: make John Mitchell [who had been the team's defensive line coach since 1994] your assistant head coach/defensive line coach. That puts him in every room. Therefore, if there's something going down that's not right, John's going to tell you about it. That gave Mike the freedom to go ahead and do that. Mike kept Dick LeBeau as the defensive coordinator and made John Mitchell assistant head coach/defensive line coach. And it worked out."

"The idea was that John wanted to have a black guy there as assistant head coach to watch Mike's back, so to speak," said Mehri.

"When Mike got that job, he easily could have said, 'We're going to run the Tampa 2,'" Minter said. "He keeps Dick LeBeau and doesn't mess with the defense. He didn't let his ego get in the way."

On January 22, 2007, Tomlin and the Steelers made it official. He signed a four-year contract with a one-year option, worth $2.5 million per season. That put him in the lower end of NFL head coaching salaries. Still, it was a huge increase from the $750,000 he received in his one season with the Vikings, and a *massive* upgrade from the $8,000 he earned at VMI a dozen years earlier.

Silver believes some of the confusion over exactly *when* the decision was made to hire Tomlin can be attributed to the fact that both the Steelers and the NFL wanted to make the announcement *after* the AFC Championship Game (that was played a day after Silver's report). Not only did the Steelers want to avoid creating a league-wide distraction, according to Silver, they also didn't want to give Tomlin an advantage in contract negotiations if he knew he was the team's choice all along.

"You've got a young, black coach during a time when the hiring inequity was so glaring," Silver said. "It was kind of a hot-button topic at that moment. If they had then tried to shake him down to take a terrible deal and he had said no and they lost him, it would not have reflected well.

"An owner I really trust told me after the fact, 'If you ever see the Rooneys and they're kind of glaring at you or giving you the evil eye, you probably cost them a million dollars or more.' They couldn't low ball him the way they would have, and he knew that."

Unfortunately, I did not witness Tomlin's historic press conference in person. Due to bad weather, my return flight from Indianapolis was delayed. In fact, neither Brown—who also experienced weather difficulties returning from Chicago—nor myself were in attendance. And we needed to be there to show our faces to the new coach, as well as try to make nice with the Steelers organization as a result of the *Trib*'s article misfire.

Tomlin gave the audience a preview of things to come. He projected a rich speaking voice, delivering each word with poise and clarity, as well as brevity. He revealed a sharp wit and low-key sense of humor.

Tomlin's introductory presser was attended by approximately fifty media members, Steelers officials and staff members, well-wishers, and Tomlin's wife, Kiya, who stood to the right of her husband at the podium next to the Rooneys. On a typically cold thirty-four-degree Pittsburgh winter day, Tomlin wore traditional Steelers colors—black suit, gold tie. He answered a total of forty-five questions.

Introduced by Art Rooney II, Tomlin opened humbly: "First and foremost, my wife and I would like to give honor and thanks to God for opening this door for my family."

When asked about erroneous media reports leading up to his hiring, Tomlin, who interviewed for one other head coaching vacancy before meeting with the Steelers, tried to make light of the situation. "Not confusing for me," he said. "The Rooneys were very upfront about the process, where it was going and how it was going. At times I thought some of the reports, the false reports, were comical. It wasn't necessarily funny when they weren't going in my favor, but it's a part of the process."

One of the keys when taking over a new team is understanding the city and legacy. Becoming a coach in the Steel City is not to be taken lightly, and showing that you not only accept—but embrace—the mindset of the fans and media is critical to future success. So, when asked about team expectations, Tomlin replied, "We intend to make no bold predictions about what we're going to do. What we are going to do is promise to have a first-class, blue-collar work ethic in how we approach our business."

Predictably, the media concentrated on Tomlin's age. He knew the questions were coming and teed off like a power hitter on a 3-0 fastball. "I don't think it will take them long to realize my goals as a coach are no different than any other coach they've ever had. I've got a job to do from a coaching standpoint. They've got a job to do from a player's standpoint. My age is my age."

One of the key questions to Tomlin was retaining LeBeau and any potential adjustments to the team's defensive scheme. "Anybody in this business knows and has a great deal of respect for coach LeBeau, and I look forward to having the opportunity to work with him. . . . I really think you just look at your personnel and what they do well and what puts them in position to win and, obviously, retaining coach LeBeau is a big part of that."

When asked *again* about the team's defense, Tomlin made it clear that there would be no direct change, but also responding that the key was getting the best out of his players. "I think part of good coaching is knowing what your guys do and what they do well. We'll maximize what they're capable of doing. And if that means setting some personal preferences and beliefs schematically aside, I'm willing to do that. X's and O's can be overrated at times. You'll find that we'll be fundamentalist in our approach, and we'll put guys in position to execute, and execute at a high level."

When asked about Tony Dungy and Lovie Smith advancing to Super Bowl XLI, and Tomlin being named the Steelers' first black head coach twenty-four hours later, Tomlin replied, "I guess we'll make true advances in this process when it's [race] no longer an issue."

Near the end of the press conference, Tomlin was asked what role, if any, the Rooney Rule played in his hire. "I personally can't answer that," he said. "Speaking to the Rooney Rule, you know, I think it's a positive thing. It gives people an opportunity to present themselves, their ideas, their visions. The decisions that people make after that I think are totally based on who they think is capable of doing the job. I think it's been an awesome experience for me. Maybe the rule itself opened a door for me that may not have been open had it not been for the rule."

The day wasn't over for reporters, who got a two-for-one news day when Art Rooney II held an unscheduled press conference following Tomlin's media gathering.

Rooney defended the Steelers' hiring process, addressing media rumors the Steelers hired Tomlin after first presenting the job to Grimm.

"They [the reports] were . . . saying we were dishonest," said Rooney II. "Our integrity means more than anything. We said all along that we were going to follow a process."

Forty-eight hours after Tomlin's hire, the story continued to gather legs. Under the headline, 'Grimm Never Got Offer, Rooney Says," Brown wrote an article contradicting the *Trib's* original story. The lede paragraph said: "[The] team never offered Russ Grimm the head coaching job despite reports saying an offer was extended."

Rooney also addressed a CBS Sportsline article by Clark Judge that appeared the same day. Judge also reported that Grimm was offered the Steelers job, citing three sources close to the team. Judge said Grimm was told he could inform those close to him he would be the Steelers' next coach.

Brown's *Trib* article quoted Rooney II saying that while the Steelers agreed on the basis of a contract with Grimm on January 20, the team made it clear he didn't have the job. A final decision was made the next day, after meeting with Dan Rooney and Colbert. He added that working out a contract agreement with both Tomlin and Grimm was part of the process.

There was no mention if the Steelers worked out a contract agreement with Rivera.

"Our intention was the numbers [for a contract] were going to be done before we made a final decision," Rooney II said.

On January 23, Grimm joined Ken Whisenhunt's coaching staff in Arizona. He told reporters he never received a firm offer from the Steelers.

"I thought I had a shot at it," said Grimm, "but whatever the details are and things like that. . . . The Rooneys did their search. I respect the decision, and it is time to move on."

Based on the team's track record, Grimm didn't fit the prototype of what the Steelers were seeking in a head coach. The last three Steelers coaches were all in their thirties when they were hired. Grimm was forty-eight at the time, fourteen years older than Tomlin.

According to a 2023 ESPN article, Indianapolis Colts owner Jim Irsay once asked Dan Rooney why he hired coaches so young. "He said, 'Jim, they don't have as much stuff to unlearn,'" said Irsay. "'They're not encumbered by these things that they've learned and gotten comfortable with. They're able to be more free in the direction they want to go.'"

During Tomlin's press conference, there was one quote that made it clear not only the type of person he was, but what he felt would put his team in the best position for success. When asked (a second time) about the hiring of assistants now that he had taken the job, and his plan on setting up a strong staff, he eloquently said, "Continuity is a factor, it's not the only factor. We're looking for good men who happen to be good coaches."

10

FIRST YEAR AT THE HELM

PITTSBURGH STEELERS
(HEAD COACH, 2007)

"Pressure is forever relevant. You're either feeling it or applying it."

THE Pittsburgh Steelers are an NFL institution. No team has won more Super Bowls; their Lombardi trophies sit proudly in six individual trophy cases on the second floor, at 3400 South Water Street . . . all of which makes Mike Tomlin's hire in January 2007 such a revelation. Tomlin arrived eleven months after the Steelers had won Super Bowl XL over the Seattle Seahawks. None of the eight previous African American head coaches hired before Tomlin in the modern era took over a team left in such good shape—only two seasons removed from winning a Super Bowl. Next closest was Chicago's Lovie Smith, who took over the Bears twenty years after the franchise appeared in its last Super Bowl. Three of those eight coaches took over teams that had never appeared in a Super Bowl. Tomlin was breathing rarified air.

In conducting his introductory news conference with the Pittsburgh media the day after being named the 16th—and first African American—coach in franchise history, Tomlin was unflappable in answering nearly four dozen questions which tested his patience and all of his communication skills. Appearing in front of the klieg lights, he didn't need to mop his brow once, even managing to crack a smile or two.

"Think about it," explained Hall of Fame linebacker Derrick Brooks, who was in the trenches with Tomlin for five years with the Tampa Bay Buccaneers. Brooks was one of three Buccaneers defenders to run back an interception for a touchdown in Tampa Bay's 48–21 annihilation of the Oakland Raiders in Super Bowl XXXVII, a game that first put Tomlin on the national map due to the outstanding performance by his secondary. "You have Coach [Tony] Dungy as one of your mentors and teachers," Brooks continued. "You go on to be the head coach where your mentor got started. You're under his coaching tree in Pittsburgh. And that's overwhelming. At the same time, he remains humble because it's no secret: a lot of people did not have him as their first choice in Pittsburgh. I can say it: a lot of people were not happy with this decision. But he never let that deter him or be a factor because, again, Coach Dungy went through that in Tampa and he shared those experiences with Coach Mike T. I think that relationship alone allowed a certain level of comfort, or a certain level of confidence that he says, 'I am who I am. I'm not apologizing about it because there's nothing to apologize for.' He didn't cry about it. He said, 'I'll earn your trust. I have that equity. At the end of the day, I'm going to set a standard and I'm going to do the best job I can as your head coach.'"

During the interview process, Tomlin presented a staff proposal to the Rooneys and Kevin Colbert about the assistants he wanted to hire. For the most part, they agreed with his choices. It was important for Tomlin to put his stamp on the team and make a statement by introducing his new coaching staff and how they aligned with his organizational vision.

Would it make sense for Tomlin to come in and blow everything up and push out Dick LeBeau—whose Cincinnati Bengals defense Tomlin watched from afar when he was a University of Cincinnati assistant coach? Tomlin understood that bringing the 4-3 alignment he coached in Minnesota and Tampa Bay to Pittsburgh would require teaching current Steelers defenders a new system, as well as acquiring players already versed in how to play the 4-3. Why do that when he could blend certain elements of his 4-3 with LeBeau's already established 3-4, which regularly ranked among the NFL's top units?

"Would I come in and blow everything up just for the sake of doing it because this is my initial plan? No, you can't do that," Tomlin said on the *Footbahlin with Roethlisberger* podcast in 2023. "You can't ask the player personnel department to all of a sudden scrap all of the players you have and try to find everything to fit automatically. In Pittsburgh, you look at the players they have and it would almost be like trying to put a round peg in square hole."

Pro Bowl nose tackle Casey Hampton was one of the round peg holdovers from the Cowher regime. "If it ain't broke, don't try to fix it. That was the smartest thing," said Hampton, who played for the Steelers from 2001 to 2012. "The defense was already ready, so it would have been crazy to make a change."

Defensive coordinator? Check.

With LeBeau already assured of returning as defensive coordinator, Tomlin, upon meeting with Bruce Arians at the Senior Bowl the same week he was hired, promoted Arians from wide receivers coach to offensive coordinator. Arians was the Cleveland Browns' offensive coordinator from 2001 to 2003. In a 2002 playoff loss at Pittsburgh, Browns journeyman quarterback Kelly Holcomb, with Arians calling the plays, threw for 429 yards and three touchdowns.

Offensive coordinator? Check.

Desiring his own quarterbacks coach to work with Ben Roethlisberger, now heading into his fourth season, Tomlin did not retain Mark Whipple, who had served for three years under Cowher. Tomlin's first choice was Rip Scherer Jr., who hired him at Memphis in 1996 and was now the quarterbacks coach for the Cleveland Browns.

Colbert, Scherer's cousin, put the kibosh on that idea.

According to Scherer, Tomlin called him after his second interview with the Steelers and before he was offered the head coaching position.

Scherer asked Tomlin how the interview went. Tomlin said, "Great," but he added a pause.

"It was something to the effect that they didn't think it would be good for Ben, the fact that Kevin and I were cousins," Scherer said.

Undaunted, Tomlin offered Scherer the Steelers' tight ends coaching position that had been held by James Daniel since 2004.

Scherer already had an NFL job coaching quarterbacks. He was appreciative of the offer, but told Tomlin thanks, but no thanks. Daniel went on to coach Steelers tight ends until his retirement after the 2020 season.

When Scherer saw Colbert at the Senior Bowl that year, he wanted to know how the Steelers decided on their quarterbacks coach.

"I said, 'Kevin, what's the deal?'" Scherer said.

"Kevin goes, 'No, Rip. It was me. I told Mike I didn't think it would be a good idea.'"

Instead of Scherer, his first choice, Tomlin selected Ken Anderson, the former Bengals quarterback who had been the quarterbacks coach and offensive coordinator for the NFL team when Tomlin was coaching defensive backs at the University of Cincinnati. Anderson, a four-time league passing champion who spent the previous four seasons as a Jacksonville Jaguars assistant, was the first quarterback to run Bill Walsh's West Coast offense. An accurate passer an excellent decision-maker, Anderson was Tomlin's logical backup choice to tutor Roethlisberger, who had thrown a league-high 23 interceptions the previous season.[1]

Former Arkansas State colleague Randy Fichtner, who exchanged phone numbers with Tomlin at a Memphis high school in 1997, was a natural to replace Arians as the wide

---

1 In his first season working under Anderson, Roethlisberger threw 10 fewer interceptions. His 26 touchdown passes were a career high and he ranked fourth in the league with a 101.4 passer rating.

receivers coach. Fichtner called plays for six years at the University of Memphis.

"I still have the message [from Tomlin]," Fichtner told Steelers. com in 2018. "The only thing it said: 'I got the job, and so do you.' I played it on the speaker phone for my wife. She started crying. I was tearing up."

Rounding out his hires, Tomlin also added former University of Cincinnati colleagues Larry Zierlein (offensive line coach) and Amos Jones (assistant special teams coach) as well as Kirby Wilson, who was the running backs coach at Tampa Bay for two of the five years that Tomlin was there.

"It shows you about the character of Mike," Rick Minter said. "He becomes a trusted friend and ally to a lot of people, and then those are the kind of guys he wants to surround himself with.

"Larry Zierlein worked for me at Cincinnati for a long time. That was Mike's first O-line coach. He had Amos Jones on the staff, he worked for me. Keith. Randy. He trusted those guys."

In total, Tomlin retained six assistants from Bill Cowher's staff, including defensive backs coach Ray Horton and linebackers coach Keith Butler, his former colleague at Memphis and Arkansas State.

Tomlin traveled from the Senior Bowl back to Minnesota for a few days to handle personal business before returning to Pittsburgh and announcing his new coaching staff featuring a Dungy twist: identifying and hiring coaches as teachers.

Tomlin told all his coaches to think like a teacher first in the classroom; that they should run their meetings like a class, like a lesson plan. Tomlin's thoughtfulness and his football curriculum was very apparent. He coached/taught with structure, and he made sure his coaches all knew the amount of information they needed to cover in meetings.

"It's not that we all think the same," Tomlin told reporters. "But guys who have the base core values that I have. As coaches, we need to be teachers. Success is built on fundamentals, muscle memory, and execution."

* * *

Standing 6-foot-3 and tipping the scales at 315 pounds, Willie Colon was entering his second NFL season and feeling good about his football future. While having high hopes for himself, Colon spent most of his time figuring out how he was going to crack the starting lineup. As a rookie, he started two games at right tackle under Cowher. Like many of his teammates, Colon concluded that Cowher was on his way out the door, as that seemed to be the theme for the entire 2006 season. As a team, the Steelers collectively rode the wave of that mindset and finished 8–8, missing the playoffs a year after winning Super Bowl XL.

Colon saw the light at the end of the tunnel regarding his Steelers future. Even with Cowher gone, the talk on the street and inside the locker room pointed to one of Cowher's lieutenants, assistant head coach/offensive line coach Russ Grimm, as his replacement. "Russ was my offensive line coach. I loved Russ," said Colon. "There was nothing that Russ could say to me that I wouldn't do. If he needed me to slaughter a cow or save a baby from a fire, I was willing to do it for him."

Cowher left a lasting impression with Colon, who viewed Grimm—who was not only the offense line coach, but also the assistant head coach—as a reasonable facsimile of the Steelers' former leader.

"When Pittsburgh drafted me and BC [Cowher] walked in the door the first time, I swear to God, there was a golden aura around him, this golden ring," said Colon, a fourth-round selection from Hofstra. "I remember saying to myself, 'Holy, shit, that's Bill Cowher.' And sitting in a room where the guys had just won a Super Bowl—they had been rocking and rolling all offseason to celebrate—the place was rowdy and loud. I just came from the Bronx, New York. How the hell do I end up in Pittsburgh, Pennsylvania?

"I'm sitting in the back of the room looking at Troy Polamalu, Ben Roethlisberger, Joey Porter, and James Harrison, and I'm kind of having an out-of-body experience, on top of coach Cowher walking in that room. When he walked in, the room goes deafening quiet. I was like, 'Woah.' He looks around the room and says, 'Men, we are the Pittsburgh Steelers and we've got a target on our backs. It's time to go to work.' Just like that, everybody zoomed out of the room. I was like, 'Oh, shit.' I couldn't help it."

Entering his seventh season and having just played in his second consecutive Pro Bowl, Hampton, unlike Colon, was no longer wide-eyed when Cowher spoke to the team. Hampton enjoyed playing for Cowher, but football to him was a business as much as it was a game. He would play as hard for the next coach as he did for Cowher. He held no personal attachment to Grimm or another one of Cowher's lieutenants, offensive coordinator Ken Whisenhunt. But like everyone else, he assumed they were the two leaders in the clubhouse.

"From what we were hearing, somebody inside the organization was going to get the job," Hampton said. "We felt like we were close to getting back. We just had a Super Bowl hangover. You know how that goes. Partying and we had a long offseason. Just enjoying it, and perhaps enjoying it a little bit too much. We didn't think we needed to make a whole lot of changes. That was kind of the consensus with the guys."

It figured to take a special coach to follow Cowher, who went by the nickname "BC" to his players. Either way, whomever replaced BC had gargantuan-sized shoes to fill.

Therefore, it spoke volumes about Tomlin's entrance and introduction to his new team; that Steeler players—regardless of personal preferences about who the coach should be—immediately locked into his message.

"To walk into that locker room after just winning a Super Bowl with a Hall of Fame coach, there may be some impression from the outside you need to get on his [Cowher's] level or you're going to be exiled," Colon said. "I don't think Mike T ever walked in with that mindset, like I need to be better than Bill Cowher. I think he walked in with the mindset that you've given me the keys to the Porsche, I'm not going to crash it. I think he was hungry to let the world know that I'm not just this token black coach for this historic football team."

According to one Steelers veteran, "My first impression was that he [Tomlin] was eager, he was hungry, and he seemed to have a pulse early on the team, which I think a lot of coaches don't necessarily have. That's [normally] something that develops over time."

The players couldn't help but notice that Tomlin was one of only five African American coaches entering the 2007 NFL season. Like many of the Steelers on a team that was predominately black—as is, and was, most of the league—Tomlin was many of the players' first black head coach at any level, dating all the way to high school or even Pop Warner.

"This dude's got a fresh edge-up, he's got a little baby fro," safety Ryan Clark, who was entering his second season with the Steelers, said on the *Pivot* podcast. "This is a real brother. This is not somebody that . . . went through the interview process and they were like, 'Oh, this feels familiar to me. I've heard guys talk like this all the time. He's just a little tan.'"

"That got my attention," Hampton admitted. "I was stunned in a way, but not. Because I know the Rooneys are going to pick the best person [based on] the way the organization is run. They got this young guy, thirty-four years old, who's never been a head coach before, he must have wowed them. They're not just hiring this guy to hire him."

Tomlin had his supporters. "He made a hell of a first impression," running back Willie Parker told reporters at the Pro Bowl that offseason. "He came and found me, and we had a big meeting in his office what he expects of me."

Tomlin also had plenty of detractors on a roster led to believe Grimm would be their new head coach. And if not Grimm, then most likely Whisenhunt. Speaking at the same Pro Bowl as teammate Parker, guard Alan Faneca said, "When Cowher retired, everybody in the league wanted two of our guys. So you'd think we would want at least one of them."

Shortly after Tomlin was hired, Roethlisberger, his franchise quarterback, invited him to lunch.

In an article appearing in *Sports Illustrated* in January 2009, Peter King wrote that Roethlisberger was the bearer of bad news. Numerous players on the Steelers—including several *key* players—weren't happy that Tomlin got the job over Grimm or

Whisenhunt. Either one of them would have sufficed, just *anybody but Tomlin*, who was young and a virtual unknown to those voicing the strongest opposition.

"You're going to have to earn the guys' respect and trust," Ben told Tomlin in the *SI* article.

With the full support of the Rooneys, Tomlin didn't seek comfort from his players.

If anything, he wanted to make his players as uncomfortable as he was.

"I resist comfort," Tomlin said on the *Pivot* podcast. "We all want to be comfortable. I realize that if you're going to have special outcomes, you've got to be comfortable being uncomfortable. I've trained myself over the years to resist comfort."

During his first spring practice with the Steelers, Tomlin introduced the uncomfortable "News" to his players, just as he did in Minnesota and learned firsthand in Tampa Bay.

During a team meeting in the spring, Tomlin flashed a pen light on one of the team's wide receivers for spiking the ball after a catch. Had the wide receiver scored a touchdown, his action would not have been penalized. But a new rule adopted for the upcoming season penalized players for spiking the ball after a non-scoring play, resulting in Tomlin putting the WR in the "News" to get his players' attention.

Thing is, the wide receiver in the "News" was none other than Hines Ward, who had been the Super Bowl XL MVP.

It did.

"I don't think guys liked the 'News' too much," Hampton said. "Sometimes it was funny. Sometimes it wasn't. But it brought accountability."

Tomlin also fined Faneca for skipping mandatory practice over contract negotiations. Faneca did not sign a new deal with Pittsburgh and became a free agent at the end of the season.

Colon said that despite Faneca's popularity on the team, he personally didn't hold Tomlin's unpopular stance against him.

"I think a lot of that was out of his hands," Colon said. "So much of the front office dictates what a coach can do or say. I think he had to let that play itself out. I think Mike T, at that time, just had to take care of the team and go with the wave. He's still a young coach. He's not going to say, 'Hey, if this guy isn't signed, that's my job.' He's like, 'Dude, I just got here. I'm still sinking my teeth in this team.' He had to trust Colbert and the Rooneys to do what's best for the team."

Coaching the Steelers extended beyond mastering X's and O's on game day. Tomlin faced a series of potential distractions which could have been overwhelming for a new coach, especially one making his head coaching debut. Tomlin, however, stood his ground each time.

After leading the team in sacks the previous season, star linebacker Joey Porter was seeking a new contract. He got a new deal, although not from the Steelers. Following his release two months into Tomlin's rookie season (in a salary cap move), Porter signed a five-year, $32 million contract with the Miami Dolphins. To some, it looked like an attempt by Steelers management to remove Porter's strong locker room presence and allow Tomlin to shape the team in his image.

"I think one of the reasons they let Joey go is because of the hold he had on the team," Hampton said. "To give Mike T the whole team to himself."

"We talked on the phone when he knew they were going in a different direction," said Porter, who recorded 98 career sacks in 13 NFL seasons. "He was a young coach. I was almost at the end of my contract and it was either going to be re-sign me or not re-sign me. We had a young James Harrison who was coming into his own. I'm still feeling like I'm the guy, so that's not even a question of how I feel I'm playing; I'm still playing at a high clip. They went in a different direction. I went to Miami. That's part of the business."

On the final day of spring practice before the players dispersed until training camp, Ward finally gave in.

"No question, when you have nine, ten years with one guy [Cowher], you're going to miss him," said Ward, who was selected by his teammates to approach Tomlin about the heavy workload during spring practice.

Tomlin's response? He took the entire team bowling and created "hat day," so the players didn't have to wear helmets.

"We all miss Coach Cowher, but we can't play this game forever," Ward said. "Players, coaches come and go, and you have to move on."

"When he's going over film, it means a lot when a coach comes in and he knows what he's talking about," Hampton said. "It ain't him just giving speeches. He got immediate respect from the guys from that standpoint."

* * *

Tomlin, warning the Steelers of what lay ahead in their first training camp together, prepared his players for all the physical and psychological hazards they would face at St. Vincent

College in Latrobe, approximately forty-five minutes from downtown Pittsburgh.

"It's going to be extremely tough," Tomlin told reporters. "I am not apologizing for that."

Tomlin scheduled fifteen days of twice-daily practices, with no days off, over the first two weeks of camp. That was more than twice as many as Cowher scheduled the previous season. To be fair, seven of Tomlin's practices were shortened and mostly for special teams players, not including the entire roster. The work overload featured the team reporting to camp four days earlier than they would have in the past, to prepare for a fifth exhibition game against the New Orleans Saints at the Hall of Fame Game in Canton, Ohio.

In 2007, NFL training camps were considered a rite of passage. Training camp at that time was hard, but for this team it *had* to be hard if they were still going to consider themselves bullies on the AFC North block. It had to be hard because the Baltimore Ravens were neck-to-neck with the Steelers for top spot in the division. It had to be hard because of the elite quarterbacks the Steelers faced during that era: Tom Brady, Peyton Manning, and Philip Rivers in the AFC; Drew Brees and Kurt Warner in the NFC. It had to be hard because Tomlin said so. That's why.

In the new coach's mind, there was no way to do it other than the hard way.

For a head coach—never mind a rookie one—the only way to find out what you had before embarking on the season is to find out who's going to crumble, who's going to rumble, who's going to stand tall, and who's going to fail. With Tomlin, you were either thriving or surviving.

"You're complaining about how bad that shit is—we're in Latrobe in the middle of August—with this black helmet on . . . . On top of that, we've got a nine-on-seven drill and our defense is number one in the league and they're trying to kick our ass," Colon said. "Or you can say to yourself, 'I'm a god-damn Pittsburgh Steeler, I'm blessed to have my feet in cleats, and I'm kicking ass today despite whoever's in front of me.' It had to be hard, because we were rock stars."

Some veterans didn't appreciate the two-a-day practices—especially when compared with Cowher's lighter training camp routine from the previous year—but they gave Tomlin the benefit of the doubt out of respect for their new coach.

"He was really hard on us," Hampton said. "Just [him] not knowing that we're a veteran team and that we know what we need to do. He was just trying to make his imprint on the team. You had to respect it. A man's got to do things his way.

"With us being a veteran team and everything that he was saying was so matter of fact and so business-like, guys really gravitated to that. He *was* making sense."

At the conclusion of the final practice of his first training camp with the Steelers, Tomlin told reporters he saw what he needed to see from his players. That, to him, was more significant than their unhappiness about the additional workload.

"It has been as good as could be expected," Tomlin said.

"We're all creatures of habit, particularly the guys that have been here a long time. Guys who were drafted here, they know one way. When you know what's going on, you never have to look at the schedule. You can kind of get on autopilot. That's what we crave. We like to be on autopilot and know what lies ahead.

"But sometimes, it's good to get out of your comfort zone a little bit and have to read an itinerary, have to keep up with the schedule and don't really know what's going on next. That's how the process has been for some people."

* * *

Employing a tactic he applied at his two previous NFL stops, Tomlin spoke individually with players, making the necessary connection to get the best out of them. Pittsburgh in 2007 may as well have been Minneapolis in 2006 or Tampa in 2001, when Tomlin planted the idea in Ronde Barber's mind that he could become the first defensive back in league history to register 20-plus career sacks.

"If that's what you need to turn the corner, he's very good at telling you about yourself—good, bad, or indifferent," Barber said. "He'll say, 'Keep doing what you're doing. Or you need to work on this. Or you do this too much.' He has no problem mincing words or fixing what he thinks will make you a better player."

When Steelers cornerback Ike Taylor heard what his new head coach did for Barber, three words came to mind: "I'm very fortunate."

Taylor was a hero in the Steelers' Super Bowl win over Seattle. His fourth-quarter interception led to Antwaan Randle-El's clinching touchdown pass. Taylor was rewarded with a five-year, $22.5 million contract prior to the start of the 2006 season, but things turned sour when Cowher benched him for five games.

After watching film, Tomlin reinserted the 6-foot-1 Taylor as the starting left corner in August, with a suggestion: lower his pad level and bend his knees in coverage.

"We talked, and it was good," Taylor said in an article I wrote for the *Pittsburgh Tribune-Review*. "We were just trying to get to know each other. Coach told me he knows what I can do. He's been with Ronde Barber; he knows what it takes."

Tomlin also returned Taylor to his more familiar role of defending the league's top receivers in single coverage, a strategy that Cowher had put in mothballs.

"Early on, Coach Tomlin was more like a player-coach. He let you do your thing until you did something bad. He wouldn't put you in check because he was trying to get to know the team," said Taylor's uncle, Herman Francois, who raised Taylor in New Orleans from the time he was in seventh grade through attending college at Louisiana-Lafayette. "Coach Tomlin made Ike better. He made him more of a 'Don't worry about your job; you're going to be alright' player."

When Tomlin took over in 2007, the Steelers were Ryan Clark's third team, signing with Pittsburgh from Washington as an unrestricted free agent in 2006 after starting free safety Chris Hope left as a free agent to sign with Tennessee. Clark, who started 50 games with Washington and the New York Giants prior to joining the Steelers, had been used primarily as a defensive back and strong safety.

He then sat down with Tomlin to discuss his future, when the new coach shared with the undrafted defender what he envisioned for the journeyman: learning the new position of free safety.

"The first time I met him, I said my goal is for you to no longer be a journeyman," Tomlin said on Clark's podcast.

Tomlin promised Clark that there would be no more moving around, going from team to team in search of a permanent home. Pittsburgh *was* his home.

"You're going to be a Pittsburgh Steeler for life," Tomlin said.

Rummaging through his motivational bag, Tomlin pulled out the emotional trigger that set Clark off.

"Every now and then, I'd called him a journeyman," Tomlin said. "That's the trigger.

"That dude needed a place to hang his hat. He needed a place to call home. He'd been on many organizations, but what organization was he going to connect with? I wanted him to connect with the experience we were going to share. I wanted to talk openly about the elephant in the room. How [we] could go about the business of working together chasing Ws."

An NFL team consists of fifty-three players. The goal of every team is to develop a strategy relative to the opposition by bringing out the best in the collective. To better manage the collective, the coach must have a handle on every individual in the collective.

Clark achieved the potential that Tomlin predicted for him. Overcoming health issues, he became a full-time starter for seven consecutive years, including a Pro Bowl appearance after playing in only six games in 2007 due to having his spleen removed because of the sickle cell trait.

Tomlin applied a different approach with Hampton, who made the Pro Bowl three times prior to the coach's arrival.

"He pretty much met with everybody individually," Hampton said. "He said, 'I really didn't have an opinion about you until

I saw film on you. You stayed on your feet a lot more than I thought. It's time for you to be a great player, instead of a good player.' He felt I was a good player who could be a lot better and hadn't reached my full potential." That season, Hampton made the Pro Bowl for the third consecutive year.

* * *

A pro football team can be defined in many ways. Of course, how a team performs on the field is its most important quality. With six Super Bowls, the Steelers are the ultimate NFL winners. But a team also can be defined, in part, by how it presents itself to the public.

Tomlin was the Steelers' most ebullient representative. He delivered motivational speeches to his players and conveyed similar messages to those inside the building who were designated conduits to the city of Pittsburgh.

Tomlin's ego-less personality and presence—call it *approachability*—helped create a culture that permeated throughout the organization.

He embraced the Steelers' culture immediately. When he interviewed with the team, he saw the Rooneys were pretty much different than any other ownership he had previously experienced.

"Mike communicates in a way that people respect and feel respected," said a former league source. "He made it an inclusive culture. And he did it without ego. He's always, 'It's not about me.' But it was about a bigger picture—the brand, what the team wants, what the team goals are. That was his goal.

"He sat down and met with everybody in every department," the source added. "Just to chat and find out what needed to be done, what the challenges were, what people were working on, and how they worked. He showed support for the non-football staff. I don't know how many coaches do that. That was new to everybody in the organization, the fact that he took the time to sit down with people and show that he cared about everyone's job."

Tomlin made everyone in the organization feel they were a part of the process, part of the Steelers being the successful NFL franchise they had become, and that everyone—on and off the field—was working together for the greater good of the team.

At the conclusion of his 17th training camp with the Steelers, Tomlin patiently answered a non-football question from the media about how well the team's playing surface staff members maintained multiple practice fields throughout camp.

"Coop and Company have done an awesome job," said Tomlin, referring to Cooper Gulley and the rest of the staff. "First presenting some quality fields for us. But also working hard to maintenance them and keep them upright as well as tear them down. I can't say enough about the service that they provided. There have been some challenges, particularly early on. We had some rain days and so forth. We had to put together a tarp crew. We just respect all the roles departmentally that make this thing go. That field group is significant."

Tomlin created a level of comfort that allowed the football side and the corporate side to develop better synergy. He took the time to speak to people. Just as important, people felt that he would listen to them. If there were events or causes he felt players should be participating in, he would get involved. He enabled *everybody* to do their respective jobs with more confidence because they knew he would support the goals of the company.

That included corporate goals, as well as community and public relations needs.

In essence, Tomlin became the Steelers de facto CEO. He knew he was going to a place that had a set culture. Yet there was an art to establishing his own culture. He took the time to communicate with people so they could understand where he was coming from. It wasn't a rah-rah speech, but rather communicating in a way that helped educate everyone in the organization that he was going to take an intellectual approach to coaching. He personified the culture; what the organization stood for. He understood leadership, saw the big picture, and conceptualized the importance of flexible thinking, of not doing everything the same way.

"I don't think Bill [Cowher] liked change as much," said the league source. "Bill wanted to keep things the same way. He was more of a 'I'm going to keep you on your toes' kind of person to keep you sharp. That was his approach. I don't think people liked talking to Bill because Bill was not a guy who would foster that kind of a culture. Mike is a guy who will speak with you, who will sit down with everybody in every department. That's what you need in a job that's so demanding and so high-profile."

"I'm gonna keep it real with you, man. Other than out on the field, very rarely did we talk football," Hampton said in describing his six-year relationship with Tomlin. "It was family talk about everyday life, the kids. Our kids were around the same age. He and Cowher were different, but they were effective in their own way. Cowher was less approachable to everybody. Guys who didn't know him were scared to approach him. But he was cool as hell."

Cowher was famous for calling players into his office to talk. "Coach T came and saw you," Colon said. "He would walk up on you. It wasn't, 'Come to my office after lunch' or 'Come to my office after practice.' Sometimes I would just be finishing my reps and he'd be like, 'Hey, Colon, let me talk to you.' And he would just spit whatever he had for me. He was never the coach that sat in the ivory tower."

* * *

Tomlin was among the first group of young coaches in the NFL. In fact, thanks to Tomlin, owners became more comfortable with the idea that you didn't have to be fifty years old before receiving your first head coaching gig—especially after Tomlin became the youngest coach—and the second African American coach—to win a Super Bowl.

In 2006, thirty-five-year-old Eric Mangini became the youngest coach in the league with the New York Jets. Tomlin became the league's youngest coach the following year, but for only a day, because the Oakland Raiders tabbed thirty-two-year-old Lane Kiffin, the son of Tomlin's former defensive coordinator in Tampa Bay, one day later. In 2009, after three seasons in New York and a combined 23–25 record, Mangini resurfaced as the Cleveland Browns' new head coach. Also that year, the Denver Broncos hired thirty-two-year-old Josh McDaniels, while Tampa Bay hired another coach with ties to Tomlin, thirty-two-year-old Raheem Morris.

Tomlin set the standard for the league hiring head coaches in their thirties. What the Steelers saw in Tomlin was a young man who, if given the reins to one of the NFL's most storied franchises, was confident enough to be himself. In New York, Mangini tried to be like his mentor, Bill Belichick. He tried to be like someone else, what worked for them. Think about the successful head coaches like Belichick and their coaching trees. You get lieutenants like Mangini and McDaniels, who tried to be like their former boss who's arguably the greatest coach in NFL history. Athletes can sniff out if you're not being genuine.

Tomlin did not come in and try to be like anyone else but himself. Some of the Steelers said it was a little bit of a challenge because he wanted them to be comfortable with being uncomfortable, seeing who in the locker room had the capability to adapt. Tomlin had to learn. He didn't know guys. Quite frankly, it's easy for an organization—especially an organization like the Steelers, which had enjoyed so much success doing things a certain way for a long period of time—to insist that Tomlin do things Cowher's way. Tomlin gave everyone a chance to prove themselves—his way. He needed to be confident in himself to come to Pittsburgh as an outsider. Otherwise, he would just be continuing what was done in the past. That didn't mean he was being weak and easier on the guys. But he didn't need to wear it on his sleeve as a badge of honor. He treated everyone like adults, as professionals, until they proved otherwise. He respected everyone as individuals. He'd listen and hear you out. You had a chance to state your case if you could properly defend your position. You're going to disagree on some things. That's human nature. It's the juggling act of any NFL head coach.

There are many different layers to an NFL head coach. Tomlin understands the psychology of dealing with the media, what the media wants to do, etc. How many times has he said during a press conference, "It's not about me." When reporters talk about his success, he always says, "It's about the men on the field."

"When he's talking to the press, he's talking to his *team*," Ed Tomlin said about his younger brother. "Those guys tune in and listen to how he does his business. He sets his tone with them. Everything he does is geared toward, in, and around them."

Tomlin came into the job understanding the role and importance of the media covering the Steelers. He also understood how to deal with the media; how to make the media work to his advantage. He didn't let an article or two rent space in his mind if someone wrote something he didn't like or disagreed with. And not that he'd forget about it, but it wasn't something he had to deal with at that moment. It could wait until a better time—his time. It's why reporters still gravitate to his press conferences. People who don't cover the Steelers *love* his press conferences. Heck, the Steelers should even charge admission to attend them.

"He reads people very well," Steelers broadcaster Bill Hillgrove said. "The way you phrase a question, or maybe the timing of it, he has that sense of, 'OK, this person is for real or this person is taking a shot at me and the franchise.' If somebody starts to ask those edgy questions, his answers get shorter and shorter. Because he knows they're out there to trap him, and he's not going to be trapped."

Tomlin lives by this axiom: "If the people can't get to you, they can't control you." It shows that he's in control of his emotions and still on top of things, although he had plenty of opportunities to go ballistic on reporters covering the team (myself included). I would attend his press conferences and watch him in action, facing a sea of mostly white faces, wondering what he was thinking, and tell myself, *No way in hell would I sit there with a straight face and not go off on that fool for asking that stupid question.*

From day one, Tomlin dealt with things on an intellectual level. There were no delusions of grandeur about what people might think or how they would react. He understood that was part of the business, that he needed broad shoulders (and he has *very* broad shoulders).

In Tomlin's case, he showed in his interviews that he could be a leader and speak to the culture of the organization. The Steelers knew that if they put Tomlin in front of the cameras, he was not going to embarrass the organization because he could speak to their values. They saw him as the face of their franchise.

* * *

As an African American coach, Tomlin couldn't get away with yelling and railing. He didn't want to be "The angry black guy." White coaches are considered to have more of a fire and brimstone personality. When you look at African American coaches as a collective, very few of them are yellers and screamers. There's a reason for that. It doesn't mean they're any less intense or caring. But they do understand how things work, and how they are viewed by the media and society in general. For instance:

In 2002, in his second season as head coach of the New York Jets, Herman Edwards responded to *New York Times* reporter Judy Battista's question about his 2–5 team not giving up on the season. Edwards's emotional response—*You play to win the game!*—overshadowed anything Edwards ever accomplished as a head coach. The Jets went 7–2 the rest of the way to finish 9–7 and advance to the divisional playoffs that year.

Four years later, Arizona Cardinals head coach Dennis Green, unhappy following his team's loss to Chicago after leading 20–0 at halftime, angrily told reporters, "If you want to crown them, then crown their ass. But they are who we thought they were! And we let them off the hook!" Green was fired after the season.

More recently, Washington Commanders first-year offensive coordinator Eric Bieniemy, who won two Super Bowls with quarterback Patrick Mahomes as the Kansas City Chiefs' offensive coordinator, came under fire from some segments of the media after Ron Rivera, his head coach, told reporters that some offensive players were concerned about Bieniemy's tough-love coaching style for an offense that has not finished higher than 20th in scoring and yards per game since 2017.

According to an ESPN article, "Bieniemy's intensity can be seen and heard daily on the practice field and, according to multiple sources, in the meeting rooms. His voice can be heard from a distance on the field, although he's as quick to praise as he is to admonish."

Such is life for black coaches in the NFL. Is it any wonder why they refrain from raising their voices at players, officials and reporters while trying to maintain self-control at all times?

Green produced winning records in eight of his first nine seasons with the Minnesota Vikings, and he was still fired after posting his first—and only—losing record with the team. That was in 2001. Green resurfaced in Arizona three years later, rebuilt the roster, and was fired the year before the Cardinals advanced to the Super Bowl for the first time. Not permitted to finish the

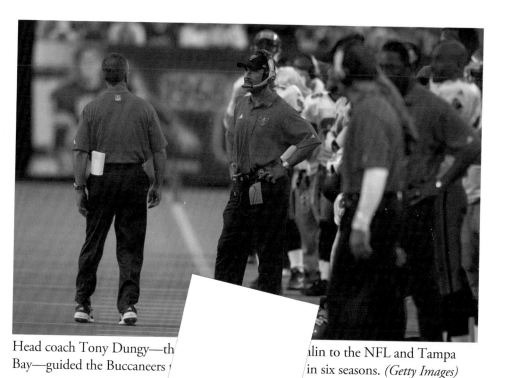

Head coach Tony Dungy—th[...]lin to the NFL and Tampa
Bay—guided the Buccaneers [...] in six seasons. *(Getty Images)*

The recommendation from Monte Kiffin—one of the greatest defensive
minds in NFL history—opened the door for Tomlin to come to Tampa
Bay. *(Getty Images)*

In his only season as Minnesota Vikings defensive coordinator, Mike Tomlin's unit led the NFL in stopping the run, among other categories. *(Getty Images)*

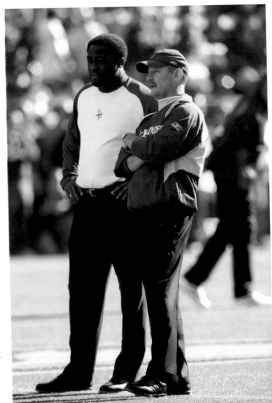

Minnesota Vikings head coach Brad Childress had enough trust in the young Tomlin to give him the keys to the team's defense. *(AP Images)*

Mike Tomlin addresses the media for the first time after becoming the 16th head coach of the Pittsburgh Steelers, on January 22, 2007. *(AP Images)*

Quarterback Ben Roethlisberger celebrates with Tomlin after the Pittsburgh Steelers defeated the Arizona Cardinals, 27–23, in Super Bowl XLIII. *(Getty Images)*

Sharing the numerous emotions that come with Super Bowl victory, Tomlin and wide receiver Hines Ward embrace in the locker room after having hoisted the Lombardi Trophy. *(Getty Images)*

President Barack Obama poses with Pittsburgh Steelers chairman Dan Rooney, Mike Tomlin, and the 2009 Super Bowl champions in the East Room of the White House, on May 21, 2009. *(Getty Images)*

Hall of Fame safety Troy Polamalu was a key figure in Tomlin's defense, and the veteran was receptive to his coach's advice during a win over the Houston Texans, on October 20, 2014. *(Getty Images)*

Linebacker James Harrison (#92) was the ringleader for what Tomlin described as the most intimidating and dominant defense in NFL history. *(Getty Images)*

In one of his first moves after taking over as head coach for the Pittsburth Steelers, Tomlin promoted John Mitchell (left) to assistant head coach. Meanwhile, Tomlin and assistant coach Keith Butler coached together for nearly two decades. *(Getty Images)*

Pittsburgh Steelers linebackers coach Keith Butler (left) and defensive coordinator Dick LeBeau. Butler replaced LeBeau when the Hall of Fame coach moved on from the team in 2015. *(Getty Images)*

Tomlin and longtime coaching colleague Randy Fichtner confer with star wide receiver Antonio Brown during a Week 11 game against the Jacksonville Jaguars in 2018. They would win the game, 20–16, for the team's sixth consecutive victory. *(Getty Images)*

In his first game against the Pittsburgh Steelers since taking over as Arizona Cardinals head coach, Bruce Arians greets Mike Tomlin following the Steelers' 25–13 victory in 2015. *(Getty Images)*

Todd Haley served as the Pittsburgh Steelers offensive coordinator under Mike Tomlin from 2012 to 2017. The Steelers advanced to the postseason in four of those seasons. *(Getty Images)*

More than two decades after coaching together at Virginia Military Institute (VMI), Tomlin and then Atlanta Falcons head coach Dan Quinn convene after the Steelers' 41–17 win in 2018. *(Getty Images)*

Former William & Mary teammates Mike Tomlin and Sean McDermott greet each other at a 2023 preseason game. *(Getty Images)*

Two of the longest tentured coaches in the NFL, Bill Belichick of the New England Patriots and Mike Tomlin of the Pittsburgh Steelers, greet after a 55–31 Pats win in 2013. Through the 2022 season, Tomlin is 3–9 against Belichick, including one play-off loss. *(Getty Images)*

Carolina Panthers head coach Ron Rivera interviewed for the Pittsburgh Steelers head coaching position that went to Mike Tomlin. Here the two meet after a 52–21 Steelers victory in 2018. *(Getty Images)*

During a tumultuous time in the US and NFL, Tomlin stands with his players on the sideline before a preseason game against New Orleans. *(Getty Images)*

Prior to a match-up with the Bengals in 2018, Mike Tomlin stands for the national anthem with (left to right) James Washington (#13), Ben Roethlisberger (#7), Ryan Shazier, and Cameron Heyward (#97). The Steelers would go on to win the game, 28–21. *(Getty Images)*

Coaching isn't easy, as Tomlin knows more than most. But no matter the case, a coach must coach, as he did with wide receiver Antonio Brown (#84) and running backs LeVeon Bell (#26) and LeGarrette Blount (#27). *(Getty Images)*

The always mercurial Antonio Brown provided Tomlin with some of his greatest and most disappointing moments with the Steelers. *(Getty Images)*

Mike Tomlin and New York Jets running back Le'Veon Bell meet for the first time since Bell's departure from Pittsburgh in 2019. Bell rushed for 72 yards in the game, with the Jets winning 16–10. *(Getty Images)*

For his first 15 years as Steelers head coach, Tomlin and Roethlisberger were intertwined. Throughout the highs and lows, they managed to set up a working relationship that led them to a Super Bowl victory and numerous winning seasons. *(Getty Images)*

Taken in the first round of the 2022 NFL Draft (20th), Kenny Pickett is the quarterback for the next generation of Pittsburgh Steelers football. *(Getty Images)*

Raymond Kaskey's Art Rooney Sr. sculpture sits outside Heinz Field, a memento to one of the greatest men—both for the game of football and American life. *(Getty Images)*

Ronde Barber, a member of the Pro Football Hall of Fame Class of 2023, receives his jacket from Tomlin during the Gold Jacket dinner on August 4, 2023, in Canton, Ohio. Tomlin was Barber's secondary coach with the Tampa Bay Buccaneers, from 2001–05, and credits Tomlin with changing the trajectory of his career. *(AP Images)*

Throughout his career, Tomlin has dedicated himself to improving his craft and leading the Pittsburgh Steelers to be the best they can be—both on and off the field. *(Getty Images)*

job he started in Arizona, Green's lasting memory as an NFL head coach is that one infamous postgame sound bite.

Edwards took the Jets to the postseason in three of his five years in New York, including his first year in 2001. Prior to his arrival, the Jets made the playoffs twice in the previous *decade*. If you're a black coach, numbers be damned. Edwards's lasting memory? *You play to win the game!*

All that Bieniemy has ever done is coach his players hard. Surely, he isn't the only NFL coach—black or white—to show his players tough love. So why does it seem like Bienemy is being singled out by the media? Is it because he's a loudmouth? Is it because of race? If Bieniemy's coaching style was good enough for Mahomes, the best quarterback in the league, it's damn sure good enough for the Commanders.

Despite some progress, the NFL still has a long way to go. Black coaches can't win because the sport won't let them. In the sixty-six-year history of the Associated Press NFL Coach of the Year award, the two winningest black coaches in league history (Tomlin and Dungy) have never won the award in their 29 combined years as head coaches. This despite Dungy going 75–21 (.781) from 2003 to 2008. Overall, a total of three black head coaches (Marvin Lewis, Lovie Smith, and Ray Rhodes) have won the award.

* * *

Before the 2007 season began, there had been talk of this still being Cowher's team. For Tomlin, it was a no-win situation.

Fairly or unfairly, the catch-22 narrative would shadow Tomlin for years, even after a Super Bowl victory.

When he won, it was because he was coaching Cowher's players. When the Steelers lost, it was because he did a poor coaching job.

"I've seen coaches come in and have a good team. That doesn't mean you're going to win," Porter said. "I've been on good teams that didn't win. You're going to blame him for winning with a good team? I don't understand that one.

"The Jerome Bettis Super Bowl team wasn't our best team. And we won it all that year. I've been on some teams who we thought, hands down, we were supposed to just win everything, and it didn't work out. I guess that's just how people are going to feel about certain situations."

On a team featuring six Pro Bowlers and three All-Pros that ranked second overall in total defense, Pittsburgh compiled a 10–6 record in Tomlin's inaugural campaign—two games better than the previous season when the Steelers missed the playoffs.

The Tomlin era opened impressively with a predictable 34–7 win over the Cleveland Browns. It was the Steelers' eighth straight victory against Cleveland, which won its last game in the series in 2003.

In the Steelers' first game in fifteen years without Cowher, Roethlisberger tossed a career-high four touchdown passes, and Parker rushed for 109 yards in 27 carries. The defense did its part, registering six sacks and forcing five turnovers.

"He really doesn't get rah-rah," Roethlisberger said about Tomlin after the game. "As a player you like that. He's calm."

Roethlisberger described one of the differences between his two NFL coaches, referencing Cowher's habit of inadvertently spitting on players when he yelled.

"You don't have to worry about getting yelled at or spit on or getting stuff thrown at you," said Roethlisberger.

Tomlin was moved after his players presented him with the game ball following his first career win.

"This win is not about me," said Tomlin. This is the story of the 2007 Steelers."

It wasn't just lip service with Tomlin, mouthing the proper words to yield the proper response. In Tomlin's world, his players always come first. A former player himself, he understands and appreciates each and every one of their efforts on a weekly basis throughout the season.

"I've got respect for what men are willing to do. I appreciate the will of man more than I appreciate talent," Tomlin said on the *Pivot* podcast.

"The story of the game of football is about the men that play," Tomlin continued. "I always felt that. I felt that when I played. So why am I going to view it differently because I coach now? The players are the product. We're the source [coaches]. We cultivate that talent. We provide the stage for that talent to show itself. And [those] dudes go out there and do that. Together, man, our families eat."

The Steelers were 3–0 when they traveled to Glendale, Arizona, to face Ken Whisenhunt and Russ Grimm, whom he beat out for the head coaching job. Tomlin may have won the war, but Arizona won the battle, 21–14, handing Tomlin his first career loss.

Tomlin faced another milestone game against New England in Week 14. The Steelers began the day allowing just 12.9 points per game which led the NFL. In Tomlin's first meeting against the Patriots since quarterback Tom Brady tossed four touchdown passes against his Minnesota Vikings in 2006, Brady again had his way, throwing four more touchdown passes (including two to Randy Moss) in a 34–13 victory. The Patriots became the fifth team in history with a 13–0 record.

The loss dropped the Steelers' record to 9–3, with three games remaining in the season. Pittsburgh lost three of its final four contests, including a home loss to the Jacksonville Jaguars (who would eliminate them from the playoffs a few weeks later).

The Steelers lost at home, 31–29, in that wild-card game.

Trailing 28–10 entering the fourth quarter, the Steelers mounted an impressive comeback to take their first lead at 29–28 on Najeh Davenport's one-yard touchdown run that was set up by Taylor's interception. However, the Steelers' defense—Tomlin's calling card all year—failed to stop Jacksonville's David Garrard on a fourth-and-2 quarterback sneak. Garrard's 32-yard scamper set up the Jaguars' winning field goal.

Roethlisberger threw two touchdown passes and three interceptions, including one returned for a touchdown. The Steelers needed a better game from Roethlisberger, who was not yet considered a franchise quarterback. They would get that—and more—from Big Ben, who was elevated to elite status in 2008.

A prevailing theme all season was player after player complaining that, starting in training camp and continuing throughout the schedule, Tomlin worked players too hard, which may have contributed to the team physically wearing down and fizzling out in the playoffs.

Tomlin said players "resisted the change." But he respected their professionalism "and not letting it affect their quality of play."

Although he didn't agree with Tomlin's methods, Hampton understood Tomlin's motives.

"Toward the end of the year, we wore down," said Hampton. "But he learned from it and did a whole lot better job of listening to guys."

"It's adapt or die for me," Tomlin said on the *Footbahlin with Roethlisberger* podcast. "I always pride myself in being open to change."

11

THE SOPHOMORE HEADS TO
THE SUPER BOWL

(2008)

"When I ring their bell, they better answer."

ENTERING his second season as the head coach of the Pittsburgh Steelers, Mike Tomlin had two important keys that would not only help his team improve, but take them to the next level: the league's top-rated defense, and a quarterback on the cusp of greatness.

Finishing 10–6 in his rookie season and at the top of the AFC North, the Steelers found a new-age head coaching commodity, a tireless strategist, innovator, teacher, and motivator who connected with his players about personnel decisions and personal matters.

Reenergizing his roster as a rookie coach and getting his players to buy in to his system, he'd help transition the team from the Cowher era to the Tomlin era. And unlike many coaches who get their first crack at a head coaching job with a subpar roster, Tomlin parlayed the winning hand he was dealt into a royal flush.

Whether it was Tomlin becoming a better head coach in his sophomore season, or his players buying what he was selling, the result was undeniably spectacular. Chalk it up to experience.

"If you've been around the track, there's no more mystical things about, 'Hey, what am I doing here?'" Tomlin said as a guest on his former QB1's *Footbahlin with Roethlisberger* podcast, in speaking about the difference between his first and second year at the helm. "What does a twelve-month calendar look like, what does this potentially lead to? What are the ramifications of this decision? There's so many unanswerable questions on that first lap. You can't answer them. What you do is you go to natural-gut killer instinct."

Knowing that he had what many saw as the "franchise quarterback," Tomlin learned to accept Roethlisberger's *breaking all the rules* playbook, which he may not have done as a rookie head coach. An instinctive and mobile passer famous for extending plays beyond their normal shelf life, Roethlisberger's penchant for improvisation took some getting used to.

"I think Year Two, the second half of that year, I was really starting to get comfortable with what happened when those plays got extended," Tomlin said on *Footbahlin with Roethlisberger*. "[Even] during the course of those two seasons, when plays got extended, he [Roethlisberger] ate."

* * *

Six months earlier, Tomlin may have set the tone for the entire season when he put a target on the back of veteran nose tackle Casey Hampton.

By reputation, Hampton was a Pro Bowl talent who traditionally worked himself into shape in time for the start of the regular season. When the bright lights came on, everybody knew "Big Hamp" would be ready to show out. But when Hampton, listed at 325 pounds but appearing much heavier, reported to training camp overweight and failed to finish the team's mandatory conditioning test, Tomlin placed him on the physically unable to perform (PUP) list.

The conditioning test consisted of eight 100-yard sprints, with a continuous running clock. On their return to the starting point, players were required to jog back fifty yards and walk the final fifty yards. Hampton completed only five of the 100-yard sprints.

"He wasn't able to finish the test," Tomlin told reporters on the day players reported to St. Vincent College. "He's overweight and not conditioned enough to participate at this point. Hopefully, it doesn't take too long, but he's not going to wake up tomorrow and be ready to go. . . . We'll just live day to day with it until he's at an acceptable level of conditioning and weight."

The next day, Hampton walked and ran around an empty field while his teammates practiced without him.

"You're all making such a big deal about it," Hampton told Scott Brown of the *Pittsburgh Tribune-Review.* "This ain't the end of the world."

It was reminiscent of two years earlier, when Minnesota Vikings defensive tackle Pat Williams, who dealt with weight issues his entire career, struggled in a conditioning test and was placed on the PUP list.

"He isn't where he needs to be," Tomlin, Minnesota's first-year defensive coordinator, told reporters in 2006. "It's disappointing for me, it's disappointing for his teammates, it's disappointing for him. As of right now, he's not up to snuff so he's got some work to do."

In 2010, a similar situation occurred when Pro Bowl defensive lineman Albert Haynesworth was in his second year in Washington. New head coach Mike Shanahan stated that all players needed to pass his conditioning test, or they would be unable to practice. Haynesworth repeatedly failed Shanahan's conditioning test and missed a lot of training camp.

All three examples featured first-year head coaches—Tomlin in Pittsburgh, Shanahan in Washington, and Brad Childress in Minnesota—new to their respective teams making an example of a veteran player and sending a message to the entire team. Shanahan, however, won two Super Bowls at his first stop in Denver before coming to Washington. Tomlin was in his second season; Childress was making his NFL head coaching debut.

Did Tomlin's ploy work?

Well, Williams made his first Pro Bowl that season. Two years later, Hampton was named to his third Pro Bowl.

Looking back, Hampton took responsibility for not reporting to training camp in shape, but wishes Tomlin had handled the situation differently.

"That was the type of deal where he didn't know me, really," Hampton said. "The coaches would tell him, 'Hamp's gonna be alright, he's gonna be in shape, he's gonna be ready when it's time to go.' It was another case of him doing things his way. I respect that because I should have had my ass in shape, no doubt about it. The only issue I had with him, and we talked about this, I let him know I thought this was some bullshit he didn't come to me first and tell me I was on the PUP list. He went to the media first. But we ironed that out. He was getting mad because I was happy to be on the PUP list. I didn't want to practice. I was really trying to get under his skin because he had pissed me off."

* * *

By his twenty-sixth birthday, Benjamin Todd Roethlisberger became the youngest starting quarterback to win a Super Bowl, survived a near-fatal motorcycle accident the offseason *after* winning the Super Bowl, led the league in interceptions, and signed an eight-year, $102 million contract extension.

In Pittsburgh's 21–10 victory over Seattle in Super Bowl XL, Roethlisberger threw for 123 yards with no touchdowns and two interceptions, making him the only winning Super Bowl quarterback to have two interceptions and zero touchdown passes. Of starting quarterbacks that played the entire Super Bowl game and won, Roethlisberger's passing yards are the lowest in the modern era and he has the lowest passer rating of any quarterback to win the Super Bowl (22.6).

An enigma as much as he was a budding superstar, the normally reclusive Roethlisberger approached the season with a one-track mind: *Do unto others as you would have them do unto you.*

My article appearing in the *Pittsburgh Tribune-Review* on Sunday, September 7, 2007, under the headline "Big Ben

Leading the Way," told the story of Roethlisberger making a conscious decision to reach out to his teammates—as well as reaching inside of himself—to achieve redemption.

> Steelers cornerback Ike Taylor didn't recognize the incoming number on his cell phone when he answered one day in late February.
> "Who is this?" Taylor asked.
> "Ben."
> It took Taylor by surprise.
> "I said, 'Wow.'"

Taylor was a fourth-round draft pick in 2003. He lost his starting job for several games under former coach Bill Cowher but has rebounded to become the Steelers' top cornerback under second-year coach Mike Tomlin.

Offensive and defensive players normally don't spend much time together because they're often in positional meetings and tend to gravitate toward players on their side of the ball.

Taylor was impressed that Roethlisberger took the time to call.

"He could have called an offensive guy to see what was going on. But he called me. That's big, coming from the quarterback," Taylor said.

Once they began talking, the two relative strangers realized how much they had in common.

"Now when we talk, it's not just about football," Taylor said. "It's, 'Hey, how you doing, how's the family?' From the time I'm in Pittsburgh to wherever (the friendship), is on."

Reaching out

That simple phone call may be one of the signs of Roethlisberger maturing—not only as a player but as a leader of the Steelers. He makes his 56th career NFL start in today's season opener against the Houston Texans at Heinz Field.

"He was one of the guys I wanted to reach out to, one of the first guys I reached out to this offseason, because I felt like Ike is misunderstood sometimes by the media and by fans because—like he said—he's a quiet guy," Roethlisberger said.

"Whether people take him as cocky or he thinks he's too good, well, let me tell you something—Ike's one of the best cornerbacks in this league. Physically and mentally, he's just a phenomenal player. I wanted to reach out to him and to try to develop a friendship.

"We're not best friends, we're not talking every day and hanging out, but I consider Ike more than just a teammate now," Roethlisberger said. "I consider him a friend and someone I would go to bat for any day of the week. If I had to play against him on Sundays, I would be afraid to throw to that side."

Steelers defensive end Brett Keisel said he's noticed a difference in how Roethlisberger interacts with his teammates.

"Ben is a great quarterback, and great quarterbacks are leaders of their offense. He understands that a little bit more this year," said Keisel, one of Roethlisberger's closest friends on the team. "He knows that [Alan] Faneca is gone, and Alan was a big leader on the offense. Someone needs to pick up the slack and what better person than the quarterback?"

The normally reclusive Roethlisberger offered rare insight into his character and subsequent personality change in a recent interview.

"People may think that I'm mean or I'm stuck-up or snotty. No. I'm just a quiet person. I'd rather know about you than you know about me," Roethlisberger said. "Once you get to know me, you realize that I can be pretty outgoing and goofy and fun."

During three weeks of training camp and the Steelers' four preseason games, Roethlisberger was a popular figure, pulling aside teammates for private conversations, or engaging them in horseplay as he did with Pro Bowl linebacker James Harrison during a recent practice.

As the quarterback, the Steelers have made a long-term commitment to me," said Roethlisberger, whose teammates voted him offensive co-captain for the first time.

"It's time to be more of a leader, but being sensitive that we still have leaders on the team—Hines Ward on offense, [James] Farrior on defense, as well as other guys. I didn't want to come in and step on anybody's toes. I easily could have.

"I know guys that have done it, that could come in and be like, 'Listen, this is my team. I'm the quarterback.

I'm the leader. You guys listen to me.' And they're hootin' and hollering. That's just not my style."

Roethlisberger said that although he has always been close with his offensive teammates, he realized he needed to reach out to more players.

"I made the conscious effort this offseason of trying to interact with everybody," Roethlisberger said. "I wanted to reach out to the defensive guys because I haven't gotten to know those guys, spend much time with them, and talk to them.

"I've been so caught up last year and the year before. Trying to learn the offense last year, and the year before trying to get back from the injury (resulting from a severe motorcycle accident). Not necessarily tune guys out, but I was so concerned with myself in trying to get right that I almost lost focus on what was important in how to be a good teammate."

Said Taylor: "Regardless of how people want to look at him or what they want to say about him, Ben's been very quiet. He minds his own business. He came into his own as being the leader of this team. Everything pretty much rides on his shoulders. Especially after signing that new contract. It's his team."

"Sometimes when I'm on the sideline or at practice, we're not always talking football," Roethlisberger said. "I'm a little more comfortable with this offense now, I know what's going on. I can afford to talk to guys, joke around. I've been able to open up to them as they've opened up to me. We've all become closer and better friends for it."

* * *

Whether a product of the roster he acquired or his skill in building defenses, the Steelers ranked No. 1 in total defense in each of Tomlin's first two seasons. In 2008, they finished first in total defense (237.2 yards per game), scoring defense (13.9 points per game), and pass defense (156.9 yards per game). They finished second in the league in run defense (80.2 yards per game), and held eight opponents to 10 points or less (all victories). Linebacker James Harrison was voted NFL Defensive Player of the Year.

The defense was already stellar, and just got better when Tomlin took over. While Tomlin did inherit a great defense, he was able to take it to the next level—a championship level.

"We wouldn't have made it to [Super Bowl XLIII] if it wasn't for the defense," Pro Bowl left tackle Marvel Smith told me in a *Trib* article. "The defense won so many games for us that year."

It was powered by defensive linemen Aaron Smith, Hampton, and Keisel. Smith and Hampton specialized in demolishing double-team blocks.

"The defense is not going to work if you can single block the defensive lineman," Hampton said. "I got double teamed the majority of the time. Aaron Smith, if you single block him, he's going to make the play every time. It was a pick-your-poison type of deal. You couldn't single block us. If you double teamed me, it was over because he [Smith] was going to eat it up every time."

In his 2010 Pro Football Hall of Fame speech, LeBeau praised his defensive front. "Guys ask me, 'Coach, what's the perfect 3–4?' 'Who would be the very ideal people at each position?'

"I said, 'Well, truthfully, you start with Casey Hampton, Aaron Smith, and Brett Keisel on the defensive line.'"

No matter how ingenious the strategy, there had to be a buy-in from the players. LeBeau's fire blitz sending five players to pressure the quarterback and dropping six in pass coverage forced opposing quarterbacks to get rid of the ball quickly. "The mentality in Pittsburgh when I was there, we just felt like if the offense gave us anything, we were going to do major things," Hampton said.

The defense was a collaborative effort between LeBeau's fire blitz and Tomlin's chess moves.

"Coach T is a player's coach, but Coach T is gonna get your football IQ all the way to Jesus," Taylor said on the *Catchin' Fades with Aqib Talib* podcast in June 2021. "Coach T used to sit down with me, [cornerback] Will Gay, Troy [Polamalu], Dickie [LeBeau], defensive staff, [assistant] coach Ray Horton, and implement. He was like, 'Y'all on the field. What y'all see . . . on tape as a coaching staff we can adjust and do?' Now, we're running through a brick wall for that. They say Coach Cowher was tough to play for, which he wasn't. He just put on that show for TV. Hell of a coach. Then you get Coach T, who can simplify football and get your IQ better, whether you're a football fan or not. Whether you're four or eighty-four, he's gonna make you understand the game. He came with a whole different perspective as far as, even though we're coaches, we still want y'all to implement what y'all seeing on the field."

In 2008, Taylor was assigned primary coverage against Hall of Fame receivers Terrell Owens and Randy Moss, in addition to Andre Johnson, Reggie Wayne, Plaxico Burress, Santana Moss, Vincent Jackson, T. J. Houshmandzadeh, and Derrick Mason.

Taylor conceded a total of two touchdown catches during the regular season.

"Simplification," Taylor explained on *The Herd with Colin Cowherd* podcast in August 2021. "You know how offensive [and] defensive coordinators, they want to re-invent the wheel? Coach T's like, 'If the wheel is round and it's been working for so long, why do we need to go back to a square wheel?' So he'll simplify. He'll sit down. He'll educate. Coach [says], 'Who's the offensive coordinator? Who's the defensive coordinator? OK, this is their personality. This is what they like to do . . . Sean McVay, Mike McCarthy. What do they like to do? They like to do this on first down. They like to do this on second down. They like to do this on third down.' Once you understand that and he simplifies that part, the game was a hundred times easier."

Players couldn't help but notice the "Tomlin Effect." Even in the locker room, considered the players sanctuary where they swapped stories, played cards, and bonded, Tomlin became a regular visitor.

Some NFL head coaches are considered mysterious and aloof by their players, who tend to have very little direct contact with their bosses. Coaches are paid to win football games. Having little else in common with their players, they often keep their personal interactions on a superficial level.

Tomlin never saw it that way.

"After practice, Mike T would walk into the locker room and go to every dude—from practice squad to main guy—and he would have something to say to them," Willie Colon said. "Good, bad, whatever. Sometimes he was checking in with a player. 'Hey, man, how's your brother, how's your mom, how's your kid doing, how's your wife?' He would do it every practice. He didn't start on one side of the room or the other. It was just wherever he went. Mind you, everything's going crazy around him. And he's like, 'Hey, man, you look a little big today. You look like you're about to be working southside security. Get the weight down.' Or he'll go over here. 'Hey, man, on this coverage this is what we're looking for. If you do this, we can get this out of that.' Boom-boom-boom. And then he'll go over here. 'Hey, man, I'm tired of talking about x-y-z; get on it, or we're going to find somebody to get on it for you.' He would have something for each guy. And it was routine.

"He would come into our meetings," Colon continued, "and not only listen to what was being taught, but also challenge guys. He would have his input. As a ballplayer, you talk to your position coach. You talk to your coordinator. Your head coach may have the overall decision whatever he feels is needed for the team. But you definitely don't get that tap-in from a head coach, specifically with your position coach. He's like, 'No, man, I want to run the air out of the football. This is what we're planning to do. This is what I would like to happen.' We heard it from our position coach. We heard it from our coordinator. This is Mike T telling us, 'Five minutes in the fourth quarter, we're pulling out the tanks. Can you handle that challenge?' That was always a good feeling, like, 'OK, if that's what's on the menu, gotta serve it.' He knew what to say, and he knew how to challenge guys— and he wasn't afraid to challenge guys."

"If you're going to lead men, you've got to know them," Tomlin said on the *Pivot* podcast. "[Shoot] him straight, don't insult his intelligence, and he'll do the rest. If you're gonna lead you better have intimate relationships, so you better be open to intimate relationships. What makes a man tick? What's his fear? What's his motivation?

"I probably have a talent for understanding people," Tomlin continued, "but is it a talent? It's not. It's listening when they're talking for real. Coaches like to think we listen. Coaches don't listen. They wait for dude's mouths to stop moving. I sensed that as a player and I hated it, so I just try to be what I wanted leading me. And so when dudes are talking, I listen. And I listen for real. It doesn't necessarily mean that it's going to produce action that's in alignment with what they want, but I listen."

* * *

Entering the 2008 season, the Steelers played what was judged to be the NFL's most difficult schedule. Based on the previous year's regular-season slate, Pittsburgh's 2008 opponents went 153–103 for a nearly .600 winning percentage. The Steelers faced both teams who played in Super Bowl XLII: the champion New York Giants and New England Patriots. They also played the Indianapolis Colts, Philadelphia Eagles, Baltimore Ravens, San Diego Chargers, Dallas Cowboys, and Tennessee Titans. The Steelers were 5–4 in those games, and 7–0 against everyone else.

Two games stood out for the Steelers in winning five of their first six matchups, beginning with a Week 4 thriller on *Monday Night Football* against Baltimore, made possible by Jeff Reed's 46-yard field goal in overtime to give the team a 23–20 victory.

The Steelers overcame a 13–3 halftime deficit, scoring two touchdowns within fifteen seconds late in the third quarter. Roethlisberger's 38-yard strike to Santonio Holmes was the Steelers' first touchdown in eight quarters, followed quickly by outside linebacker LaMarr Woodley scooping up a Joe Flacco fumble created by a Harrison sack and rumbling seven yards for the score.

Bouncing back strong six days later, the Steelers won a 26–21 grinder at Jacksonville in another primetime matchup on Sunday night. The result was huge for a team that had lost twice to the Jaguars the previous season, including the painful wildcard playoff defeat. Trailing 21–20 in the fourth quarter, it all turned out well when Roethlisberger, who didn't practice during the week due to a sore shoulder, connected with Hines Ward on a short fade route for the winning score with just under two minutes remaining.

It was a vintage performance for Roethlisberger, who tossed three touchdowns after throwing a total of two touchdown passes over his first four games. Stout as usual, the Steelers defense limited Jacksonville to 38 rushing yards. Filling in for banged-up running backs Willie Parker and rookie Rashard Mendenhall, backup Mewelde Moore, who was with Tomlin in Minnesota, gained 99 yards on 17 carries.

"We're coming from Pittsburgh, where it's forty-something degrees," Colon said. "We're in Jacksonville. It's ninety degrees. It's humid. Feels like somebody was breathing back in our mouths it's so humid. It was my right guard Darnell Stapleton's first game starting [for Kendall Simmons]. I'm standing all of 6-foot-3. Darnell's 6-foot-3. We're going against Marcus Stroud (6-foot-6). John Henderson (6-foot-7). These dudes are monsters. I remember saying to D-Stape [Stapleton], 'We're gonna bang, bro.' It was just a gritty, dogfight of a game. I can remember walking off the field with Mike T pumping his fist to the crowd like, 'Yeah!' It was like a prizefight when nobody counts on you to win the fight and you come out of it even though you're beaten and battered and you're standing up and you're like, 'Hell, yeah!' I can remember the pride he had on his face. Just as much as it meant to us to say, 'How ya like me now?' To see him wear that too was a cool moment."

The Steelers' season was taking on a familiar pattern with the defense setting the tone nearly every game. Coming off a 38–10 victory at Cincinnati, the Steelers, despite allowing just one touchdown and four field goals, suffered a 21–14 loss to the New York Giants. New York added a safety when Harrison, filling in for long snapper Greg Warren, who suffered a torn ACL in the third quarter, snapped the ball out of the end zone. "That's a championship-caliber football team," Tomlin said about the Giants after the game.

The same couldn't be said for his team, which blew a 14–9 lead midway through the fourth quarter. Roethlisberger threw four interceptions for only the second time in his career. He was constantly under duress, sacked five times, and finished with a 38.5 passer rating.

Now 6–2 after taking down Washington, 23–6, this Steelers team would no longer be judged by easy wins against Cincinnati and Washington, but rather how they performed against playoff-caliber opponents to determine whether they were on the right track to contend for another championship.

They failed to put away another quality opponent at home, faltering late to the Indianapolis Colts, in Week 10, 24–20, after building a 17–7 lead in the second quarter. This time, the Steelers' normally reliable defense was outmatched, as quarterback Peyton Manning threw three touchdown passes. With Roethlisberger, who had reinjured his shoulder in Washington the previous week, tossing three more interceptions and no touchdowns, the Steelers fell into a tie with Baltimore for the division lead.

With the defensive looking for a bounce-back performance, they welcomed the struggling Chargers to Heinz Field. It turned out that, thanks to their destructive defense holding another opponent in check, the Steelers didn't need to score a touchdown to win. Three Reed field goals, including the game-winner with 32 seconds to play—plus a safety courtesy of raging bull pass rusher Harrison, who stripped the ball from quarterback Philip Rivers in the end zone—was all the Steelers needed to hold off San Diego in the first 11–10 final in NFL history.

As previously mentioned, it's one thing to beat mediocre teams, but another entirely to beat those expected for success. So to go into New England and throttle the Patriots, 33–10, for Pittsburgh's first win at New England in eleven years—and Tomlin's first NFL win over Bill Belichick—set the Steelers on a playoff run of historic proportions.

After losing Hall of Fame quarterback Tom Brady to a knee injury in the first game of the season, the Pats had rallied around backup Matt Cassel and sat at the top of the AFC East standings with a 7–4 record. Not to be deterred by the aura of New England, the Steelers sacked Cassel five times and intercepted him twice. Harrison forced two fumbles. Roethlisberger threw multiple touchdown passes for the first time in six games. Led by a healthy Parker and the unheralded Moore, the Steelers rushed for 161 yards—their highest total since the second game of the season. At 9–3, Pittsburgh remained a game ahead of Baltimore in the AFC North.

A week later, Tomlin's leadership was put to the test when Parker, who carried the ball 12 times for only 25 yards in the Steelers' 20–13 home win against Dallas, suggested the team should employ a fullback to boost the running game.

There didn't seem to be any cause for alarm, considering the Steelers won the game and were 10–3, winning four in a row. To the contrary: it was naïve for Parker—who was inactive for five games and averaged 3.5 yards per carry with three 100-yard performances in the other eight contests—to think he could voice his complaint to reporters and Tomlin wouldn't notice. Sure enough, the next day Tomlin put Parker on blast. While the coach had preferred to handle these types of situations outside of the public eye, his running back had now forced him to speak publicly about the matter.

"The issue for us has been and will continue to be winning," Tomlin told reporters at his daily briefing. "That's my interpretation of Steelers football. Every morning when I come to work, I walk past five Lombardi Trophies, not five rushing titles."

Advantage, Tomlin. Game, set, match.

Parker's words, spoken in the heat of the moment, were no longer an issue. Tomlin cleverly called a truce when he named Parker team captain for the next game at Baltimore.

It didn't hurt Parker's case that he gained 47 yards on 14 carries against the Ravens' rugged run defense. Or that the Steelers rallied for a 13–9 victory on Roethlisberger's red zone touchdown pass to Holmes on a bang-bang play that needed a replay to confirm. It was all about proper timing: The Steelers were about to embark on their hottest stretch of the season.

Winning three of their final four games—and six of their final seven—earned the Steelers a bye in the playoffs for the first time since 2004. They awaited the outcome of the Chargers-Colts wild-card matchup. But instead of facing Peyton Manning and the 12–4 Colts, they would be going up against an 8–8 San Diego team who stunned Indianapolis on Darren Sproles's 22-yard touchdown run in overtime, setting up a Steelers-Chargers rematch in the divisional round.

In the Steelers' earlier game against San Diego, Roethlisberger enjoyed one of his best performances of the year, throwing for 308 yards against the NFL's worst passing defense. However, the Steelers did not score a touchdown, partly because they committed 13 penalties for 115 yards. Parker carried the ground game with 115 yards for a 4.6-yard average.

With Roethlisberger recovered from a concussion he suffered two weeks earlier, Parker licking his chops for another shot at San Diego's run defense, and Holmes freed from Tomlin's doghouse after being suspended for a game because of a misdemeanor marijuana charge in October, the Steelers rolled over the Chargers 35–24 to record Tomlin's first career playoff victory.

San Diego concentrated on shutting down Roethlisberger, holding him under 200 passing yards, That left Parker free to score two touchdowns and gobble up a season-high 146 yards for the franchise's highest individual postseason rushing total since Franco Harris gained 153 yards against the Baltimore Colts in the 1975 divisional round.

After an early touchdown pass from Philip Rivers to Vincent Jackson, Holmes made it 7–7 only five minutes later when he replied with a 67-yard punt return for a touchdown, his second career playoff TD in as many postseason games. His playoff run was just getting started.

As for the defense, the Steelers held San Diego—a team that averaged 107.9 yards per game—to *15* yards rushing. One thing that definitely worked in their favor was the absence of future Hall of Fame running back LaDainian Tomlinson, who had torn a tendon in his groin during the team's win over the Colts. While Darren Sproles had done a stellar job against Indy, he was no match for Pittsburgh. The anemic total was two yards fewer than Pittsburgh's Steel Curtain allowed the Minnesota Vikings in Super Bowl IX.

If the Steelers defeated Baltimore for the third time in one season in the AFC championship Game, they would advance to Super Bowl XLIII in Tampa.

"What else would you expect? Us and the Ravens," Tomlin said at his postgame press conference before a larger-than-usual media contingent, which now included national reporters. "It would be a big game if it was a scrimmage. It just happens to be the AFC Championship Game."

The hate was real between the Steelers and Ravens. Former Steelers cornerback Bryant McFadden recalled the time a Pittsburgh elementary school student was sent home for wearing the jersey of Ravens Hall of Fame safety Ed Reed.

"I can't remember what year it was, but we were playing the Ravens and we were both competitive," McFadden said on Pittsburgh radio station 93.7 The Fan. "I remember watching the news when I came home from practice and I saw one school in Pittsburgh, it was 'Wear your favorite team jersey to school day.' One student wore an Ed Reed jersey and they sent him home. You know that's one of the proudest moments of my life in Pittsburgh? Not on the football field, but away from it. When I saw that, I said, 'I know I'm in the right city.' They sent this poor little innocent child home because his favorite team was the Ravens and he had the guts to wear their jersey to a Pittsburgh elementary school, and they sent him home. I said, 'You gotta love Steeler Nation.'"

What transpired in the AFC title game was another head-knocker between two franchises that respected—but truly despised—one another. After two first quarter field goals by Jeff Reed, "Big Play Holmes" made it 13–0 in the second quarter on a beautiful 65-yard catch-and-run that began with him snaring a pass on the right side of the field after Roethlisberger, who scrambled to his left to extend the play and threw off his back foot, appeared to throw the ball away. The pass sailed over the head of Baltimore defensive back Fabian Washington, who slipped in coverage on the broken play. Upon making the catch, Holmes veered left to avoid two defenders, collected blocks from tight end Heath Miller and wide receiver Nate Washington, and dove into the end zone just ahead of Ed Reed.

"I remember scrambling left and looking back to see if anyone was coming and no one was," Roethlisberger said. "I stepped up and was getting ready to throw it away. I knew Santonio was over there. I was going to throw it over his head and at the last minute the guy's back was turned and I just threw it where he could make the play. When you get him the ball, he'll do the rest."

Said Holmes, "I kind of felt he was throwing the ball away. He felt like he was throwing the ball away. I got lazy and let the defender feel like the ball was going to be thrown out of bounds. When I saw it [was] short, I reacted quicker to the ball than he did, and I had a group of guys that were running with me."

With less than ten minutes left in regulation, it looked like Baltimore had swung the pendulum in its favor. After a rushing touchdown by Willis McGahee, the Ravens forced Pittsburgh into a quick three-and-out, which included a false start by Colon and a sack on Big Ben by Terrell Suggs for a fourth-and-17.

Not to be deterred, the Steelers' defense stepped up once again. After a big sack by Woodley on Flacco that forced a third-and-13, Troy Polamalu jumped a route on a pass intended for Derrick Mason and twisted his way 40 yards for a pick-six that put the Steelers back up, 23–14.

Yet even with the back-and-forth match-up, no play defined the sheer brutality of the Steelers-Ravens rivalry more than Ryan Clark's devastating hit on Baltimore running back McGahee. With Baltimore attempting a desperation rally, Flacco delivered a short pass to McGahee, who turned upfield. Clark left his feet to deliver the blow, knocking McGahee out cold and resulting in a fumble recovered by the Steelers. Both players lay on the field after the collision as their teammates and coaches gathered around them, some falling to their knees in prayer. McGahee, who told doctors he felt significant neck pain after the hit, was carted into the locker room. Clark was helped to the sideline.

"I thought he passed on the football field. I'm not lying," McFadden said after the game on 93.7 The Fan. "When Ryan

Clark hit McGahee, and I knew McGahee coming out of high school being from South Florida, I thought he died.

"On the football field, it sounded like a cannon. Like a cannonball being shot out of a cannon like *boom*.

"And when it happened, everything kind of went silent . . . people weren't really trying to attack the fumble because we were concerned about the two bodies that were laying on the football field."

After a three-and-out by Pittsburgh after McGahee's fumble, Tyrone Carter intercepted Flacco with 1:20 left, delivering a 23–14 win and a trip to the team's seventh Super Bowl, the first for Tomlin as a head coach. "It is not my story; it is our story—the story of the 2008 Steelers," Tomlin said. The game was the highest-rated television show on any network during the fall season. CBS reported the game attracted 40.64 million viewers, the highest total since the previous year's Super Bowl between the Giants and Patriots.

"Without a doubt this is the best defense that I've ever played on," Polamalu said. "This team had to rely more on the defense. We had to make a lot more big plays."

* * *

Super Bowl XLIII featured a soap opera–like coaching rematch between Tomlin and Whisenhunt, whom Tomlin beat out for the Steelers job. Tomlin also beat out Grimm, who was now Arizona's assistant head coach.

Tomlin and Whisenhunt had met for the first time in the fourth game of the 2007 season. Arizona rallied for two touchdowns in the fourth quarter to defeat the Steelers, 21–14, marking Tomlin's first loss as an NFL head coach.

TOMLIN

For those in Pittsburgh, what could be worse than Tomlin los-ing to Whisenhunt and Grimm in the Super Bowl?

Nothing.

Tomlin was at his diplomatic best when discussing his coach-ing adversaries from the desert. "We played those guys last year," Tomlin said, selecting his words carefully. "They are a well-coached outfit. It is obvious that they have a great deal of belief in what they are doing. They are playing great football. You don't get to this game unless you are. We respect them, we also respect the process that we believe will get us ready for combat. We tend to focus on the things that we can control. That is our prepara-tion, and ultimately our play, in respect to those guys."

Ed Tomlin discovered during the 2008 regular season that his younger brother was *persona non grata* to Whisenhunt. As direc-tor of sports marketing for Under Armour, the older Tomlin rep-resented Arizona defensive back Dominique Rodgers-Cromartie, whose team was scheduled to face Washington on September 21 at FedEx Field, and arrived in town early for the game.

"I went over to their practice," Ed Tomlin said. "[Whisenhunt] found out who I was. He made everybody leave because he didn't want me there. He was still salty I guess."

"That game was big. Really, really, huge," Cyrus Mehri said of the Super Bowl XLIII matchup. "There was a lot of pressure on the Fritz Pollard Alliance because if Mike had lost, all the nay-sayers in Pittsburgh would have come out full force. That was high stakes for the movement."

If Tomlin never won another game in the NFL, he *had* to win this one.

"Oh, my goodness," said John Wooten. "If Ken Whisenhunt wins that game, think about the people in Pittsburgh. I'm talking about the fans. What are they going to say? 'We could have had this guy and Dan Rooney went for the other guy.' Just think about what that would have meant. What it would have done to Mr. Rooney. And I know he did that [interview Tomlin] because of me. I know that he went to Minnesota because of me. He would not have gone if I didn't say that to him, because I asked him. I didn't say you need to do this and that. All I'm asking is for you to do me a favor and go see the kid in Minnesota."

I co-authored a Super Bowl diary with Steelers linebacker James Farrior for the *Trib* that week. It was considered a coup for the newspaper to secure Farrior, who may have produced his greatest season with a team-high 146 tackles for the NFL's top-rated defense. The idea was to find a player willing to take a few minutes out of his busy schedule each day to share his thoughts and insights leading up to the big game. I would interview Farrior and transcribe his quotes.

This was the last entry of Farrior's Super Bowl diary. He shared with *Trib* readers how Tomlin delivered his pregame speech at the team's final practice.

Saturday, January 31, 2009
TAMPA, Fla.

Revved up
We had a good practice [on Friday]. The tempo was good. Everybody's starting to get into it and get excited. It's really starting to get down to it. Guys are getting wired up.

Keeping it tight

Coach Tomlin doesn't get too emotional when he gives his pregame speech. He usually keeps it real lighthearted. He usually just tells us something funny that you can relate to football, usually about his two sons [Michael Dean and Mason]. He talks about them a lot and how he tries to develop them into being great young men and the things they go through and the things they think about when they're little kids. You just look back on it, how we were all at this point at one time. Stories like that. Then he'll get down to football and tell us what we need to do to win. Sometimes he talks [long]. It depends. I don't know if I should tell you this, but me and Casey [Hampton] have bets on how long he's going to go. We've done it a few times and Hamp beat me every time. I thought it was going to be longer than it was and Hamp was pretty much on point.

Game-day routine

The day of the game, I wake up, go eat breakfast, go back to the room, take a shower, get dressed, and watch a little TV, usually the news. Sometimes I watch the pregame shows to see what the commentators are saying.

Differing opinions

I really don't pay too much attention when I'm on there because I have a good idea what I was talking about. I've seen myself plenty of times on TV. I just like to see what the commentators say before the game and then what they turn around and say when the game is over.

It's just funny sometimes how the tables turn and they go the opposite way. One week this guy's the best, the next week it's another guy.

Music selection
I usually catch the last bus to the stadium, because I don't really need a lot of time to get ready. I don't need a lot of tape and all the extra stuff. I get my iPod ready with my pregame music, from the time I get into the locker room until I warm up. Probably at least thirty to forty minutes. I listen to old-school, hardcore hip-hop, like Public Enemy. It's like the heavy metal of rap. It gets me started.

Making an impression
The funniest thing to happen this week was the guy at media day on Wednesday with the raccoon hat. That dude was funny. He was sitting right beside me. He was asking me stuff about Steeler Nation and the fans. Then he had some words of wisdom, some type of poem that he wrote down for me, to inspire me for the game. He was a character. No, he didn't ask me for my autograph.

Despite motivating and elevating the Steelers to play in Super Bowl XLIII in his second season with the opportunity to become the youngest coach to win a Super Bowl, nobody hailed Tomlin as a coaching genius. All Tomlin had done, it seemed, was coach the roster he received from Cowher. One thing, though: Tomlin had to convince the same roster of players that finished 8–8 in Cowher's final season to wake up and smell the coffee.

Tomlin shook up the Steelers in his rookie year with a super hard training camp, only to ease up in his second season.

Did he push his players too hard initially? Call it a necessary evil. "We didn't like it sometimes, but it was something we had to deal with," Farrior said after the Steelers defeated Baltimore in the AFC Championship Game. "This year [Tomlin knows] when to push our buttons and when to lay off."

Tomlin moved on, as did his players. Not only did he not lose the team, he gained a *new* team, in a manner of speaking. Asked to compare the Steelers' last two Super Bowl teams—one under Tomlin, one under Cowher—Parker told reporters attending Super Bowl XLIII Media Day, "It's a different team, both sides of the ball. It's not about what you did in the last game; it's a different task."

If, in fact, Tomlin was a good coach benefitting from great talent, his mind-numbing defense in 2008 was the best in franchise history since the days of Joe Greene, Jack Lambert, Mel Blount, etc.

Not only tasked with winning the sixth Super Bowl in the history of the franchise, Tomlin, as stated earlier, couldn't afford to lose to Whisenhunt and Grimm, the two former Steelers assistants he beat out for Pittsburgh's head coaching position. How's that for pressure?

"It took a lot of work to get to this moment," Tomlin told reporters five days before the Super Bowl. "We're not going to fight this. We're going to embrace this and enjoy this part of the game. Ultimately, we know that on Sunday the ball is going to be kicked off and we've got to play. We're going to make sure we do what we need to do between now and then to make sure we're at our best."

Tomlin's coaching counterpart was playing it close to the vest and carefully choosing his words about the pending matchup. "They don't allow themselves the luxury of getting caught up in that stuff," said Cardinals special teams coach Kevin Spencer, referencing Whisenhunt and Grimm.

Not everyone in Arizona was taking the high road. Phoenix mayor Phil Gordon blew his nose into a Steelers' Terrible Towel and threw it on the ground at a Super Bowl send-off rally for the Cardinals.

Entering the contest as seven-point favorites after winning their division featuring the two teams in the AFC Championship Game—Arizona was a wild-card playoff team in the NFC—the Steelers received the opening kickoff and moved down the field on a 71-yard scoring drive that featured two chunk yardage plays. Roethlisberger followed up a 31-yard pass to Ward, who was playing on a sprained knee, with a 21-yard strike to tight end Miller at the 1. On third down, Roethlisberger appeared to score on a scramble, but the play was overruled by a replay challenge; Roethlisberger was down before crossing the goal line. Reed's short field goal made it 3–0.

Reserve back Gary Russell's 1-yard touchdown on the second play in the second quarter extended the lead to 10–0 and established the Steelers as the first team to score on its first two possessions since the Denver Broncos in Super Bowl XXXII.

The Steelers led 10–7 late in the second quarter when Harrison made what many consider to be the best play in Super Bowl history. After the Steelers scored the first two times they touched the ball, Arizona responded with a short Kurt Warner touchdown pass to Ben Patrick, and was ready to tack on another score in the final minute of the first half when the football gods looked down favorably upon the Steelers.

Following an interception by Karlos Dansby on a pass intended for Holmes, the Cardinals had the ball with two minutes left in the half, on the Steelers' 34 yard line. With 18 seconds left, and on first-and-goal from the Steelers 2, Warner, working from the shotgun, threw a quick pass to the goal line toward wide receiver Anquan Boldin. With the defense showing blitz, Harrison—who faked like he was going to rush the passer—dropped back in coverage and snagged the interception.

What occurred next was something for the record books. Harrison, surprisingly spry for a man of his physical dimensions (6-foot and 243 pounds), ran down the right sideline, nearly stepping out of bounds but staying inside the white lines as he picked up steam and a convoy of blockers. Harrison broke a tackle shy of midfield and hopped over a teammate to avoid falling, while making another potential tackler miss. Still stumbling, bumbling, rumbling, and losing speed with every step, Harrison carried Arizona receivers Steve Breaston and Larry Fitzgerald into the end zone to complete the 100-yard interception return, which at the time was the longest play in Super Bowl history.

"We were on a max blitz," said Harrison. "Kurt had to throw a quick slant and he threw it straight to me. After that it was about my teammates helping me get to the other end.

"[The field] got short when I first started and then it got long again and then it got a little shorter towards the middle and then I was just, 'I am already here there is no need to stop.' I'm not going to lie, it was a quarter tank. But I ended up making it."

Harrison's pick-six was an unforgettable momentum changer which, instead of becoming a Warner touchdown pass resulting in a 14–10 Arizona halftime lead (with Arizona receiving the ball in the second half), completely turned the tables and gave the Steelers, who were 10–1 during the season when holding a lead at halftime, a 17–7 advantage at the break.

The special sauce behind Harrison's return was how aggressively and willingly Pittsburgh's defenders blocked to keep their teammate upright. No less than seven Steelers delivered or attempted to make a block, with Woodley blocking guard Reggie Wells two different times on the play.

How Harrison's wall of blockers materialized was no accident. Tomlin and LeBeau stressed to their players in their three final Super Bowl practices that a play didn't end with an interception. Their emphasis: *Look for someone to block.*

During the week of Super Bowl XLIII, Tomlin predicted the Steelers would need a play like Harrison's to defeat Arizona. He planned accordingly.

"We had a practice prior to the game, we picked off maybe five or six passes," Tomlin said during a 2009 interview with NFL Network. "I'm watching [the] practice tape, I can't sleep, and I decide to make a cutup of every interception that we had in that practice. I noticed that we weren't rallying and getting offensive. So when we met on Thursday, I ran that cutup . . . didn't say much, other than the fact that this performance is probably not going to be enough. We're gonna have to get out in front of people, and we're gonna have to run one back, or maybe two back."

Tomlin reminded his team that the last time he coached in a Super Bowl as Tampa Bay's defensive backs coach in Super Bowl

XXXVII, that defense ran back three interceptions and scored 21 points in a 48–21 victory over the Oakland Raiders.

"And I thought that was a great defense," said Tomlin, who motivated his players by laughing when delivering the message. "They didn't think it was as funny as I did, but for the rest of the week, when we picked the ball off, they got out in front of one another, and ran it back."

"We're like, 'OK, we're going to do what coach says to do,'" McFadden said on his *All Things Covered* podcast on CBS Sports in 2021. "From that point on, every time someone caught an interception, it didn't matter if it was the first group, second group or the third group, whoever's on a football field, if you caught an interception, you better go find someone to block and you return it all the way to the house.

"'Yo, that's why great coaches, coach great teams. They put you in position to be successful, you just gotta listen.'"

Arizona defensive back Antrel Rolle said he considered tripping Harrison during the return as he watched from the sideline.

"What I [paid] attention to on the interception is the blocking," Rolle said on the podcast. "Y'all beat our players up. Y'all manhandled everybody who was trying to get him. Larry Fitzgerald got bumped out of bounds and, unfortunately, I happened to be in that space, and he ran into me . . . If he hadn't run into me, he definitely would have caught him."

Though heading into the locker room on a down note, Arizona knew the game was far from over. After a 21-yard field goal by Jeff Reed in the third—the only scoring of the quarter that brought the score to 20–7—the Cardinals turned the heat up.

After a three-and-out by both Arizona and Pittsburgh to start the fourth, the Cardinals went 87 yards on nine plays that ended with a one-yard touchdown reception by Fitzgerald. It was now 20–14 with a little under eight minutes left in regulation.

With another three-and-out from the Steelers' offense, the Cardinals had big receptions by Boldin and Breaston to put them on the Pittsburgh 26 yard line. But after a holding penalty on tackle Mike Gandy, the offensive faltered, resulting in a punt.

Concerns began to mount as the Cardinals downed the ball on the 2 yard line, but Harrison—who ended the first half with a bang—lost his composure and received a personal foul after repeatedly hitting Arizona defensive back Aaron Francisco. Thankfully for the Steelers, the play happened after the change of possession, as the penalty could have given the Cardinals the ball back and closer to taking the lead. Even the hard-nosed former coach and iconic broadcaster John Madden had issue with the play, saying during the television broadcast, "He ought to be thrown out for that. . . . I like aggressiveness, I like tough football, but that's overboard."

With the ball on their 1, the hope for Pittsburgh was to get the ball moving and keep possession. So after an incomplete pass and a Parker run for no gain, Big Ben hit Holmes for a huge 19-yard reception that would have put them on the 20 . . . but there was one issue: center Justin Hartwig was called for an offensive holding in the end zone, causing a safety. Now, with just under three minutes left, the Steelers' lead was cut to four, 20–16, with the Cardinals receiving the ball back.

Having the defense head back onto the field would put most Steelers fans at ease, but the momentum had completely swung in the opposite direction. After an incomplete pass, Warner hit Fitzgerald down the middle, splitting the defense and sprinting 64 yards for a touchdown that put Arizona up 23–20 with just under three minutes to play.

After 16 unanswered points and being down for the first time in the game, it seemed that, for one of the rare times in his head coaching career, Tomlin was stunned into silence. He was shellshocked.

"I was paralyzed for a split second like everybody else," Tomlin said on the *Pivot* podcast.

At that moment, Tomlin, the coach who was comfortable being uncomfortable, was silently seeking comfort. Thankfully for him, it would not come from a coach, or a teammate, or anyone else associated with the team. Instead, it would be the most effective type for Tomlin: familial comfort.

"I had my brother down there on that sideline. My brother is five years older than me. And like certain things you need when stuff gets really thick, I wanted my brother on the sideline in that Super Bowl." Tomlin, in an amazing moment of candor, said on the *Pivot* podcast. "I just needed that, that familiar, that home, that's what I think about when Larry Fitzgerald caught that ball and went down the middle of the field on us. But my big brother walked by me, he hit me on my hip and that woke me up. He didn't say anything because he was scared to death . . . I wasn't looking for anything substantial from him but his presence because that's my big bro. . . . I had great books because my brother always wanted better for me than he wanted for himself . . . I felt he needed to be there and so . . . I got him down there, but you don't know the purpose of someone's presence, and my brother was there to hit me on the hip when Larry

Fitzgerald went down the middle of the field, because that's really all he did. He didn't say nothing."

That's because Ed Tomlin was also shellshocked by the sudden turn of events.

"I was messed up, too," Ed said. "I was like, 'Slim, we might lose this game.'

"It was one of the few times I could ever get him to admit to seeking comfort," he continued. "I was like, 'I got you, man. Don't even worry about it.' He was like, '[Forget] you, man.' I slapped him on his hip, just messing with him, because I knew where his head was. Or maybe I didn't. He said it woke him up. I'm in Tampa the whole week but I didn't get a chance to see him until Saturday for the family dinner. We're talking all week. I'm like, 'Bro, is this what it looks like?' He was like, 'This is what we're built for. We're supposed to be here.' It was crazy because so many games that year ended that way."

Down 23–20 after giving up 16 straight points, Roethlisberger huddled up the offense at the Cardinals 22 with 2:30 remaining.

The end zone was 78 yards away. Pittsburgh needed a touchdown to take the lead, or a field goal to tie.

"Tone [Holmes] was walking on the field," Ed Tomlin said. "He was like, 'Let's go be great.'"

"I said that I wanted to be the guy that made the plays," said Holmes. "Great players step up in big-time games and make great plays."

But the drive didn't start out the way they planned, as a holding penalty pushed them back 10 yards. It was either now or never.

Then, in a flash, Holmes caught three passes for 67 yards. And just like that, the Steelers had first down at the Arizona 6 with 49 seconds remaining.

"I said, 'Seven [Roethlisberger], I want the ball,'" Holmes told ESPN's Jeremy Fowler in 2019. "He never said anything. He just threw it to me."

Roethlisberger drilled a bullet pass to Holmes in the left corner of the end zone. Holmes was open but the ball zipped through his outreached hands.

Roethlisberger had other options, like Ward, the MVP from Super Bowl XL. Instead, he went right back to Holmes—*Mr. Let's Go Be Great*—the very next play. Holmes ran a corner route to the right side. He needed to clear the linebacker, read the safety, and beat the cornerback. He did all three and looked back for the ball.

"When I saw him pointing, I wasn't sure if he was pointing to me," Holmes said. "Didn't see the ball until it came out of his hands."

Roethlisberger pump faked to maneuver Arizona's defenders around the end zone like pieces on a chess board. He delivered a ball that only Holmes could catch before the receiver fell out of bounds, leaning on a 90-degree angle, both feet positioned inside the white line with toes pointed down like a ballerina's.

Steelers 27, Cardinals 23.

Ballgame.

After the kickoff, and with the ball at the 23 yard line and 29 seconds left, the question was if Arizona had any more miracles left.

Kurt Warner, who already had 344 passing yards on the day, hit Fitzgerald for 20 and J. J. Arrington for 13, using their two remaining timeouts after each reception.

With 15 seconds left and 44 yards from the end zone, the Steelers were in a prevent defense, having only three defenders on the line . . . but that was all they needed. Under immediate pressure, Warner scrambled and wound up for a last-second heave when Woodley shoved back tackle Levi Brown and stripped the ball from Warner before he could get the ball out of his hand. Keisel recovered the fumble and, just like that, the Steelers became six-time Super Bowl champions.

And with the offense getting into victory formation, Keisel delivered another gift—this time directly to his head coach—with the ceremonial Gatorade bath.

Not only did Tomlin dodge an Arizona bullet, he also became the youngest coach to win a Super Bowl.

His counterpart took it all in from the opposite side of the field.

"It's one of the most difficult things you could ever imagine," said Whisenhunt. "This was not just in a regular game. It was the Super Bowl."

Indeed.

In one of his proudest moments, Tomlin presented another Lombardi Trophy to Rooney, who didn't succumb to public pressure and instead hired who he knew to be the best man to coach his football team.

"We had the toughest schedule in the league. They kept going under Mike Tomlin's direction and it was great," said Rooney. "Mike has just done a marvelous job . . . We'll make room [in the trophy case]."

"I'm extremely blessed," Tomlin said when asked if he felt he was in over his head when he replaced Cowher. "No, I had great belief in the Rooneys and their decision making. They know what they're doing. My comfort rested in their decision making and all I wanted to do was prove them right."

Tony Dungy, the coach who provided Tomlin with his first NFL coaching job and who gave him a glowing recommendation to Rooney, attended the Super Bowl as a member of NBC's broadcast team. The irony was not lost on Tomlin, who succeeded Dungy as the second African American coach to win a Super Bowl.[1]

"[Dungy] paved that road," Tomlin said. "I just got to walk down it. I benefit from the sacrifices and the challenges of those that have come before me; him being one of them. It makes it all the sweeter that I consider him a personal friend."

---

1 Tomlin is one of only four coaches to win a Super Bowl in their second season with a new team (Barry Switzer with the Cowboys in Super Bowl XXX, Brian Billick with the Ravens in Super Bowl XXXV, and Doug Pederson with the Eagles in Super Bowl LII). He was also the youngest head coach to win a Super Bowl until Sean McVay won with the LA Rams in Super Bowl LVI.

12

A SUPER BOWL HANGOVER AND A JOURNEY BACK TO THE PROMISED LAND

(2009–10)

"Don't seek comfort."

IT isn't easy being a head coach in the NFL, let alone for the Pittsburgh Steelers. Take into account replacing a future Hall of Fame coach in Bill Cowher, who had brought a Super Bowl trophy to the Steel City in 2006. Then to come in and gain the trust, respect and, allegiance of a veteran football team—especially with no previous head coaching experience? But that's just what he did and, from that point forward, his word was bond.

"I wouldn't say that *any* coach could coach our team," said Casey Hampton. "The right coach had to coach it. He had to have a strong personality, because we were a veteran team. We had a *great* team; our coach just retired. We didn't look at it like, 'Oh, we're sorry and we just got a new coach.' With us being a veteran team and him being so matter-of-fact and businesslike, guys really gravitated to that."

Every year is different. One year you're Super Bowl champion, the next year you're 8–8 and miss the playoffs. Out of nowhere, your coach resigns. The following season you finish 10–6 with a new coach who did a 180 from the old coach and lose in the first round of the playoffs . . . but at least you're back in the postseason, right? The following season, after making all the proper adjustments, you win another Super Bowl—second in four years; take a bow. But don't celebrate too long. In the NFL, life is a box of chocolates.

Quite frankly, 2009 was Tomlin's biggest challenge in his first three years as an NFL head coach.

"Every year, he'll have something he has to go through," said former Steelers linebacker Joey Porter. "He'll be down players or something else will happen, but you never hear him cry about the hand he was dealt. When shit gets tough, he just rolls up his sleeves and keeps grinding."

"Something else" appeared in the form of the Steelers being forced to answer difficult questions about their franchise quarterback before stepping onto the field for their first game of the season.

On July 21, 2009, a civil lawsuit was filed in Nevada, where a woman alleged sexual assault from Roethlisberger in a hotel penthouse in July 2008. In his first public comments about the allegations, Roethlisberger read a statement at the Steelers' practice facility. He spoke for less than two minutes and didn't respond to questions.

"[Saturday] was the first I heard of her accusations," said Roethlisberger, who was accompanied by Tomlin (who represented the Steelers), his agent, Ryan Tollner, and his attorney, David Cornwell. "Her false and vicious allegations are an attack on my family and on me. I would never, ever force myself on a woman."

The woman filed that she was working as a VIP casino host at Harrah's Lake Tahoe, where Roethlisberger was attending a celebrity golf tournament. After being called to Roethlisberger's room with a complaint about a broken television, the complaint alleges that Roethlisberger blocked the door when she tried to leave. According to the lawsuit, Roethlisberger grabbed her and tried to kiss her.

Roethlisberger denied these accusations.

"As much as I'd like to answer everyone's questions," Roethlisberger said, "I'm going to respect the legal process, and I'm confident that the truth will prevail."

The lawsuit was seeking a minimum of $440,000 in damages from Roethlisberger, and at least $50,000 in damages from Harrah's officials, along with an unspecified amount of punitive damages. According to the lawsuit, the woman didn't file a criminal complaint because she was concerned Harrah's would side with Roethlisberger and she would be fired. Law enforcement officials in Nevada said they didn't plan to open a criminal investigation. Roethlisberger never faced criminal charges. An out-of-court settlement was reached in 2011.

Nine days later, Roethlisberger met with reporters at training camp. He made it clear he would not address the allegations: "Any other football questions? I can walk away if we want."

Roethlisberger apologized to his teammates at the first team meeting of the year.

"It means a great deal," said Hines Ward. "You really don't know all the stories behind it, but he apologized to the team and gave his side."

Tackle Max Starks said Roethlisberger's apology was meant to eliminate "potential distractions."

"It was an apology for us," said Starks, "because when you come to training camp, your main focus is football and to have something like this on top of that, that's what he was apologizing for."

Roethlisberger was encouraged by his teammates' support. "It's good because they have my back and I have theirs." He added that this Steelers team was better prepared to avoid another Super Bowl hangover, which they were unable to do in 2006. That summer, Roethlisberger was involved in a motorcycle accident and had an appendectomy that caused him to miss the season opener. The Steelers lost six of their first eight games and finished 8–8 in Cowher's final season.

"It helps to have been there before because you know what to expect and how to deal with it," Roethlisberger said.

Unfortunately for Tomlin and the Steelers, it was just the first in a series of distractions that had the coach putting out fires all over Allegheny County.

"I understand it's that time of the year, and it's something to talk about, but it's not going to be an issue for us, it's really not," Tomlin said. "If this derails our football team, then we've got a lot more problems than this story."

* * *

Right away, the Steelers saw some things that revealed the season after winning Super Bowl XLIII was going to be different—and *difficult*. After a 13–10 overtime win over Tennessee at home, they followed that with losses at Chicago (17–14) and Cincinnati (23–20), posting a losing record (1–2) for the first time in Tomlin's career. While the team countered with a bounce-back five-game winning streak, the wheels just as quickly fell off, as they followed that with an unthinkable five-game losing streak (including back-to-back overtime losses against the Chiefs and Ravens, respectively).

Sitting at 6–7 and seeing their season slipping away, the Steelers' former record-setting defense seemed to have taken an extended vacation after the Super Bowl. Through 13 games, six opponents had scored 20 or more points. But it wasn't all from lack of effort, as injuries played a large role in their struggle. All-Pro safety Troy Polamalu missed 10 games and more than half of two others, while defensive end Aaron Smith spent 10 games on injured reserve. The defense also lost cornerback Bryant McFadden, who joined the Arizona Cardinals as a free agent. Linebacker Larry Foote signed with his hometown Detroit Lions.

The role reversal provided a revealing glimpse inside the Steelers locker room. They were a veteran team, which meant their tried-and-true defense was growing old together. Along the front seven, Smith was thirty-three, Hampton, thirty-one. Brett Keisel was the youngest defensive line starter at thirty. Backups Chris Hoke and Travis Kirschke were thirty-three and thirty-four, respectively. Their advanced age resulted in the team selecting defensive end Ziggy Hood in the first round of the 2009 draft. At linebacker, James Farrior was thirty-four, James

Harrison, thirty-one. The good news was that LaMarr Woodley (25) and Lawrence Timmons (23) were entering their prime. In the secondary, safety Tyrone Carter (33) and cornerback Deshea Townsend (33) weren't getting any younger. Polamalu was banged up, playing in only five games; in 12 NFL seasons Polamalu played in all 16 games only six times. Anthony Smith, the team's third-round pick from the 2006 draft—expected to provide additional depth at safety—had signed with Green Bay. The Steelers' plunged from the league's top-ranked pass defense to sixteenth.

Offensively, the Steelers boasted a 4,000-yard quarterback, two 1,000-yard receivers (Santonio Holmes and Hines Ward), and a 1,000-yard running back (Rashard Mendenhall) for the first time in franchise history. They ranked seventh in total yards and fourth in time of possession. However, they dropped down to twenty-first in red-zone efficiency: great between the twenties, unpredictable inside the twenties. In both losses to Cincinnati, the Steelers were 1-for-7 in the red zone. Their gaudy offensive numbers were deceiving. Among the ten teams with quarterbacks who passed for more than 4,000 yards, Roethlisberger and Dallas's Tony Romo tied for the fewest touchdown passes (with 26).

The wheels were wobbling on the Super Bowl bandwagon after the Steelers lost to Kansas City (27–24 in OT), Baltimore (20–17 in OT), Oakland (27–24), and Cleveland (13–6) in a span of nineteen days. The last thing the team needed was another distraction.

Prior to the Steelers' loss at Baltimore in a Sunday night nationally televised game on NBC, Ward, in a pregame interview on the network, questioned Roethlisberger's toughness.

Ben, who suffered a concussion the previous week at Kansas City, was advised by the team not to play against the Ravens.

Third-string quarterback Dennis Dixon got the start after Roethlisberger and backup Charlie Batch left the game against the Chiefs with injuries. The twenty-four-year-old Dixon, who had completed just one pass in two years and was appearing in his first game of the season, completed 12 of 26 passes for 145 yards, with one touchdown and an interception. His 24-yard touchdown run gave the Steelers a 17–14 lead with 6:24 to play in regulation, but he threw a pick in overtime, leading to Baltimore's game-winning field goal.

In an interview broadcast the night of the game, Ward said the Steelers locker room was divided on whether Roethlisberger should play against the Ravens.

"This game is almost like a playoff game," Ward said, as the team went into the week with a 6–4 record. "It's almost a must-win. I could see some players or teammates questioning, like, 'It's just a concussion. I've played with a concussion before.'

"It's almost like a 50–50 toss-up in the locker room," Ward continued. "Should he play? Shouldn't he play? It's really hard to say."

Roethlisberger passed every concussion test during the week. He told Tomlin on Friday he was having headaches, and on Saturday team neurosurgeon Dr. Joseph Maroon advised coaches not to play him. Tomlin made Roethlisberger the emergency number three quarterback, with no plans for him to get on the field.

Afterward, Ward expressed regret in separate conversations with Roethlisberger and Tomlin. He later apologized on his Facebook page:

Ben and I are cool and always will be. We will not let this come between us . . . I didn't mean to cause such a stir. My frustration was . . . this was a big game for us to stay in the playoff picture . . . I was frustrated because there was no indication of Ben not being able to play.

After their Week 14 loss to the Browns, the Steelers won their final three games against Green Bay (37–36), Baltimore (23–20), and Miami (24–22) to finish the regular season at 9–7. They missed the playoffs for the third time since 2000—and first time under Tomlin—in a four-way tiebreaker with the Jets, Texans, and Ravens. Baltimore had clinched the wild-card spot by winning at Oakland on the final weekend.

With Polamalu and Aaron Smith missing for much of the season on an aging defense, without the same overall team focus from the previous season, and with an offense featuring too many peaks and valleys—plus some unexpected distractions—the Steelers suffered through their second Super Bowl hangover in four years.

* * *

For the second time in nine months, Roethlisberger read from a prepared statement at the Steelers' practice facility, in response to a sexual assault claim by a woman. The first time, Roethlisberger was joined at the front of the room by Tomlin and Colbert, in a show of support for their franchise quarterback. A year later, Roethlisberger stood alone after NFL Commissioner Roger Goodell suspended the team's quarterback for six games for his actions in Milledgeville, Georgia, where a young woman accused him of sexually assaulting her. Roethlisberger was not charged with a crime, becoming the first NFL player suspended by Goodell not charged with a crime. The suspension was later reduced to four games.

"I am truly sorry for the disappointment and negative attention I have brought to my family, my teammates and coaches, the Rooneys, and the NFL," Roethlisberger said in his prepared statement.

Team president Art Rooney II, who considered trading Roethlisberger but decided to give him another chance, said, "I agree and support the decision the commissioner made." Rooney wanted to discipline Roethlisberger but decided to wait, as the players' union could challenge a team suspension but wouldn't be able to do so if Goodell levied the punishment.

The Steelers contacted several teams about trading a top-10 pick for Roethlisberger, an NFL source told ESPN Insider Adam Schefter. The Steelers called the Rams, 49ers, Raiders, Bills, Jaguars, Seahawks, and Browns, with the Rams and Bills the most interested teams, the source said.

Tomlin hadn't handpicked Roethlisberger, who was the quarterback of record when he arrived, but Roethlisberger was his *guy*. That meant Tomlin had to embrace Big Ben's game-winning touchdown pass in Super Bowl XLIII, along with facing the harsh realities of his QB1 being forced to defend his character while refuting sexual assault allegations in two of Tomlin's first four seasons in Pittsburgh. Roethlisberger wasn't charged in either case, but the public's perception of the franchise quarterback was much less complimentary on a national level than it was in Pittsburgh proper, where most of the local media protected Ben's blind side like an All-Pro left tackle. On many teams, the quarterback is the "face of the franchise." But not on this team, where the Steelers have been identified by three individuals—Noll, Cowher, and Tomlin—since 1969. It was a tough and unfair burden for a young head coach—particularly a young *black* head coach—to bear.

It also meant Tomlin looked the other way when necessary.

"He'd always say, 'I'm going to treat everybody fairly, but I'm not going to treat everybody the same,'" Willie Colon said. "And he meant that. He knew where the money was at."

Roethlisberger had an assigned parking space at the Steelers practice facility. There was a sign on the fence where his car was parked that read RED HAWKS ONLY, referring to the nickname of Roethlisberger's alma mater, Miami University of Ohio. "There's a lot of coaches that wouldn't permit that," said Bill Hillgrove, who has been the Steelers play-by-play announcer since 1994. "But Mike realized a franchise quarterback is only going to come along every so often. There are some coaches who would make him take the sign down. Mike knew he had a great one."

The day before Roethlisberger's apology—and a week before his suspension was announced—the Steelers traded Holmes, the MVP of Super Bowl XLIII, to the New York Jets for a fifth-round draft pick. Holmes was facing a four-game suspension for violating the league's substance abuse policy—this after Tomlin suspended him for one game for marijuana possession in 2008, a charge that was later dropped. As a rookie, Holmes was charged with disorderly conduct and another time for choking a former girlfriend, but was not convicted on either charge. Holmes was currently facing a civil suit in his home state of Florida, when a woman accused him of throwing a glass that cut her above her eye in an Orlando nightclub.

You could argue the Steelers traded Holmes when his value was at its lowest, resulting in the front office giving away a Pro Bowl–caliber receiver for such a low draft pick.[1] However, multiple media outlets reported the Steelers were so fed up with Holmes that they were prepared to release him if no trade partner was found.

"I was very shocked at first," Holmes said on a conference call with reporters.

A few days later, former tackle Marvel Smith voiced a popular opinion in the Steelers locker room.

"I'm not going to say Ben gets away with a lot, but he's held to a different standard," Smith said on SiriusXM NFL radio. "If they plan on using Santonio as a scapegoat, they are going to have a huge issue in that locker room. Guys already feel like, I guess you can say, they put Ben on a pedestal. He gets away with more than any other guy on the team would."

The way Hampton viewed it, Tomlin was his coach, but Roethlisberger was Tomlin's *guy*. There are no secrets on a football team. When it came to who made the front page of "The News" and who didn't, every Steelers player understood that Roethlisberger—warts and all—sat atop the totem pole.

"You've got to put everybody on 'The News,'" Hampton said. "I think when you ain't putting everybody on 'The News,' it ain't the same. Everybody didn't make 'The News.' I'm gonna leave it at that.

"Ain't nobody more important than nobody else," Hampton continued. "We really felt that way. Everybody was the same.

---

1   Hall of Fame receiver Randy Moss was traded from the Raiders to New England for a fourth-round pick in 2007.

That was the different style between [Tomlin] and Cowher, and both [styles] worked. Cowher kind of treated everybody more the same than [Tomlin] did. Everybody's treated fine, but everybody ain't treated the same. I get that.

"[Tomlin] told me, 'Hamp, I'm gonna tolerate you.' Other players get days off. 'Hamp, you ain't *never* getting no day off.' It's not a big deal though. My [position] coach [John Mitchell] took care of me."

Several days after appearing on SiriusXM NFL radio, Smith granted me a phone interview. My *Trib* column, written around Smith's on-the-record quotes, was published on April 22, 2010, under the title "Steelers Fed Ben's Sense of Entitlement," and took readers inside the Steelers locker room.

No team owners more entrusted a player with the keys to their franchise than the Rooneys did with Ben Roethlisberger—and it resulted in a sense of entitlement for the team's $102 million quarterback.

Comments by Steelers president Art Rooney II before Roethlisberger received a conditional six-game suspension Wednesday indicated the team placed so much faith in Roethlisberger's character that Rooney didn't have a serious discussion with him after the first allegation of sexual assault in Nevada. But Roethlisberger betrayed his team's trust after a second allegation of sexual assault surfaced in Georgia, complete with sordid details in a police report that have been bandied about from coast to coast.

Former Steelers tackle Marvel Smith described Roethlisberger's relationship with the team under coach Mike Tomlin as one in which the quarterback had complete freedom during games and wasn't reprimanded for mistakes. According to Smith, who was with the team from 2000 to 2008, Roethlisberger could do no wrong when Tomlin replaced Bill Cowher before the 2007 season.

"I saw the transition from when Ben ran the plays he was told and when he started talking about plays he didn't want to run," Smith told the *Tribune-Review* in a phone interview.

When asked about the change in offensive coordinators, from Ken Whisenhunt to Bruce Arians, Roethlisberger responded, "It will be nice to know Bruce isn't going to handcuff us." Roethlisberger later apologized to Whisenhunt.

In 2009, Roethlisberger became the first Steelers quarterback to throw for 4,000 yards in a season.

"I remember me and Ben talking about the differences between the coaching staffs—how he wasn't allowed to do certain things with the other coaching staff that he was allowed to do now," Smith said. "He kind of felt like he was treated as a rookie even in his second and third year in the league."

Smith painted a picture of Tomlin propping up Roethlisberger at the expense of teammates while giving players the impression that Roethlisberger was receiving preferential treatment.

"We all have bad games here and there, but I remember when Ben would have a bad game that clearly affected the outcome and the coaches wouldn't say nothing to him directly or even address the fact he might have had three or four interceptions that game," Smith said.

"They would address the other bad [stuff] that happened but not address the glaring issue of throwing a pick in a drive. . . . We'd talk about turnovers, and [coaches] said we had this amount of turnovers, but they don't address it like, 'Have better ball security [or], read the safety instead of instead of throwing it straight to him when he's double-covered.'

"When you do that in front of the whole team, that sends a message he's on a different level. It creates a division within the team. You can't sit there in front of the whole team and not say something to one player that clearly had a bigger impact than anybody else on that game and not even address it."

Roethlisberger was treated more like the rest of his teammates during his first three NFL seasons, said Smith, a big fan of Cowher.

"It wasn't like that with Coach Cowher and Whisenhunt," Smith said. "We addressed all the issues a number of times throughout the season.

"Ben wasn't the one that was making us win. It was a team effort. We wouldn't have made it to [Super Bowl XLIII] if it wasn't for the defense. The defense won so many games for us that year. We put the defense in so many bad situations. The offense made that last play that everybody remembers, but the defense got us there.

"The defense always wanted us to run the ball because they know it kept them off the field. I'm sure the last two years I was there, when they went through the transition of passing the ball more, the defense didn't like that by any means."

When the Steelers opened training camp, Pittsburgh-area reporters were joined by reporters from ESPN, NFL Network, and the *New York Times*, who descended upon sleepy Latrobe to question not only Roethlisberger, but Tomlin and Steelers players about the impact the franchise quarterback's absence would have on the season.

There were an estimated ten thousand fans at St. Vincent College to watch the Steelers' first practice open to the public. Concerned at how he would be received considering his off-season troubles, Roethlisberger was encouraged by loud cheers from well-wishers wearing black and gold.

"It was good to be out here," said Roethlisberger, who signed autographs for thirty minutes after practice. "I walked out, and they cheered pretty loud. It was neat to hear everybody cheering and seeing my jersey."

Roethlisberger would eventually meet with Goodell, who reduced the six-game ban to four, during the commissioner's training camp tour. "It's going to be a challenge," Roethlisberger said. "Football is my escape, my getaway."

Offensive coordinator Bruce Arians told reporters assembled at camp what they already knew: Roethlisberger was the starting quarterback when he returned from his suspension. Ben split reps during training camp with former Jaguars starter Byron Leftwich, who had been the team's backup in 2008, and was re-acquired in a trade with Tampa Bay to provide more depth during Roethlisberger's absence. Big Ben participated in training camp and preseason games, but was not permitted to be around the team once the regular season began.

Tomlin had no control over his quarterback's situation, other than finding a suitable replacement among Dixon, Charlie

Batch, and Leftwich during the first quarter of the season. He did make several coaching changes, including promoting Randy Fichtner to quarterbacks coach when Ken Anderson retired. Tomlin also cut ties with Larry Zierlein, who had been the offensive line coach and was a longtime associate of Tomlin's from their days at the University of Cincinnati. His replacement was Sean Kugler, who had been coaching in the league since 2001. Scottie Montgomery stepped in for Fichtner as the wide receivers coach, while Al Everest took over for Bob Ligashesky as the special teams coach.

Working in lockstep with Kevin Colbert, Tomlin laid the groundwork for the future with one of the most impactful draft classes in franchise history.

They started with the offensive line, with the team taking Florida Gator Maurkice Pouncey with the 18th overall pick. The first center selected by the Steelers in the first round since 1937, Pouncey would be a mainstay on the offensive line, starting all 16 regular season games as a rookie. The Steelers initially moved Pouncey to guard with plans to eventually move him over to center. "As a young guy coming in, it's probably easier coming in at guard," Tomlin told reporters. It was reminiscent of two decades earlier when the Steelers played Hall of Famer Dermontti Dawson at guard his rookie season before switching him to center, where he started for twelve years.

The Steelers also drafted a pair of wide receivers, selecting SMU's Emmanuel Sanders in the third round and Central Michigan's Antonio Brown in the sixth. The pair combined for 44 receptions and scored three touchdowns as rookies. Tomlin described the competition between Sanders and Brown as, "two dogs, one bone."

Covering that training camp for the *Trib,* I'll never forget the day when Montgomery admonished the entire wide receiver group. Some of the receivers, Sanders included, literally hung their heads in the face of Montgomery's scathing criticism, which was in full view of reporters. I couldn't help but notice the Brown kid from Central Michigan stood tall, took in every harsh word, and never flinched. I didn't realize it at the time, but I was looking at a future All-Pro wideout who scored a touchdown the first time he touched the ball in an NFL game.

A former college wide receiver, Tomlin's Steelers have drafted several talented receivers on his watch. Originally the team's director of football operations who was promoted to general manager, Colbert's overall role in drafting players may have technically been greater than Tomlin's, but the pair regularly attended college pro days and the NFL Combine together. Once asked to define his role in the draft process, Tomlin told Pittsburgh reporters, "I take responsibility for the players we have drafted since I've been here . . . because it's the truth." The list of receivers drafted since Tomlin's arrival includes not only Brown and Sanders, but also Mike Wallace, Martavis Bryant, JuJu Smith-Schuster, Diontae Johnson, and George Pickens, the latter catching 52 passes for a 15.4 yard average as a rookie in 2022. Another wideout, Chase Claypool, was traded for a second-round draft pick during the 2022 season.

"His mindset and attitude and experience with receivers, he had a special knack for that," Ed Tomlin said about his brother's ability to identify talented wideouts.

Prior to the Steelers' selection with the 195th pick in the sixth round, Tomlin indicated it was time to draft Brown, who caught 305 passes for 3,199 yards in the Mid-American Conference.

"You like your little one-cut guy here?" Tomlin asked Arians in an ESPN article by senior NFL national reporter Jeremy Fowler. Tomlin marveled at Brown's underrated ball skills and his ability to separate.

"I love him right here," Arians said.

There was a lot to love, but also signs that there may be issues down the line. For instance, Brown was benched for the first game of the season due to missing a team meeting, though the Steelers would edge the Falcons in overtime, 15–9. Yet in Week 2 at Tennessee, Brown was on the field for the opening kickoff, and after taking the ball from Mewelde Moore on a reverse, returned it 89 yards for a touchdown in the Steelers' 19–11 win. Overlooked in the victory was the rebirth of the Steelers' defense, which registered its most turnovers (seven) in a game since 1997.

Despite injuries that caused Leftwich and Dixon to miss playing time, the Steelers won three of their first four games in Roethlisberger's absence. The defense, which returned to its 2008 form following an uncharacteristic slump the year before, yielded a paltry 12.5 points during that stretch (allowing just four touchdowns over sixteen quarters). Miami was the first team to score 20 points against the Steelers in the sixth game of the season. The Dolphins, who were averaging 115.9 yards on the ground, totaled 64 yards on 21 attempts. Roethlisberger had his best performance in his second game back from the suspension, completing 19 of 27 passes for 302 yards, with two touchdowns with no interceptions in a 23–22 victory.

In his first 54 regular-season games as an NFL coach, Tomlin, who was still only thirty-eight years old, won twice as often as he lost for a .704 winning percentage. He opened his fourth season with a 5–1 record despite not having his franchise quarterback for the first four games. While there were still 10 games left in the season, the Steelers appeared to have hit their stride and it looked like Tomlin was on his way to registering his third double-digit win campaign.

Tomlin was charged with the difficult task of continuing the Steelers' winning tradition while at the same time reshaping the roster in his own image; putting to bed the perception that his early success was limited to Cowher's players. For example, Mike Wallace was drafted the year before Holmes was traded, and led the NFL in yards per catch as a rookie (19.4). That following year, Wallace, in Holmes's absence, had 1,257 receiving yards and led the league with seven 100-yard receiving games. Mendenhall's arrival downsized the contributions of Willie Parker, who was signed as an undrafted free agent in 2004. In 2009, Parker's final NFL season and Mendenhall's second, the young back rushed for over 1,100 yards and seven touchdowns. Parker's output was reduced to 389 yards on 98 carries. In Mendenhall's third season, he ran for 1,273 yards and 13 touchdowns, both career highs.

"We lost Santonio, but we lost other guys that were also significant pieces," Colon said. "Guys were not unfocused, but the level of detail we had kind of wavered a little bit. Mike T had to adjust and reinstate, 'We've got to go back and do this again.' On top of that, we've got to do it with guys who [didn't] help us do it the first time.

Colon continued: "How do you do that? How do you talk to a young Mike Wallace? How do you continue to motivate James Harrison? How do you continue to let this all-world defense stay hungry with guys who helped him get to the promised land who are no longer there?"

Tomlin knew his players. He knew their motivations and what drove them. He also understood how injuries can weaken and sidetrack a team. And in Colon's case, how injuries can affect a player's psyche.

Put simply, the Steelers offensive line was in a constant state of flux. Right tackle Colon missed the entire season with an Achilles injury and was replaced in the starting lineup by the thirty-five-year-old longtime Dallas Cowboy, Flozell Adams. Left tackle Starks went on injured reserve after seven games and was replaced in the starting lineup by Jonathan Scott. Versatile backup Trai Essex appeared in twelve games, starting five. Not to mention the coaching staff's decision to start Pouncey as a rookie.

"Those guys are survivors," Tomlin said of his embattled players.

Being unable to play because of injury took a toll on Colon, both physical and mental. Not one to miss games, he had started 48 consecutive regular season games in the Tomlin era and manned his position with a warrior's mentality that the head coach demanded from his offensive linemen.

"When I hurt my Achilles before training camp, I was devastated," said Colon. "I got hurt when I felt like I was about to enter my prime. I had a lot of anxiety. I was angry. But Mike T wouldn't allow me to sit at home and sulk. Not only did he allow me to travel with the team, he let me work out at the facility. He was like, 'I want you here. I want you to be a part of this. These young guys need your guidance and advice and know-how. I need that culture in this room.' It meant a lot. He kept me out of the dark hole I easily could have climbed in.

"I was drinking. Hanging out. I was very bitter," he continued. "I wanted to run away. Mike T and Sean Kugler wouldn't allow me to sit at home on weekends and sulk. I needed to be around football in some fashion. They treated me as if I was getting ready to play on Sunday. I'm forever grateful to Mike T and Sean Kugler for not closing the door."

Offensive line issues aside, not having their franchise quarterback for the first four games, while losing two other quarterbacks to injuries at various times, shifted more pressure to Wallace, who had to adjust to catching passes from four different quarterbacks—no easy task, especially from a second-year receiver. On top of all the injuries, the final shoe to drop was Harrison, the Steelers' All-Pro linebacker, considering retirement during the season.

"We overcame a lot more obstacles than we have in the past," Polamalu said.

During a 28–10 home victory against Cleveland, Harrison, the 2008 Defensive Player of the Year, knocked two Browns out of the game with vicious hits. In the middle of the second quarter, Harrison drilled former college teammate Josh Cribbs with the crown of his helmet into the side of Cribbs's helmet. Then with two minutes left before the half, he flattened Mohamed Massaquoi after a catch, delivering his forearms to the player's face. "I kind of laid off on him," Harrison told reporters after the game. Both Cribbs and Massaquoi sustained concussions.

Two years earlier, the NFL had passed a rule to prevent hits to the head and neck area. While there was no penalty on the Cribbs hit (as he was considered a runner and not in a defenseless position), neither was one called on Massaquoi's hit because he caught the ball and wasn't considered a "defenseless receiver" (though it would be considered so by today's rules). That led

Harrison to believe he was in the clear regarding a fine. "I'm not worried about getting fined," he said. "If I get fined on that, it's got to be a travesty. They didn't call [penalties]."

He was wrong.

The NFL fined Harrison $75,000 two days later for his hit on Massaquoi, referring to him as a "repeat offender" after the league had previously fined him $5,000 for unnecessary roughness on a roughing the passer penalty against Tennessee quarterback Vince Young in the second game of the season.

After going on a national radio show in which he contemplated retirement, Harrison returned to practice and met with Tomlin, who told reporters Harrison didn't like the perception he was a dirty player. Tomlin gave Harrison the day off with instructions to return to practice the next day.

In a statement released to the media, Harrison defended his play.

"I want it to be known that I have never and would never intentionally try to injure any player. I believe that my statements, along with the hits that happened in other games this past Sunday and the subsequent media storm, are the reasons I was fined on what I know was a clean hit.

"I will not retire from the NFL. I will continue to play the game with the same passion, intensity and focus with which I have always played and let the chips fall where they may. I have never given up, quit or walked away from anything in my life and I am not about to start now. I will not let down my family, friends or the Steelers Nation."

As head coach, Tomlin's ultimate goal was to win football games. To achieve that goal in 2010, he needed Harrison to continue to sacrifice his body for the good of the team.

After allowing Harrison to blow off steam, Tomlin did what separated him from many of his coaching peers, with his ability to look inside his players and determine what made each of them tick.

Harrison didn't miss a game and produced another Pro Bowl campaign, with 70 solo tackles, 10.5 sacks, six forced fumbles, and two interceptions, while racking up a whopping $125,000 in fines.

Call it a gift, a knack, or just plain luck. Whatever it is, Tomlin not only knew how to connect with his players, but what was needed to get them to play at their best.

"James is a very disciplined and very regimented player and is also a very emotional player," Tomlin said. "Once the emotions wore off from the initial shock of some of the things he had to deal with, he generally quickly gets back to focus on what it is he does, which, of course, is play outside linebacker extremely well. So not a lot was needed to be done with James other than maybe give him a day off and let itself burn out like I knew it would, and he did."

Of all the elite defenses Tomlin coached in Pittsburgh and Tampa Bay, the 2010 unit ranks as his favorite. It was an intimidating group that permitted a league-low 1,004 rushing yards—third-lowest total in league history (for a 16-game schedule) to Tomlin's 2006 Minnesota defense—led the NFL with 48 sacks, ranked second in total yards allowed, and third in opponents scoring (on only 25.7 percent of their drives).

"I just thought the [2010] group beat you up," Tomlin said on the *Footbahlin with Roethlisberger* podcast. "Just in terms of physicality without a doubt. The [2002 Tampa Bay] group was a splash play group . . . You're talking about a bar fight and you're talking about football. [2010] created . . . what we know now as the player safety initiative. The powers that be watched them play and said this is not good for the future of football."

With the comfort level of Harrison no longer an issue, the Steelers' defense had only one misstep down the stretch, occurring in a 39–26 loss to New England in Week 10. Overall, Pittsburgh won seven of its final nine regular-season games, including impressive road wins against Cincinnati (23–7), Buffalo (19–16 in OT), and Baltimore (13–10).

Unlike their last trip to the playoffs, the Steelers didn't finish the regular season as the No. 1 seed despite posting an identical 12–4 record. New England held the top spot in the AFC with the Steelers at No. 2. If the teams met in the AFC Championship Game, New England would be home, along with having a first-round bye.

Heading into the divisional round, the Steelers would face off against their nemesis, the No. 5 seeded Baltimore Ravens. They had split during the regular season, with each team winning on the road. Two years earlier, the Ravens stood in the way of the Steelers advancing to Super Bowl XLIII. Now, the Ravens were trying to prevent the Steelers from playing in their second conference title game in three years.

Ryan Clark was the story of the game, the inspiration behind the defense's big-play mentality. He personally accounted for two Baltimore turnovers, precipitating a 14-point third-quarter explosion. Heading into the second half down 21–7, Clark tackled running back Ray Rice, causing a fumble recovered by Woodley on Baltimore's 18-yard line. Roethlisberger capitalized with a short touchdown pass to Heath Miller, slicing the Ravens' lead to 21–14. Clark was at it again two series later, picking off a Joe Flacco pass and returning 17 yards to the Ravens' 25. Another short Roethlisberger scoring toss, this time to Ward, tied the game. Baltimore's turnover fest continued on its next drive, when Flacco fumbled the center snap, recovered by Brett Keisel at the Baltimore 23. Shaun Suisham's 35-yard field goal pushed the Steelers to a 24–21 lead with 12:15 left in the fourth quarter.

While Pittsburgh held the momentum, the pendulum swung when Ladarius Webb returned a Jeremy Kapinos punt 55 yards to the Steelers 10-yard line. A holding penalty on the play moved the ball back to the 29-yard line, and while Baltimore was unable to get into the endzone, a Billy Cundiff field goal tied the game at 24–24 with just under four minutes left in regulation.

After two incompletions to start the drive, Ben hit Hines Ward on third-and-10 for a first down. With a fresh set of downs, he was then sacked by Cory Redding and Paul Kruger, and after another incomplete pass, Roethlisberger faced third-and-19 at his own 38. If the Steelers failed to move the chains, they would be forced to punt and ask their defense, which held the Ravens to 126 total yards, to once again save the day.

What to do? Super Bowl and playoff hero Holmes was long gone. How about Ward, or perhaps Miller—each of whom scored a touchdown in the game? Nope. Perhaps Brown, the rookie who clearly gained his quarterback's trust in the clutch? Coming out of their time out, and with 2:07 left to play, Brown slipped behind coverage along the right sideline to snag Roethlisberger's bullet pass, holding the ball against his helmet to complete the 58-yard catch. Brown went out of bounds at the Baltimore 4 yard line.

The Steelers now sensed that this was their game. At worst, they could kick a short field goal for a three-point advantage.

A seven-point lead would be much better. On third down, Mendenhall's one-yard scoring burst capped a furious second-half rally, resulting in a hard-fought 31–24 victory.

"Styles make fights," said Tomlin, who improved his record against the Ravens to 7–3 [regular season and playoffs]. "Those two teams are Hagler-Hearns. It was great for the game of football."

Even greater for Pittsburgh was New England's 28–21 upset loss to the sixth-seeded New York Jets. Instead of traveling to face their nemesis for the conference title, the Steelers would play host to the upstart Jets.

The Jets were a confident ballclub. Not only did they topple New England on the road to advance to within one game of their first Super Bowl appearance since 1969, they had also handled the Steelers at Pittsburgh in Week 15, 22–17.[2] The Jets rushed for 106 yards, most against the Steelers all season.

"They beat us at our place. We're going to have to play better than we did the last time," Tomlin told reporters, also sending a message to his team.

Jets head coach Rex Ryan sent the league a message before the season even began, writing, "Soon To Be Champs" on an ESPN bus during training camp. Two days before the title game, Ryan said he wanted to see green and white confetti fall, signaling a Jets' victory over the Steelers.

It would certainly be no cake walk in Pittsburgh, as the Jets had already eliminated Peyton Manning and the Colts in Indy for the wild card (on a field goal as time expired), and done the

---

2 This was also the first time the Jets had won in Pittsburgh and only the fourth
   win against the team in 19 total games, going back to 1970.

same in New England to Brady and the Pats. Now they were headed to Heinz Field in the hopes of a third road victory in the AFC Championship to send them to Dallas.

With a game plan to stifle Roethlisberger, the Jets' defense failed to account for Mendenhall, who ran wild for a career playoff-high 126 yards and one score.

In their 24–19 win, the Steelers made one big play after another, highlighted by William Gay's fumble return for a touchdown in the second quarter. The Jets, who rallied from a 24–0 deficit, needed one stop on third-and-six to give the ball back to their offense to complete the comeback. They couldn't pull it off against a Tomlin-influenced offense that once again rose to the occasion. For the second week in a row, the Roethlisberger-to-Brown connection struck in the clutch.

It was a pass play, of course, designed for Ward, the franchise's career leader in receptions, but that option was taken away when Ryan, rather than calling for a blitz to collapse the pocket, dropped potential pass rushers into coverage. Improvising, Roethlisberger did what Brady and Manning were unable to do against the Jets: he scrambled to give himself more time to find an open receiver, and a 14-yard completion gave them the first down. The only thing left to do was get into victory formation and take a knee three times and they'd be on their way to face the Green Bay Packers in Super Bowl XLV.

Four years, two AFC titles, and two trips to the Super Bowl later, no head coach ever coached the Steelers so well as quickly into his tenure as Tomlin.

"It's probably about two Super Bowls too short in my vision," Tomlin said. "That's just me. I'm not in a reflection mode. We've got a good football team—guys who are not only talented but selfless . . . we are trying to maximize the opportunity we have. . . . We're excited about it. It's not going to paralyze us. We're not going to dwell on it or over-analyze it. We are simply going to prepare and ultimately play. Maybe later in life when we're old, maybe we'll sit down and reflect a little bit."

* * *

On the same day their chartered flight touched down at Dallas-Fort Worth International Airport—six days before Super Bowl XLV—the Steelers made headlines, once again, for something that had nothing to do with the game.

The Steelers were escorted from the airport to the Omni Fort Worth Hotel, located about twenty-five miles away, by several police officers. Later that evening, a blog article in the home-town *Dallas Morning News* reported that Ward, Ike Taylor, and other Steelers teammates were seen at a popular gentleman's club about thirty miles from the team hotel.

Although the optics weren't great, the players violated no team rules. Whether their actions would create a distraction for the team was an issue for another day.

"What typically happens [with newspapers] when a Super Bowl is in your town is kind of all-hands-on-deck," said Gromer Jeffers, a political reporter at the *Dallas Morning News* who wrote the blog article. " You go to Super Bowl parties, you go to all the events. The paper's not going to assign anybody to go to a strip club, right? I got wind of it. I had been to the spot before.

"On Monday nights, there's a local radio station that does a promotion. I heard they were going to have the Steelers and the Packers there," Jeffers continued. "At first blush you think, 'Yeah, right. They're just trying to get people in there.' I dropped by after work just to hang out. I see them coming in and I'm like, 'That's Hines Ward. That's Ike Taylor.' There were linemen I couldn't recognize because I didn't cover the Steelers. The women are dancing all over them and giving them lap dances. Money was being thrown around, making it rain. Twitter was just starting. I didn't have a Twitter account, so I wrote a blog about it."

When asked about the Steelers' "boys night out" at the gentleman's club, Tomlin said the team treated Super Bowl week like any other week during the regular season.

"I understand things may be viewed and be reported differently, but that's not our concern," Tomlin said. "I am not concerned about that one iota."

Super Bowl week was classic Mike Tomlin. It was standing room only at his media sessions, and, in typical fashion, he did his best to deflect attention away from his players and put it on himself.

When repeatedly pressed about Roethlisberger's controversial season in the aftermath of his four-game suspension, Tomlin didn't run from the questions or ask why the Roethlisberger-Aaron Rodgers matchup between the franchise quarterbacks wasn't receiving more attention.

"Ben is a highly respected member of our football team, not only because of what he's done this year, but just as large, his body of work and the person that he is," Tomlin said. "We all fall short of perfection, we all make mistakes. His are well-documented. He's doing the best he can in terms of moving forward with it, as are his teammates."

Tomlin had spoken. His succinct explanation about how the Steelers' compartmentalized Roethlisberger's four-game absence over a sixteen-game schedule while holding the team together highlighted the origins of their culture.

"It's not broken, so I wasn't going to try to fix it," Tomlin said. "It's sound, it's time-tested, and it's proven. I didn't have any deep or philosophical thoughts regarding it. I was more interested in what I needed to do to add to that legacy.

"We believe in building through the draft. I don't think that's a big secret. Equally as important is that we believe in paying our own players—those who are deserving—and simply adding to and supplementing that. That's our business model. It's worked for a long time prior to me getting here. I think it creates an atmosphere where guys care about one another. They care about the organization. They understand it is bigger than them."

In the sixties, Green Bay was the go-to franchise in professional football. Coached by Vince Lombardi and quarterbacked by Bart Starr, the Packers won the first two Super Bowls in history to uphold the reputation of the established NFL against the fledgling AFL. By the time the Packers won their third Super Bowl twenty-nine years later, the NFL-AFL rivalry was a thing of the past. To win their fourth Super Bowl, the Packers faced the ultimate test in the Steelers, who were vying to become the first team to win seven Super Bowls.

To defeat the Packers, who were 3.5-point favorites, the Steelers needed a vintage performance from Roethlisberger, who was 10–2 in the postseason but whose first two Super Bowl performances were met with mixed reviews. This game was his opportunity to break the tie and join an exclusive club of quarterbacks with three or more Super Bowl victories.

Pittsburgh's top-rated defense was great all year, sure. But not even the Steelers' latter-day "Steel Curtain" could overcome Roethlisberger's two first-half interceptions, including Nick Collins's pick-six return, giving Green Bay a 14–0 lead in the first quarter. Both interceptions were thrown into double coverage.

"We just turned the ball over too many times," said Roethlisberger, "and it's my fault."

In two of the Steelers' four losses during the regular season, they trailed at intermission, raising the degree of difficulty for a team needing to overcome a 21–10 halftime deficit against the Packers—in the Super Bowl of all games.

Attempting to stage the biggest comeback in Super Bowl history, the Steelers pulled within four, 21–17, on Mendenhall's eight-yard touchdown run in the third quarter. But what Mendenhall gave, he also took away. On the first play of the fourth quarter, linebacker Clay Matthews delivered a jarring hit, knocking the ball clean from Mendenhall's grasp.

"I just got hit, and the ball came out," Mendenhall explained. "It just happened, and it should not have happened." Mendenhall did not carry the ball again after the fumble.

Green Bay's offense responded with an eight-play, 55-yard drive that ended with a Greg Jennings touchdown reception from Rodgers. The score gave the Packers a 28–17 lead with less than twelve minutes remaining.

Roethlisberger's 25-yard touchdown pass to Wallace and ensuing two-point conversion made it 28–25, but it was too little, too late. Green Bay's offense responded with a 10-play drive that ate up more than five minutes, ending with a field goal to increase their lead to 31–25.

With barely two minutes left and one time out, it was now or never. After completions to Miller and Ward, Roethlisberger threw three straight incompletions to end any hopes of a comeback.

"Usually when you lose, it's because of turnovers," said Tomlin, whose team turned the ball over three times, resulting in 21 Green Bay points. "But they made plays. It's probably less about what we were unable to do than what they were able to do."

Art Rooney II addressed the Steelers after the game.

"I just said, 'Thanks,'" Rooney said. "They worked hard and they got us close to winning a seventh championship. That's pretty impressive."

13

THE TEBOW EFFECT AND TWIN .500 SEASONS

(2011–13)

"Excuses are tools for the incompetent."

AFTER winning Super Bowl XLIII in 2008, the question going into the next season was if the team would suffer from a SB hangover. But is it the same for teams who lost the Super Bowl?

Super Bowl XLV was a game the Steelers very easily could have won. Should have won, perhaps? That's a debate with no expiration date. Green Bay quarterback Aaron Rodgers was at the top of his game and made every big play. On the other hand, Roethlisberger, who survived a landmine of a season, made his share of big plays—including some for the other team.

Roethlisberger's biggest victory moving forward may have been entering 2011 with a clean slate. For the first time since Tomlin's first Super Bowl season, the start of training camp wasn't marked by players and coaching staff alike performing damage control and defending their franchise quarterback about his off-the-field issues. It had been a drain on the entire team, but also a tribute to Tomlin for keeping his team focused and in contention to win the franchise's seventh Super Bowl right up until the final minutes.

More importantly, Tomlin had the support of the front office, which went out on a limb to bring him into the fold in what was, at the time, one of the most scrutinized head coaching hires in league history. Succumbing to the dreaded Super Bowl hangover, the Steelers won their final three games to climb out of a rabbit hole and finish 9–7 in 2009. Refocused, they bounced back to play in Super Bowl XLV the following year.

Other teams would still be celebrating after winning the Super Bowl, much less be thinking about the possibility of their head coach losing his team. Not the Steelers, who viewed every season as an opportunity to play in *another* Super Bowl.

With Dan Rooney serving as United States Ambassador to Ireland since July 2009, Art Rooney II assumed daily control of the franchise. In an interview with the *Pittsburgh Tribune-Review* after losing to Green Bay in the Super Bowl, he shared his feelings about Tomlin's job performance: "It showed something about Mike that he's not going to let a team give up on itself."

The Steelers displayed public support for Tomlin after their latest Super Bowl appearance by signing him to a two-year contract extension that would keep him in Pittsburgh through at least 2012.

Tomlin was a players' coach, but his patience with teaching, delegating responsibility among his coaches, and imposing his will behind the scenes was his strong suit.[1]

His selfless mentality allowed him to look the other way regarding the Roethlisberger-Arians dynamic. Other people might not have wanted to give him credit, but Tomlin was secure enough as leader to understand that whatever success was generated by that pairing would be shared by him as well . . . along with any blame. He had no ego hangups.

It was not within Tomlin's nature to make himself the center of attention. Instead, it was Rooney who told several Pittsburgh media outlets that he and Tomlin agreed the offense needed to run the ball more efficiently.

Roethlisberger and Arians made good on Tomlin's request. After running the ball 44.2 percent of the time and not making the playoffs in 2009, they increased their production on the ground to 47.4 percent in 2010, and made a return trip to the Super Bowl.

Clearly, Tomlin, Arians, and Roethlisberger were on the same page. But for the offense to continue to evolve and conquer, Roethlisberger and Arians—the offensive coordinator signed a one-year extension before the season—had to evolve together. That meant not necessarily calling more running plays, but running more on passing downs and vice versa.

What began as a professional relationship became personal, expanding the dialogue even further between offensive coordinator

---

1 Through the 2022 season, over the past twenty-five years, of teams losing the Super Bowl, 16 of 25 had a winning record, with 14 of 25 making the playoffs. Only the Patriots—losers of Super Bowl LI—not only made the SB the following season, but also won.

and franchise quarterback. In other words, Roethlisberger didn't mind having Arians inside his head. They played golf together and visited each other at their offseason homes in Georgia. "I can talk to him about anything," Roethlisberger said.

The no-huddle was a Roethlisberger favorite in which he ran Arians's plays, but on his terms. By making it difficult for the defense to substitute more linebackers and defensive backs for fewer run stoppers, the no-huddle became Roethlisberger's security blanket. With this method, Arians still had control over play calling but Roethlisberger had more freedom and flexibility to run plays he was comfortable with.

With Hines Ward in his new role as possession receiver, the emergence of Mike Wallace as a legitimate deep threat and Antonio Brown's promise as the other wideout was a testament to the Steelers' uncanny ability to identify a need and reload quickly. The passing game fed off a strong running game manned by Rashard Mendenhall, whose back-to-back 1,000-yard campaigns made folks forget about Willie Parker. If the passing game struggled, it wouldn't be because Roethlisberger didn't have enough quality weapons at the skill positions.

Based on his aging defensive roster, Tomlin figured to squeeze at least one more terrific season from a unit featuring seven full-time starters thirty years or older, including four *starters* thirty-three and older. Four AFC Championship Game appearances, three trips to the Super Bowl, and seven years later, the Steelers defense was still regarded as a group that should go down in history as one of the league's finest.

Despite overflowing with championship talent, the reality was unavoidable: this defense, particularly the defensive front, was on borrowed time. In response to Father Time, the Steelers selected defensive linemen with their first-round selections in two of the previous three drafts.[2]

It's not a situation where we're looking to tear things apart and start over," Rooney said in the same interview with the *Trib*. "I think there are a lot of pieces in place. Getting younger on defense is a process that already started."

* * *

There was another, darker side to the Steelers advancing to two Super Bowls and reaching the postseason in three of Tomlin's first four seasons. It was difficult for a team to play all those extra playoff games (seven, nearly half a season), lose quality free agents as a result of that success, select at the bottom of the first round in two of those years, and remain consistently good, if not great. Due to the Steelers' success, the team's average pick in the first round since Tomlin's arrival has been 21.8 out of 32 selections. There have been more hits than misses. The year after Tomlin's first Super Bowl appearance, the Steelers dipped to 9–7 the following year. Would attrition and complacency strike again in 2011?

It would be easy to buy into that narrative considering the team's performance in their season opener at Baltimore. They looked old, overwhelmed, and old. The 35–7 defeat was their first opening day loss in eight years. The Steelers trailed 14–0 after the first quarter and 27–7 at halftime before the Ravens called off the dogs.

---

2 In 2009 they drafted Ziggy Hood (32nd overall) out of Missouri, and in 2011 drafted Cameron Heyward (31st overall) out of Ohio State.

Baltimore harassed Roethlisberger into throwing three interceptions and losing two fumbles outright. Another fumble was lost on the center exchange. The Steelers committed a total of six turnovers in the second half. Terrell Suggs sacked Roethlisberger three times. Baltimore safety Ed Reed had two interceptions. The Steelers' defense managed only one sack against Joe Flacco who, along with three touchdown passes, won for the first time against the Steelers with Roethlisberger in the lineup. Ray Rice became the first 100-yard rusher against Pittsburgh in two seasons.

"We got beat into submission," linebacker James Farrior said in the locker room after the game.

Everything that could go wrong did go wrong for the Steelers, but it was only one game. Roethlisberger took a beating and played poorly, but he was already looking ahead to next week. As he did following every game, win or lose, home or away, Roethlisberger did a group interview with reporters. "I'd rather this be a Week One loss than a Week 13, 14, 15 loss," Roethlisberger said.

The Steelers got back on track with wins against Seattle (24–0) in their home opener and Indianapolis (23–20) on the road. Then, surprisingly, they fell to 2–2 following a loss at Houston (17–10), a team that had only a single winning season since joining the league in 2002.

While the defense seemed to be regaining its form after the opening-day setback, the offense was held to a total of two touchdowns in the two losses. Could they snap out of their early-season funk?

Tomlin's calling card has always been his ability to rally the troops. In 2009, after two losses in their first three games, the Steelers won five straight. Then, after the bottom appeared to fall out, resulting in a five-game losing streak, the team finished the season on a high note, winning their final three games. In 2010, following a 5–1 start, the Steelers lost two of their next three games. They then proceeded to win four straight and six of their final seven.

For the third consecutive year, the Steelers looked to Tomlin for answers. In a 38–17 home win against Tennessee, Roethlisberger, playing on a sprained left foot, threw a season-high five touchdown passes, including two to Ward. Next up was Jacksonville and a re-commitment to the run. Mendenhall, who had missed the previous game with a hamstring injury, carried the ball 23 times for 146 yards and a touchdown in a 17–13 victory. In week seven, three years after Super Bowl XLIII, the Steelers and Arizona met again with the same results. Roethlisberger tossed three more touchdown passes—giving him nine in three games—in an easy 32–20 road win.

Sitting at 5–2, next up were the 5–1 New England Patriots. Tomlin was 1–2 against the Patriots and head coach Bill Belichick.

"One of my favorite things [Tomlin] said to us that I think is very true. We were losing games because we were just being dumb at times with penalties," said Colon, who signed a five-year, $29 million contract prior to the start of the 2011 season, but was limited to only one game because of an injury. "He said, 'I'll put the Pittsburgh Steelers against any team in the NFL in a parking lot fight hands down and we'll beat the hell of them.' The difference between us and the New England Patriots is they have that same mentality but they don't beat themselves and they play a lot smarter than we do. It was so real because it was right.

"There wasn't a time in my NFL career, no matter what away game it was—from Baltimore to San Francisco, from Detroit to Tampa—where we weren't going to try to just kick the living crap out of teams physically. And I know for a good portion of my Steeler career we made a lot of teams tap [out]. But we also watched New England play as tough as us, have the same type of swagger, but from the neck up they kicked a lot of [butt]. And that's what we lacked. [Tomlin] was very real about saying that. From the neck up, we've got to be smarter. That just wasn't on the players, but on the coaches, too. He never doubted the armor we wore. He never doubted our toughness. He made adjustments in practice to make sure we honed in on that."

The Steelers walloped New England, 25–17, for their fourth consecutive victory and first place in the conference. Roethlisberger outdueled Brady, passing for 365 yards and two touchdowns. Brady tossed two touchdown passes of his own, but was limited to 198 passing yards against a defense that was missing starting linebackers Farrior and James Harrison. Brady was sacked three times, twice by Woodley, who departed the game with an injury. NFL receiving leader Wes Welker was held to just six catches for 39 yards by Ike Taylor, who followed Welker all over the field and guarded him in the slot on third downs. The Steelers held a decisive advantage in time of possession (36:22 to 20:38), translating to having the ball 60 percent of the time.

"We talked about how that group was going to be tested," Tomlin said in explaining how his banged-up defense performed against an explosive New England offense that was averaging 30.8 points per game (and was held under 20 points for the first time all season). "They were tested tonight and passed the test."

What emerged from the first half of the season was a revitalized Steelers ballclub that discovered offensive balance and rediscovered a crunching defense. At 6–2, the team would only lose two more games the rest of the way. One of those defeats was telling, however, and prevented the Steelers from capturing their third division title under Tomlin and the opportunity to host a playoff game.

A week after sticking it to Brady, Belichick, and the Patriots, the Steelers had Baltimore trapped against the ropes after wiping out a 10-point deficit and holding a 20–16 advantage after a Roethlisberger to Wallace touchdown pass late in the fourth quarter. A few strategic body blows from the Steelers' second-ranked defense, and the Ravens were poised for the knockout after forcing a quick three-and-out.

After going 20 yards on six plays, Pittsburgh punted the ball back to Baltimore with 2:34 left on the clock and no timeouts. Instead of another quick three-and-out, the Ravens delivered a devastating counterpunch when Flacco capped a 13-play, 92-yard drive with a 26-yard touchdown pass to rookie Torrey Smith with eight seconds remaining. Baltimore's 23–20 comeback victory knocked the Steelers out of first place and pushed the Ravens into a first-place division tie with Cincinnati. It was Baltimore's first season sweep of the Steelers since 2006.

"I felt good about where they were," Tomlin said after the game. "We had a four-point lead, and our defense was on the field."

The game marked the return of Harrison after a four-game absence from a broken orbital bone and he picked up as if he hadn't missed a game, recording three sacks. The secondary, however—in a switch from the New England game—played man-to-man instead of zone and left open real estate for Baltimore's receivers. The Steelers' struggles in single coverage, particularly against the deep ball, would resurface again in the postseason.

After a 24–17 win over the Bengals that sent them into the bye, they kept up with their winning ways, going 5–1 down the stretch to finish the season with a 12–4 record.

As they did in Tomlin's first year, the Steelers did not receive a first-round bye. Though finishing with similar 12–4 records with the Ravens, Baltimore had won both regular-season matchups for sole possession of the division. As such, Pittsburgh would have to play in a wild-card game against Denver. The Broncos ended the regular season on a three-game losing streak and finished the season at .500, with an 8–8 record. Compare that with the Steelers, who won six of their last seven.

Though winning the division and heading to the playoffs for the first time since 2005, Denver's season did not begin on a high note. After starting 1–4, the decision was made to replace quarterback Kyle Orton with former Heisman Trophy winner and second-year pro Tim Tebow. With Tebow now at the helm coming out of the bye week, the Broncos reeled off seven wins in eight weeks, including six consecutive (with three of those wins coming in overtime).

In his first eight starts, the former Florida product, taken 25th overall in the 2010 draft with questions on if he would fit as an NFL quarterback, threw for 1,211 yards with 10 touchdown passes (against two interceptions), along with 480 rushing yards. Yet during the Broncos' three-game losing streak at the end of the season, Buffalo, New England, and Kansas City kept the mobile quarterback in the pocket and forced him into making bad throws. Pittsburgh figured to mimic that strategy against the second-year player who struggled to read defenses and was clearly overmatched against the veteran LeBeau heading into the wild card.

What resulted was shocking to all involved. After a 20-point second quarter lead for Denver, Pittsburgh needed to battle the rest of the way to tie the game at 23 apiece, sending the game into overtime.

Now in extra time, the Broncos won the toss and would receive the ball in the hopes of going the length of the field to move on to the next round.

However, nobody expected that they would only need a single play to do so, when Tebow connected with Demaryius Thomas on an 80-yard touchdown pass to give the Broncos a 29–23 victory. On the play, Tebow faked a handoff to running back Willis McGahee, dropped back, and rifled the ball to Thomas on a quick slant. Thomas shook off Taylor's attempted tackle near midfield and ran away from Taylor and safety Ryan Mundy for the score.

Not only did the inexperienced Tebow throw for a career-high 316 yards, but he picked the Steelers' defense apart downfield, averaging 31.6 yards on his 10 completions. Thomas had four receptions for 204 yards, including receptions of 51, 58, and the game-winning 80-yard catch.

"If you don't get Tim on the ground, he's going to make his plays," Taylor said three days after the game on the *Ike Taylor Show* (of which I co-hosted) on TribLIVE Radio. "He is a running back who can throw the ball."

"He threw the ball pretty well," Farrior said. "We hadn't really seen that out of him on the tapes we watched in preparing for him."

Entering the game, the Steelers prioritized attacking Tebow with pressure from the front seven and trusting their defensive backs to cover man-to-man as they did in the second Baltimore game. Not only did the Steelers fail to record a sack, but they didn't switch coverage to account for the lack of a pass rush.

"Whatever they call, I'll roll with it. I would never make an excuse," Taylor said. "I'm behind coach LeBeau all the way. . . . Unfortunately, one of my worst games of the year came at the wrong time."

It didn't help the Steelers' aging defense when Ryan Clark couldn't play due to his sickle cell condition. Casey Hampton and Brett Keisel departed the game with injuries. All three starters were over thirty years old on a unit that performed superbly all season but let the team down in the playoffs. They were sorely missed.

Denver's high altitude affected Clark's medical condition. When the Steelers played in Colorado in Tomlin's first season in 2007, Clark played and ended up losing his spleen and gall bladder because his major organs were deprived of oxygen. When the Steelers returned to Denver in 2009, Tomlin did not allow Clark to play.

"I met with him and informed him I am not going to allow him to play in the game," Tomlin said. "It was an easy decision for us. When looking at all of our data, we came to the determination he is at more risk so we are not going to play him. It's that simple."

Actually, it's not that simple. The Steelers needed Clark in the secondary against Denver. That became apparent on the Broncos' winning touchdown when after eluding Taylor to make the catch across the middle, Thomas was met with nothing but open field on his way to the end zone—Clark's territory.

Only a few minutes after his season ended, Tomlin conducted a master class on how to orchestrate a press conference following a loss:
1. Praise your opponent.
2. Deflect blame from your players.
3. Present a positive front.

Tomlin opened by presenting a positive front. "I'm proud of our guys and the way that they fought," he said. "But obviously we're not into moral victories. It wasn't enough."

"Coach, can you talk about Ike [Taylor]?" Tomlin was asked by a reporter. "It seems like he really struggled against Thomas."

Tomlin knew the question was coming. "They did a nice job," he said. "I'd be remiss if I didn't compliment Demaryius Thomas and the other guys that made the significant plays. More than anything, it's good, tough challenge catches by them and some run after. Nice job by those guys."[3]

Another reporter asked Tomlin to describe what occurred (i.e., assign blame) on Thomas's 80-yard touchdown catch. His answer was to hold his entire defense accountable, as opposed to pointing the finger at a specific player (or players). "He got inside our cornerback," said Tomlin, again not mentioning Taylor by name. "Of course, we had a number of people committed to the run. He made a nice catch, he was able to break free. The catch is less of an issue than his ability to break free

---

3 Tomlin never mentioned Taylor by name, thereby giving the reporter no ammunition to bury Taylor based on Tomlin's response. Instead, he praised Thomas. If you don't think Tomlin had a few choice words for Taylor after the game, you'd be mistaken. But if the Pittsburgh media was going to criticize Taylor for his performance—and it did—Tomlin wasn't going to help by throwing Taylor—one of his personal favorites—under the bus.

and to run after. The run after was significant not only on that play but in several instances."

Tomlin chided another reporter who wanted to know if injuries impacted the loss.

"You know better than that," Tomlin said. "We don't live in that world. We don't make excuses. . . . The guys who we put on the field were capable of doing the job. The reason we didn't do the job is because we didn't perform well enough from a coaches' standpoint, from a players' standpoint."

* * *

Despite posting back-to-back 12–4 seasons and the defense setting new standards for excellence, a playoff exit in the wild card round was still considered below expectations.

The Steelers made it clear they were not stuck in a romantic fantasy with their glorious history. Soon after their season ended with the playoff loss at Denver, the team released defensive stalwarts Farrior and Aaron Smith, along with Ward, the franchise's career leader in total receptions, receiving yards, and touchdown catches. Combined, the trio started an incredible 496 NFL games with the franchise.

Ward had two years remaining on his contract worth $4 million annually. The team leader in receptions for eleven consecutive seasons, Ward released a statement to the media. "This isn't how I wanted this chapter of my career to end," Ward said. "I did everything in my power to remain a Steeler and finish what I started here fourteen years ago."

Smith played his entire thirteen-season career in Pittsburgh. After not missing a game from the day he moved into the starting lineup in 2000 until seven games into the 2007 season, he didn't play in more than six games in 2009, 2010, or 2011, due to a torn biceps, torn triceps, and rotator cuff surgery in three different seasons. He was due to make $2.1 million in the final year of his contract.

Signed as a free agent in 2002, Farrior—who was named to two Pro Bowls and led the Steelers annually in tackles—played in all but six games in his decade with the team. He had one year remaining on the five-year extension he signed in 2008.

"Both Aaron and James have given their all during their time in Pittsburgh and we appreciate their efforts and leadership," Art Rooney II said in a statement released on Steelers.com.

Viewed through a different prism, the Steelers presented all three veterans with the opportunity to earn nearly *all* the money from their third contract, a rarity in the NFL.

"Guys don't want to leave Pittsburgh," Hampton said. "Anybody who left for the money, when you go back and talk to them, they said they wished they would have stayed. Larry Foote came back. B-Mac (Bryant McFadden) came back. The grass ain't greener all the time."

"A lot of guys go for the money, and I get that," Taylor said on the *Ike Taylor Show* on TribLIVE Radio. "The James Farriors and Casey Hamptons told me, 'Ike, if you stay, no question, you're probably going to stay for less [money]. But you'll [receive] all your money. There won't be any [head] coaching changes. You're going to have some stability.' When I signed my second deal in 2006, Omar Khan (promoted to Steelers GM in 2022) told me, 'Ike, your third deal is going to be better than your second.' I wound up finishing my third deal out, which is rare with one team."

The Steelers reasoned that retaining some of their key veterans who contributed so much to the team's success, even for one more year, was detrimental to players behind them on the depth chart. A clean sweep was not the answer. For example, Harrison was thirty-four but remained a major force at linebacker. But players such as Ziggy Hood, Antonio Brown (wide receiver), and Foote/Lawrence Timmons (linebacker) needed to have expanded roles and required more playing time.

Those changes extended beyond the playing field, when the Steelers announced that offensive coordinator Bruce Arians, fifty-nine, was retiring after five years in a one-paragraph statement.

Tomlin addressed Arians's departure with his own statement.

"I appreciate his efforts over the past five years as the team's offensive coordinator and for helping lead our offense to new heights during his time with the Steelers," Tomlin said. "I am grateful to Bruce for contributing to our success and wish him nothing but the best in his retirement."

Ten days after the announcement, the Indianapolis Colts officially hired Arians as the team's new offensive coordinator, though he would take on the role as interim head coach for the season, due to Chuck Pagano's leukemia diagnosis. He would lead the team into the playoffs, and was named Coach of the Year. All this left the Steelers with egg on their collective faces. So much for Arians's retirement.

Some people in Pittsburgh loved Arians, some people hated him. As the Steelers' offensive coordinator, he was a polarizing figure.

When Tomlin promoted Arians to offensive coordinator in 2007, Arians created a new playbook that replaced a blocking fullback with multiple tight ends. Instead of running to set up the pass, the Steelers now passed to set up the run with two tight ends and two wideouts or three wideouts and one tight end. Instead of a straight handoff, Roethlisberger would pump fake a receiver screen and give the ball to the running back on a delay. Arians turned Ben into a five- and seven-step quarterback completing long developing routes to his receivers.

Holding on to the ball contributed to Roethlisberger being sacked 40 times in 2011—Arians's final season in Pittsburgh. Critics argued that Arians allowed Ben to throw as often as he wanted. Which resulted in him holding on to the ball too long, which led to too many sacks.

Following Arians's curious departure, the Steelers introduced Todd Haley as their new offensive coordinator. Haley, who worked under Bill Parcells with the New York Giants and Dallas, emphasized a short passing game with the quarterback releasing the ball quickly—totally opposite from Arians, who built a strong relationship with Roethlisberger; the two would golf together in their down time. Ironically, Haley passed on Cowher's offer to coach Pittsburgh's wide receivers in 2004; the job which eventually went to Arians. Haley's father, Dick, had been the Steelers' personnel director from 1971 to 1990.

"All my early memories in life revolved around the Steelers," Haley, who was 19–26 as head coach of the Kansas City Chiefs from 2009 to 2011, said at his introductory press conference. "Those things stayed with me and are a part of who I am and what I am. In my mind, this is the greatest organization and greatest team in the NFL, and that comes from the heart."

Haley's personal connection to the Steelers led to media reports that Rooney made the unilateral decision to let Arians go and hire Haley against Tomlin's wishes.

A few weeks later at the NFL Owners Meetings in Palm Beach, Florida, Tomlin, in his first interview since the end of the season, said he alone made the decision regarding both the old and new offensive coordinator.

"I thought it was time for a change," Tomlin said. "More than anything, I'm not going to apologize for change. That's football. I think all of us in this industry understand that, and our intentions are that it changed for the better."

Additionally, Tomlin denied any involvement by Rooney. "I don't know where some of those perceptions come from. And I hired Todd Haley as well, which is your next question, which is another funny one to me. And don't get me wrong, of course, Art Rooney owns the football team, he can do what he wants to do, but those directives did not happen."

In a 2021 interview with Sam Farmer of the *Los Angeles Times*, Arians explained why he believed the Steelers let him go. "Got fired because I was too loyal to Ben," Arians said. "If that's a problem, you've got the problem. I get very close to my quarterbacks."

Rip Scherer Jr., Kevin Colbert's cousin who hired Tomlin at Memphis and served as Tomlin's mentor for more than a decade, suggested there was an organizational shift when Art took over the day-to-day operations from his father.

"Personally, I thought Dan let Mike do whatever he wanted to do," Scherer said. "When Art took over, my outside opinion, just watching from afar, he's more involved."

Now entering his sixth season, Tomlin said his new offensive coordinator fit the Steelers' narrative for up-and-coming skill players such as Wallace, Brown, and Emmanuel Sanders.

"We're moving into a situation where we have an opportunity to grow and develop some young talent offensively," Tomlin said.

Tomlin also noted that the AFC North, which the Steelers had dominated for years along with Baltimore, was becoming a more balanced division with the emergence of Cincinnati as a legitimate playoff contender. In past seasons, posting a winning record in the division usually meant a trip to the postseason. According to Tomlin, division wins would be harder to come by in 2012. Haley's offense would present a new look for division opponents.

"It's awesome to have an opportunity to maybe have the division of some common opponents—people who get comfortable with how you play football—get uncomfortable," Tomlin said. "That's what's going to happen to us this year. We're excited about that."

"There's a lot of talk about systems, offense and defense, and I believe you do what gives you the best chance to succeed," Haley said. "If the best chance to succeed is running 63 times a game, you run 63 times a game."

Wide receiver Mike Wallace's ability to take the top off opposing defenses made him critical to the offense's success. But Wallace, who was eligible for a $2.7 million first-round franchise tender and was absent from OTAs in want of a new contract, was absent when Haley began installing the team's new offense.

Serving as an intermediary, Taylor hinted on his radio show that Wallace was unhappy over the lack of progress in his negotiations.

"There's a lot of frustration with Mike right now," Taylor said after the New Orleans natives spent Memorial Day weekend in Las Vegas. "He wants to be here . . . but at the same time, he wants his paper [money]. Mike feels like he outperformed his last contract. But he's dealing with a monster, and that's the

Pittsburgh Steelers . . . they are not going to let you dictate to them how you feel."

Frustration was evident on both sides when, shortly after Colbert confirmed the Steelers would not continue with negotiations until Wallace signed his tender and reported to training camp, the team signed Antonio Brown to a five-year, $42.5 million contract extension. It was an incredible deal for the sixth-round draft pick who was the first player in NFL history with 1,000 receiving and 1,000 return yards in the same season. Brown's signing meant that Wallace would most likely become an unrestricted free agent after the season.

Only a few days after signing his new deal, Brown got into the first of two training camp fights with Taylor. On both occasions, the players had to be separated by teammates and, in the case of the first fight, Colbert also intervened. The players made up, and Brown even appeared on Taylor's radio show in a public display of goodwill.

While it is normal for players to scuffle during training camp, the fights for the Steelers were only a small preview of the many spats Tomlin and his team would endure from their star receiver over the next several years.

* * *

In 2012, after a promising 6–3 start, the Steelers finished 8–8 and missed the playoffs for the first time since 2009. Normally playing their best football in the second half of the season, Pittsburgh lost five of their remaining seven games. Between 2007 and 2011, the Steelers were 31–17 (.646) after Week 8 and 32–17 after the bye week (.653). It was their first non-winning campaign since Bill Cowher's final season in 2006. The Steelers placed third in the improved AFC North behind first-place Baltimore and Cincinnati, who represented the division in the playoffs.

Though teams will tell you that injuries are a part of the game and never an excuse, they were a major distraction—and disruption—to the team's 2012 campaign. Defensively, James Harrison, LaMarr Woodley, and Troy Polamalu missed a combined 12 games. Ike Taylor fractured his right ankle in the team's Week 13 win over Baltimore and would miss the final four games of the season (in which the team went 1–3), ending his consecutive game streak at 135 games. Still strong against the run and pass, the Steelers' defense became vulnerable in the scoring department, giving up 19.6 points per game compared with the previous season, in which they allowed only 14.2. Though scoring was up from 20.3 in 2011 to 21.0 in 2012, the point differential from one season to the next was the difference between going to the playoffs and going home.

Statistically, the Steelers were a superior passing and running team in Arians's final season. Under Haley, however, Roethlisberger—who suffered shoulder and rib injuries in a *Monday Night Football* overtime win against Kansas City in Week 10—recorded the lowest interception total of his career (eight). It was a testament to Haley's new system and Roethlisberger making fewer ill-advised passes into coverage.

Haley's preference for the short passing game resulted in the lowest career yards per catch averages for Wallace and Brown. Wallace, with his numbers declining (recording his first season under 1,000 yards receiving since his rookie campaign) and already unhappy because of his contract uncertainty, was as good as gone at the end of the year. Fewer big plays in the passing game placed more emphasis on the run game, which predictably sputtered when Mendenhall was slow to recover from an ACL injury he received in the final game of the previous season. Clearly not at full strength coming off such a major knee injury, Mendenhall, who also injured his Achilles in the fifth game against Tennessee, was limited to 51 carries for 182 yards and no touchdowns in his contract year, clouding his future with the team that drafted him in the first round in 2008. A one-game suspension—for "conduct detrimental to the team"—didn't help his case.

Mendenhall did not attend the Steelers' 34–24 loss to San Diego after his coaches informed him he would not be activated.

"Last Sunday he was not at the game," Tomlin told reporters. "I deemed those actions a detriment to our efforts. I stated as such when I met with him and there were going to be repercussions. . . . I require that all guys remain professional regardless of personal circumstance. He didn't meet the standard in that regard and accepted the consequences. . . . We had a good visit, he accepted it."

If anything, Tomlin set the bar so high, averaging eleven wins in his first five seasons, that anything less was unacceptable.

With media rumblings as to the team's future—especially after his recent contract extension—Tomlin had a huge job ahead of him in 2013. As an organization, the Steelers never referred to themselves as "rebuilding." After all, when Roethlisberger is your quarterback, quite naturally a team believes—rightly or wrongly—it can contend for a championship. But, like it or not, the Steelers were in the throes of a rebuild. For the first time in Pittsburgh, as one after another of the players who helped the team win Super Bowls XL and XLIII departed, Tomlin was coaching with a target on his back.

Defense, which had always been the backbone of the Steelers, was fast becoming a weakness. Two of the team's standout defensive starters from the good ol' days, James Harrison and Casey Hampton, would not be on the roster entering the 2013 season. After a dozen years in black and yellow, the Steelers decided to part ways with the thirty-five-year-old Hampton, a beloved locker room presence whose pregame ritual featured his teammates trying to tackle him during warmups. Signing Steve McClendon to a three-year contract, the free agent Hampton was not offered a deal to return for a thirteenth season.

Harrison, who would be thirty-six at the start of the season, was a different story. The Steelers wanted to keep the 2008 NFL Defensive Player of the Year who was named to five consecutive Pro Bowls. However, they couldn't agree on the size of the pay cut Harrison was willing to accept. "I appreciate everything [Harrison] has done in my six years as head coach and wish him nothing but the best in the future," Tomlin said. Rubbing salt in the wound, Harrison, the Steelers' best pass rusher along with Woodley, signed with division rival Cincinnati.

Losing Wallace to free agency (signing a six-year, $50 million deal with the Miami Dolphins) was no surprise. The Steelers began preparations for Wallace's departure during his final season when the coaching staff identified him and Sanders as co-starters in November. The refurbished wide receiver room had anointed itself "The Young Money Crew" two years earlier. With Wallace gone and Ward retired, the remaining original members were Antonio "Cash Money" Brown and Emmanuel "Easy Money" Sanders.

The running back room also underwent a much-needed face-lift when the Steelers—who finished a lowly 26th in rushing—selected Michigan State's Le'Veon Bell with their second-round draft pick. A three-year starter, Bell started 19 consecutive games for the Spartans and led the Big Ten in rushing with just under 1,800 yards in his junior season, adding 32 catches. Tomlin, who had dinner with Bell at Michigan State's Pro Day, planned to insert the rookie as the team's feature back, especially after the free agent Mendenhall signed with Arizona prior to the draft.

"It puts us at a place where we can have a chance to run the ball and throw the ball out of the backfield successfully," Haley said.

* * *

In 2013, Tomlin's seventh season at the helm, Ben Roethlisberger played all 16 games for the first time in five years, throwing for 4,261 yards, 28 touchdowns, and 14 interceptions. His 64.1 completion percentage was his best to date. And yet Roethlisberger's heroics didn't prevent the Steelers from finishing 8–8. It was the first time the Steelers missed the postseason in back-to-back years in more than a decade, going back to the 1999 and 2000 seasons. To add insult to injury, the team's 0–4 start was the worst since 1968, when rookie coach Bill Austin led the team to a 1–2–1 record to begin the season (and 5–8–1 record overall).

The list of negatives went on and on, overshadowing Brown's breakout campaign of 110 receptions for 1,499 yards and eight touchdowns. After a foot sprain during a preseason game against the Redskins forced Bell to miss the first three games of the season, he still led the team in rushing with 244 carries for 800 yards and eight touchdowns, along with 45 catches for 399 yards. The Steelers were on their way to forming their own set of Triplets with Roethlisberger, Bell, and Brown.

But woe, unto the defense.

After too many years of carrying the team on its back, the defense finally broke down in a big way. Veteran departures plus underperforming new faces equaled embarrassing performances. After giving up 40 points to the Bears in Week 3, a 55–31 loss in Week 9 against the Patriots put the Steelers behind the eight-ball at 2–6. New England's total points and total yards (610) were the most against a Steelers defense in franchise history. Brady threw for 432 yards and four touchdowns. "As a defense, we let the team down," Ryan Clark said.

Still, the Steelers, who entered the game ranked 31st in pass defense, gave themselves a chance, rallying from 14–0 and 24–10 deficits to make it 24–24 with 7:10 remaining in the third quarter.

That was it for the good news. Now for the bad news: New England scored 31 unanswered points on its final five possessions.[4]

"I've never been a part of anything like that in my life," Polamalu said.

Echoing Polamalu's sentiment, Tomlin never wanted to be a part of anything like that ever again.

"I am angry, disappointed," Tomlin said. "Those people who are lacking in effort won't be playing. We will look at every aspect of what we're doing and who we're doing it with. We can't have performances like that."

---

4 In their final five possessions, Big Ben went 12-for-25 for 171 yards, with one touchdown and one interception, along with two sacks. Bell had two rushing attempts for a total of 13 yards.

To their credit, the Steelers heeded Tomlin's words, winning three straight and six of their final eight games after the New England loss to finish 8–8 for the second consecutive season.

Among those two setbacks was a memorable 22–20 loss at Baltimore on Thanksgiving night, a game in which Tomlin's unexpected and out-of-character actions during a critical moment overshadowed the outcome.

Following the Steelers' first score of the game that made it 13–7 against the defending Super Bowl champions, Baltimore's Jacoby Jones fielded the kickoff at the goal line and broke clear along the Pittsburgh sideline toward an apparent touchdown. But a funny thing happened on the way to the end zone when Jones suddenly had to swerve to avoid Tomlin, who stood in the restricted area between the sideline and the playing field with his back to the action and his right foot inexplicably blocking Jones's path. Tomlin moved out of the way just in time to avoid a collision, but the adjustment in Jones's stride allowed Cortez Allen to drag him down 27 yards shy of a touchdown. Baltimore settled for a field goal.

Tomlin's actions didn't affect the result . . . but what if it had? Surely that possibility factored into the league's decision, after reviewing the play, to fine Tomlin $100,000 for stepping onto the field. It was the second-largest fine for a head coach in NFL history, topped only by the $500,000 administered to Belichick for his role in "Spygate." The league later admitted that Tomlin should have been penalized 15 yards for unsportsmanlike conduct.

"I thought I'd break from my normal routine and do what's appropriate under the circumstances," Tomlin said during his weekly press conference five days after the game. "My description of my actions on that play are a lot of things—embarrassing, inexcusable, illegal, a blunder . . . I take full responsibility for my actions . . . I acknowledge that my actions unfortunately became part of the play. I also embrace that as head coaches, we're held to the highest standards of conduct, and I realize that blunder fell woefully short of that expectation . . . I also understand that with my position comes the charge of preserving and protecting the integrity of the game of football. My biggest error was not realizing that play jeopardized the integrity of the game from a perception standpoint."

In speaking on the *Pivot* podcast, Tomlin went into a bit more detail on his error, while expressing his love for the game and how he truly felt about potentially impacting the result.

> People that know me and know the level of respect that I have for the game and the men that play it, then I don't feel a need to explain it to them. And those that don't know me, I just assume they think the worst to me. I don't care.
>
> [There] was one Jumbotron in that stadium. And I like to see the contour of the coverage unit and the kick return unit come together. And so, I'm routine. . . . I stand on the line. I watch the ball get kicked. I make sure that we're not offsides. And then I watch the Jumbotron. And so in that instance we were kicking left to right, and the Jumbotron was behind our kick unit.
>
> And so we kicked the ball off, and I'm looking up at the contour of the deal. And somebody falls down. And so when somebody fell down, I almost like leaned in on the Jumbotron. And then I saw a double team block, and I said,

"Oh, no!" And so I'm walking at the Jumbotron like I'm watching a horror movie. Like, "Oh, no. Oh, that's bad."

What people don't talk about is the stuff that's on the Jumbotron is backwards. It's flipped. And so I'm watching the Jumbotron, and on the Jumbotron it looks like he's running up the right sideline. But actually he's coming up our sideline. And so I'm processing it. . . . Once the ball got kicked, I'm locked in on the Jumbotron. I'm watching the structure of it break down, and it has got my attention. . . . And in my mind I'm thinking he's going up their sideline because the Jumbotron picture is backwards. I didn't realize I was in danger until I saw myself on the Jumbotron. I dodged Jacoby because I saw myself—I never saw him. I was like, "OH!" and he went by me. I saw myself as he was running down the sideline, I came into the Jumbotron . . . and I paid a hundred thousand dollars for that mistake.

Considering how their season began with four straight losses, the Steelers still managed to put themselves in playoff contention, competing with Baltimore, Miami, and San Diego for the final playoff spot. But after San Diego defeated Kansas City in overtime of Week 17, it secured their postseason berth and ended Pittsburgh's chances.

"There are no woulda couldas," Taylor said in a perfect wrap to an imperfect season. "It's the humblest sport. You have your ups and downs. This year, for the most part, we've just been consistent in being inconsistent. When you play in the NFL, you have to be consistent."

14

REBOUNDING

(2014–16)

"The standard is the standard."

I T stands to reason that in a league where the rules now favored the offense, the Steelers underwent a philosophical change, transitioning from a team with a legendary defense to one shaped by its ability to manufacture points. Tomlin was now taking a more active role in the offense. The fact that he replaced Bruce Arians with Todd Haley as offensive coordinator was a glaring example that Tomlin wanted to move the offense in a different direction.

Hence, the increased emphasis on the offensive side of the ball. All but conceding the obvious decline on the defensive side of the ball, Tomlin and Company should have adopted the slogan: "If we can't stop you, we'll outscore you." In 2014, the 11–5 Steelers, following back-to-back .500 seasons, established a franchise record for points per game, averaging 27.3. This despite the defense conceding 23.0 points per game a year after giving up 23.1. Not since 1988, during a 5–11 campaign when opponents averaged 26.3 points, had the Steelers yielded such a high scoring average.

Lawrence Timmons, Ike Taylor, and Troy Polamalu entered the season as the only three starters left from the 2012 defense that ranked No. 1 in the NFL in fewest yards allowed. Timmons became the team's oldest linebacker at age twenty-seven, following the release of LaMarr Woodley, the fastest Steelers defender in history to reach 50 sacks (he signed with Oakland following his release); and Larry Foote, who became a starter in Arizona following his release. James Harrison, who was released by the Steelers the year before, was added late in the season following his release by Cincinnati to bolster an anemic pass rush.

Starting all 16 games in consecutive seasons for the first time in his career, Ben Roethlisberger, no longer pushing back against Haley's insistence that he get rid of the football quicker, amassed a career-high 4,952 passing yards and equaled a career high with 32 touchdown passes. His 67.1 completion percentage was also a personal best. Roethlisberger's favorite target was Antonio Brown, who caught a franchise-record 129 passes, with 1,500 yards and eight touchdowns. Rookie Martavis Bryant was a surprising revelation, averaging 21.1 yards per reception with nearly a third of his catches resulting in touchdowns (eight) despite not dressing for the first six games. Bryant picked up some of the slack left by Emmanuel Sanders, who had signed with Denver as a free agent.

Le'Veon Bell was outrageously productive, averaging 4.7 yards per carry and leading the AFC with 1,361 yards rushing. He also set a franchise record for Steelers running backs, with 83 receptions. Unfortunately, Bell injured his knee against Cincinnati in the final game of the regular season and did not play in the team's playoff loss to Baltimore.

Finishing atop the AFC North after a five-game winning streak to end the season, the Steelers opened the postseason against the Ravens, their division rival who they split the season series against. With Bell missing from the lineup, the Steelers couldn't generate a balanced attack, accumulating only 68 yards rushing in a 30–17 home playoff loss. Baltimore knew this, and pressured Roethlisberger the entire game, sacking him five times to go along with two interceptions. The Ravens' strategy was to force the Steelers to pass more than they wanted (Roethlisberger completed 31 of 45 passes for 334 yards and three touchdowns). A balanced offense had also been a key to Pittsburgh's season, as the team was 6–0 when Ben threw 35 times or less, but 5–6 when forced to throw 36 times or more.

The Steelers concluded their season ranked first in the NFL in passing offense and second in total offense. They were the first team in league history with a 4,500-yard passer, a 1,500-yard receiver, and a 1,300-yard rusher in the same season. Roethlisberger, Brown, Bell and Pouncey were all named to the Pro Bowl. Statistically, they were great. But something was amiss from the team that advanced to the Super Bowl four years earlier. But as the saying goes, "Defense wins championships," and this team just didn't have that. Now heading into his ninth season, it was Tomlin's job to search for answers and fill in the blanks.

"It's very painful," Tomlin said at his end-of-the-year press conference. "When the journey comes to an end, it should be elation or bitter disappointment, and it is that. We don't run away from that. I embrace that."

* * *

Before the season even started, Bell and fellow running back LeGarrette Blount were arrested on their way to the airport for a preseason game after police said they found marijuana in Bell's car during a traffic stop. Bell was suspended by the league for the first two games the following season. Between repeated injuries and too many off-the-field issues, Bell was sometimes more trouble than he was worth for Tomlin, a problem solver who valued his running back's elite-level talent but certainly could do without all the extracurricular distractions.

Bell would become troublesome for Tomlin. A steal in the second round, Bell's skillset was first rate—when he was healthy. Between injuries, off-the-field issues, and, ultimately, an unresolved contract dispute, Tomlin loved Bell's talent but disliked the constant baggage that came along with him. If need be, Tomlin could do without Blount who arrived in Pittsburgh bearing a warning label from his college days and was suspended at Oregon for punching an opposing player in the jaw. Not so with Bell, a legitimate franchise running back, who was a risk Tomlin was willing to take.

Turning their attention to reconfiguring the defense through the draft, GM Kevin Colbet and Tomlin settled on speedy Ohio State linebacker Ryan Shazier with the 15th overall pick. Shazier was credited with 22.5 tackles for losses and six sacks in his final college season.

"Bigger than positional needs, what we needed was a defensive playmaker," Tomlin told reporters following Shazier's selection. "When you start talking about guys at the linebacker position running sub-4.5, that's rare air."

Seeking a young, defensive playmaker, the Steelers bypassed drafting a defensive back in the first round despite a growing need at the position with Taylor in his 12th season. Instead, the Steelers settled on Shazier, even though they drafted another linebacker, Jarvis Jones, with their first-round pick the previous year. Shazier had the speed and coverage skills of a defensive back, and he could also rush the passer with the ability to make plays behind the line of scrimmage.

"As offenses continue to spread out, you need speed; you need speed at linebacker, you need speed at secondary, you need speed everywhere," Colbert said.

The Tomlin-Colbert dynamic worked so well because Tomlin, as the visible face of the organization—compared with Colbert's behind-the-scenes presence—was secure enough in his position on the team to allow Colbert to do his job and not feel threatened by it.

Back in 2000, a power struggle between Bill Cowher and then-GM Tom Donohoe resulted in the latter—who played a role in hiring Cowher and turned down an offer from Seattle to remain in Pittsburgh for less money—resigning under pressure after the Steelers were forced to choose between the two. "In some ways, you could say we looked at it that way," Art Rooney II said. "Both men said, 'If I'm the problem, I'll resign.'

They both felt it was a problem, and the only solution was for one of them to leave, and in the end we felt that way, too."

Tomlin's willingness to work in lockstep with Colbert may have factored into the Steelers' decision to hire him. "[Colbert] was established when I got here," Tomlin said on the *Bleav in Steelers* podcast with Taylor shortly after the 2022 draft. "His willingness to be open about my presence and my views was the catalyst or foundation for our relationship."

Their relationship wasn't about the coach or GM talking to the public. They figured out a formula that worked not only for them, but one that also benefited the entire organization. Tomlin talked about personnel decisions to the media during the season and didn't talk as much in the offseason. Colbert was just the opposite: he talked more during the offseason, letting Tomlin speak for the team during the season.

"Mike used to tell me all the time how Kevin Colbert was able to distinguish the values between different positions," Ed Tomlin said. "Is this guy a better tight end than this guy is a tackle? It's been a learning experience for him in that regard. I'm sure Kevin had a lot do with that from a talent evaluation standpoint."

To assist linebackers coach Keith Butler, Tomlin brought back a familiar face: Joey Porter. His official title was defensive assistant but, make no mistake about it, Tomlin didn't hire Porter—a four-time All-Pro who registered 60 sacks in his eight seasons with the Steelers—to coach defensive backs.

In his own words, Tomlin's decision to bring Porter back into the fold after he departed as a free agent in the coach's first year in Pittsburgh, had a personal feel to it. Porter signed a one-day contract after announcing his retirement in 2012 so he could officially retire as a Steeler.

Porter's hire made sense. The Steelers invested first-round money in Jones, who was struggling to grasp the defense. In a surprising admission, Butler revealed that teammates had to tell Jones, who recorded only one sack as a rookie, where to line up. Porter brought an attack-mode ferociousness to the outside linebacker position, which the team was hopeful he could impart to Jones.

"We are excited about having Joey back with the Steelers family," Tomlin said upon Porter's hiring. "Joey spent a number of years with Pittsburgh as a player, and now he's back to assist the coaching staff."

When Porter reached out to Tomlin after serving as a volunteer assistant at his alma mater, Colorado State, he didn't know what to expect.

"I talked to Mike at the Senior Bowl. He was like, 'I'm busy handling some stuff. I'll get back to you,'" Porter said. "There were a lot of people down there looking for jobs. When they see a guy without a job, they kind of avoid you. I remember leaving there saying it was a wasted trip.

"Mike called me back a couple weeks later. They flew me out. He hired me right there on the spot.

"I wasn't in a space where I was crossing paths with him," Porter continued. "When he first got the Steelers job, he told me they were going in a different direction. And it wasn't in a bad way. I played against him when I was with the Dolphins and in Arizona, but we weren't having conversations like that. To think that somebody's about to hire you when you don't have a relationship with them, to bring you back in the building that you once were a part of, I was like, 'I would love it, but I don't know how it's gonna go.' When I say he brought me in, it was with open arms."

Tomlin opened some eyes with the addition of Mike Munchak, his fourth offensive line coach in eight seasons and the third former head coach on Tomlin's staff, joining Dick LeBeau, Haley and himself. A Hall of Fame offensive lineman, Munchak was 22–26 as head coach of the Tennessee Titans. Refusing to comply with management's request to fire his offensive and defensive coordinators following a 7–9 campaign in 2013, Munchack was let go and replaced by Whisenhunt, who had been fired in 2012 after six seasons in Arizona. Highly sought after on the free agent market, Munchak interviewed for head coaching vacancies in Cleveland and Detroit. When those opportunities failed to materialize, Munchak resurfaced in Pittsburgh.

Thanks to Bell, whose unorthodox, herky-jerky running style was becoming the talk of the NFL, Tomlin became eager to install Munchak's specialty: zone blocking. Instead of offensive linemen blocking specific defenders vertically and straight ahead, zone blocking required them to caravan toward the sideline and push back whatever defenders are in the way. The Steelers attempted to convert to zone blocking under Jack Bicknell Jr. the previous year, but scrapped the idea when Pouncey injured his knee eight snaps into the season opener. Now with a healthy Pouncey and every offensive line starter returning, Munchak was a welcome addition.

Following a home loss against Tampa Bay that left the Steelers with a 2–2 record—two weeks after a loss at Baltimore—Tomlin addressed what had become a sore subject for him as a black head coach in the NFL: his perception as a "players' coach."

Scott Brown, my former colleague at the *Trib* now covering the Steelers for ESPN, wrote an insightful article about Tomlin responding to being called a "players coach" during a pregame interview on FOX Sports prior to the Tampa Bay loss.

During the interview, Tomlin said longtime defensive coordinator Dick LeBeau isn't referred to as a players' coach because he is "an old white guy."

At his weekly news conference two days later, Tomlin told reporters, "Sometimes when they couple 'players' coach' with questions about how I wear my hair or what I choose to wear on the sidelines or what type of music I listen to, then it gets kind of old and falls into that category for me. I'd like to think the manner in which I do my job, whether it's positive or negative, has very little to do with my haircut or the clothes that I wear or the type of music I listen to, and that's when I get annoyed with that line of questioning."

* * *

It was another busy offseason for Tomlin, who didn't have to look far for a new defensive coordinator with the departure of LeBeau. Tomlin finally got around to rewarding Butler, his coaching buddy from Memphis and Arkansas State who remained loyal to the Steelers despite being considered for other defensive coordinator vacancies. The Steelers took care of Butler prior to his promotion, enticing him to stay with three-year extensions instead of the usual two-year deals offered to assistant coaches.

Pittsburgh led the NFL in total defense in five of LeBeau's thirteen seasons and finished in the top 10 five times. But LeBeau's defense was losing traction, falling to 18th in total defense *and* scoring defense in 2014. The Steelers had become uncharacteristically vulnerable on the back end, giving up 15 plays of 40 yards or longer.

Don't call his departure a retirement, LeBeau, seventy-seven, cautioned. "I'm resigning this position, not retiring," LeBeau told the *Urbana Daily Citizen* in Ohio.

Tomlin had now replaced his original offensive and defensive coordinators. If they weren't before, the Steelers had become a team made wholly in his image. "We want to thank Dick for his many years of service with the team and all that he has done for this organization," Tomlin said in a statement released by the Steelers shortly after LeBeau's announcement. "His coaching helped lead us to many successful seasons and championships."

Reading between the lines, LeBeau's departure had a similar feel to how Arians left the team; the Steelers announced it as a "retirement" . . . until Arians joined the Indianapolis Colts as their offensive coordinator. LeBeau said he still had plenty of coaching left in him, and he proved it a few weeks later when the Tennessee Titans made him their assistant head coach of the defense.

The Steelers also said goodbye to three more LeBeau disciples: Polamalu, Taylor, and Brett Keisel. Loyalty to LeBeau had nothing to do with their departures; they simply grew old together. Polamalu and Taylor—who were drafted the same year and retired within a few days of one another—were both thirty-four; Keisel was thirty-six. The trio started a total of 396 games in the black and yellow.

In actuality, the secret to the Steelers' defensive success wasn't really a secret at all. The team drafted and shopped the free-agent market intelligently and cheaply—only Polamalu, Casey Hampton, and Timmons were first-round picks among the core group from 2007 to 2014 under Tomlin. Those players, immersed in LeBeau's system, performed at a high level until they couldn't.

"It was playing with the same guys for a long period of time, guys getting accustomed to each other," Hampton said. "I played with three D-linemen at least ten years each. I played with my middle linebacker ten, eleven years. Just over time, man, doing the same things over and over. It was easy for us."

Tomlin could never replace his blast-from-the-past defense. Free agency didn't allow teams—or *entire* defensive units—to stay together for years at a time. What he could do, however, was build the defense back to respectability with regards to rule changes now favoring the offense.

"In this day of free agency, it's rare to play for one team," Taylor said in announcing his retirement after twelve seasons on the *Ike Taylor Show* on TribLIVE Radio. "For me to have this opportunity says a lot about how they felt about me, what I gave back to the organization."

In his sendoff to the Hall of Fame safety, Tomlin praised Polmalu's vast contributions to the Steelers.

"Troy is a shining example of a football man in the way he loved the game, the way he respected the game and the way he played the game."

Polamalu did not like the way he found out he was being released, according to Mike Freeman of *Bleacher Report*. Freeman reported Polamalu was upset that Tomlin did not deliver the message in person. As Freeman wrote in his column:

> Early in 2015, Polamalu received a voicemail from Tomlin. The 12-year veteran was being cut, went the

message, according to a person familiar with the call. Tomlin apologized and then hung up.

Polamalu was angry Tomlin didn't deliver the news in person. Rather than trying to catch on somewhere else after spending his career in Pittsburgh, Polamalu retired that April . . . [Polamalu] has told Steelers players and others he will never return to the team until Tomlin is gone.

* * *

Everything considered, Tomlin did a masterful coaching job in 2015. How the Steelers qualified for the playoffs with a 10–6 record can only be described as a miracle.

After a tough year for the defense, the Steelers entered a new season without three defensive starters from their glory years. They had also parted ways with their longtime defensive coordinator.

With the hopes of coming in with a clean slate and working to build a new persona, the train began to come off the tracks early. Star center Maurkice Pouncey, who the team had given a five-year, $44.12 million contract extension the season before (making him the highest-paid center in the NFL)—suffered a broken fibula during a preseason game against the Packers and would miss the entire year. The suspension of Bell from the previous year would also go into effect, resulting in him missing the first two games of the season. Upon returning to the lineup, Bell played five games and was leading the league in rushing with 511 yards. Then in the team's eighth game of the season against the Bengals, he tore his MCL and was lost for the season.

Second-year receiver Martavis Bryant was suspended for the first four games for also violating the league's substance abuse policy. Not one to be left out, Roethlisberger missed four games with a right shoulder injury only to miss more action later in the year with a foot sprain, as well as left tackle Kelvin Beachum, who suffered a season-ending ACL tear in October.

At 4–4, the Steelers were faced with a win-or-else ultimatum: go 6–2 the rest of the way, or go home.

The following week in a must-win home game against Oakland, DeAngelo Williams, who replaced Bell in the lineup, carried 27 times for 170 yards and two touchdowns against the league's No. 2 rush defense in the Steelers' 38–35 victory. "He's delivered for us time and time again," Tomlin said in describing Williams's performance to reporters.

Tomlin's resourcefulness was evident as his backup running back operated behind a patchwork offensive line featuring center Cody Wallace, who prior to stepping in for Pro Bowler Pouncey in preseason had started a total of six games in six years; and tackle Alejandro Villanueva, who had no NFL snaps prior to replacing Beachum.

To top it off, Roethlisberger, who had just returned to the lineup the previous week, suffered a foot injury in the fourth quarter and was replaced by Landry Jones who, with less than two minutes remaining, drove the Steelers from their 20 to set up Chris Boswell's game-winning field goal with two seconds on the clock.

"You can waste a lot of time focusing on the guys who aren't available to you," Tomlin told reporters after the game. "You're just focused on the guys who are and how we can put together the right mix to be successful, how we can utilize their skills, how we can work to minimize their weaknesses individually and collectively.

"Injuries are as much a part of the game as blocking and tackling," continued Tomlin. "It's unfortunate, we don't like it, but we embrace the challenge that comes with it."

The week after the Oakland game, the Steelers had 13 players on their injury list. The only week when the Steelers had fewer than five players on their injury list in 2015 was the opening week of the season. With Roethlisberger back in the lineup, Pittsburgh defeated Cleveland, 30–9, to improve to 6–4.

Guard Ramon Foster said in the locker room after the Oakland win that it would be easy for the players to feel sorry for themselves with so many injuries. "I joke around with it," said Foster. "I say, 'I don't know who (ticked) off the football gods, but they're definitely letting us have it this year. You can lose one or two guys, but this has been off the charts. We could write a book about it."

And, yet, in spite of everything, Foster told reporters that the Steelers, who were basically following the lead of their head coach, still believed they were good enough to advance to Super Bowl LX—even if no one outside their locker room did.

"We don't want to sit at home in January," said Foster. "We still have a lot of guys who are capable of doing it. We have the talent to still make a push and be in [Santa Clara]."

Throughout the season, Tomlin improvised but never compromised the Steelers' chances of winning.

Take for instance when Tomlin signed thirty-five-year-old Michael Vick, thought to be past his prime as an insurance quarterback in late August when longtime backup Bruce

Gradkowski was lost for the season with a hand injury. Vick went 2–1 with Pittsburgh in what turned out to be the final starts of his NFL career.

In his first start for the injured Roethlisberger against Baltimore, Vick performed poorly in a 23–20 overtime loss. Tomlin stuck with Vick the following week at San Diego, and the 13-year veteran delivered, rallying the Steelers from second-half deficits of 17–10 and 20–17. Vick's 72-yard touchdown pass to Markus Wheaton made it 17–17 with 7:42 to play. After San Diego reclaimed the lead at 20–17, the Steelers took over at their 20 with 2:38 left. Vick completed two passes to Darrius Heyward-Bey for 24 yards. Still mobile despite his advanced age, Vick scrambled for 24 yards to the San Diego 17. Vick then passed to tight end Heath Miller for 16 yards to the 1.

With five seconds remaining, not only did Tomlin eschew a quarterback sneak or traditional running play, he called for Bell to carry the ball out of the non-traditional Wildcat formation. Bell's touchdown gave the Steelers a 24–20 victory.

Taking a scene straight out of *The Godfather*, Tomlin told reporters, "It was time to go to the mattresses."

Explained Tomlin, "We got to play to win, I'm not going to overanalyze it."

Even so, the *Post-Gazette* was quick to note their feelings on the decision, even though it worked out for the Steelers. As Ed Bouchette wrote, "The call to go to Bell, rather than, say a quick quarterback sneak, would have raised the hackles of those who believe Tomlin has poor clock management if he did not score. But he did, and that was all anyone cared about afterward."

Tomlin inserted Jones for Vick in the next game against Arizona. Jones completed 8 of 12 passes for 168 yards and two touchdowns, including an 88-yarder to Bryant. As for his decision to go back and forth with Jones and Vick, who combined to go 2–2 in Roethlisberger's absence, Tomlin said he based his decisions the same way for every player, regardless of position. "We did what was required to win," said Tomlin. "Guys just didn't let go of the rope."

Nor did Tomlin, who, from the very start, accepted every challenge head-on. When informed by Roethlisberger soon after accepting the job that some of his players didn't want him, he won them over anyway.

The relationship between Tomlin and Roethlisberger was one built on mutual respect and was mostly rooted in a strong desire by both men to win football games. Tomlin left it up to Arians and Roethlisberger to golf together; that wasn't his thing. Tomlin was a football lifer who believed Ben gave him the best opportunity to *win*. That was their common bond.

"Ben and I are obviously very different people, but we shared a couple things that were critical in terms of us being able to have a great working relationship for an extended period of time," Tomlin told the *Bleav in Steelers* podcast with Taylor a few months after Roethlisberger's retirement.

"Ben is a sick competitor . . . Ben's gonna kill you at everything—at ping pong, bowling, it does not matter.

"I'm cut in a very similar way," continued Tomlin, "and I always appreciated that about him, and that's something that was unchanged from the time he was twenty-three to the time he was thirty-nine. . . . [T]hat component of it, that competitive spirit, is a tie that binds, and allowed us to deal with the things that come up when you have the role that I have and the role that he had."

In 2012, Roethlisberger was critical of the play-calling in a 27–24 overtime loss at Dallas which was a direct reflection on Tomlin and his first-year coordinator Haley, who he entrusted to run the offense in the first year after Arians, a Roethlisberger favorite. Specifically, Ben didn't think Haley called enough plays to get Miller the ball in the second half.

"I don't think we called the right plays to get [Miller] the ball," Roethlisberger told reporters after the game. Roethlisberger also said the lack of use of the no-huddle was "disappointing."

At his weekly news conference two days later, Tomlin told reporters he met with Roethlisberger about Haley's play-calling the day after the game. "I'm sure if anything was read into his comments, it was just that," said Tomlin, who routinely met with Rothlisberger on Monday to review video of the game. "I met with Ben yesterday, and he's ready to move forward. . . . It's just about finding the necessary combination to win." On this occasion, Roethlisberger met with Haley and Art Rooney II during the video review session.

The day after Tomlin's news conference, Roethlisberger spoke with reporters. "I came in and apologized to Todd and I apologized to Mike and Mr. Rooney," said Roethlisberger. "I'm just apologizing for the storm that I created and caused."

Tomlin entered into his relationship with Roethlisberger with both eyes wide open.

"I'm gonna have bumps in the road along with the way," Tomlin said in the *Bleav in Steelers* podcast. "That's just life. But I never questioned his will; I never questioned his intentions being successful and having a desire to win and doing whatever's required for us to be in play that way. And that's what made working with him so fun for so long."

From his first meeting with Roethlisberger, and from there attempting to get the best out of guard Alan Faneca who no longer wanted to play for the Steelers in what would be his final year in Pittsburgh, Tomlin, given no choice, quickly became an expert at putting out fires.

Faneca told reporters at the Pro Bowl after Tomlin was hired that he was disappointed Grimm or Whisenhunt didn't get the job. Faneca, who had one year remaining on his contract, announced at minicamp it would be his last year as a Steeler. Tomlin didn't take it personally because he understood Faneca wanted a new deal. "Sure, it's an issue," Tomlin told reporters at his first Steelers minicamp. "More than anything else, it's got to be a lesson for us as a football team that no season is without its ups and downs. Adversity is part of it, distractions are part of it, and this is an opportunity to grow in that area and deal with some things and go out and play football."

"There was skepticism," Farrior told reporters three years after Tomlin took over the Steelers. "He had never been a head coach. It's always a process when you get a new coach, but I don't think it took a long time for him to establish himself and develop a good relationship with the players."

The ups and downs that Tomlin faced in his first year in 2007 or his ninth season in 2015 were no different than any other year for the head coach who, after becoming the youngest to win a Super Bowl and failing to make the playoffs the following year, led his team to back-to-back 12–4 records. And who then posted back-to-back 8–8 records and missed the playoffs two years in a row for the first time since the turn of the decade, only to win the AFC North the following season.

Now this.

After winning the next two games before going into the bye and then dropping their Week 12 matchup in Seattle to bring their record to 6–5, the Steelers rallied to win four of their next five and finish 10–6, good enough for second in the AFC North behind the Bengals.

So not only did Tomlin steer another team into the postseason for the sixth time in nine seasons, the Steelers faced the same Cincy team that captured the AFC North title. Entering the game as favorites, the Bengals, who had not won a playoff game since 1990, were looking to break the streak against their division rivals.

Yet heading into the fourth quarter, you would have thought the opposite. With three field goals by the rookie Chris Boswell and a touchdown pass from Ben to Bryant, the Steelers were up 15–0 (after missing on their two-point conversion).

Undaunted, Cincinnati scored 16 straight points, taking a 16–15 lead (following an A. J. McCarron touchdown pass to A. J. Green) with 1:50 to go.

One reason for the turnaround may have been the loss of Roethlisberger, who left the game with a shoulder injury following a big sack from Steelers' nemesis Vontaze Burfict at the end of the third quarter (and whose sideline tackle ten weeks earlier knocked Bell out for the season). After just two completions on his first two drives, and with less than two minutes remaining, Jones was intercepted on his first pass of the drive, setting up the Bengals at the Steelers 26. Miraculously, on the very next play, Shazier stripped the ball from running back Jeremy Hill. The Steelers had the ball back with all three timeouts remaining, but with the ball at the 9 yard line had a lot of work ahead of them.

With their backs against the wall, Tomlin went with his gut instinct, reasoning that a banged-up Roethlisberger who could barely throw the ball was a better option than a second-string Jones.

And it looked at the start like he might have been right, as the offense moved the ball to their own 34 yard line. With 28 seconds remaining, the Steelers faced a fourth-and-3. As he had done so many times, Ben was able to hit Brown for a 12-yard gain and the first down. It was his sixth reception of the game, giving him 107 yards on the day.

With no timeouts left, 22 seconds on the clock, and on the Cincinnati 47, the Steelers needed to either get into the end zone or get a few more yards for a potential game-winning field goal.

On the next play, going back to his go-to guy, Ben zipped a pass to Brown . . . which was too high and out of reach. But with an illegal hit by Burfict, who could have avoided contact with Brown on the incomplete pass but instead delivered a blow to Brown's head, resulting in a concussion—along with *another* personal foul on cornerback by Adam "Pacman" Jones for making contact with an official, the Steelers now had the ball on the Cincy 15 with 18 seconds to go. Boswell, who had already hit three field goals on the day, nailed his fourth—this time a 35-yarder—to give Pittsburgh an 18–16 lead with just 14 seconds on the clock.

"It was dire," Tomlin said. "Ben and I have been together nine years. We looked at each other and kind of said, 'Now or never.'"

Minus Brown, Bell, Pouncey, Beachum, and DeAngelo Williams, who led the team in rushing in Bell's absence—the Steelers headed to Denver for a divisional round match-up. Yet with all the injuries, their defense had kept the Broncos out of the end zone and clung to a 13–12 lead heading into the fourth quarter. To be in position to defeat Denver on the road one game from playing for the AFC championship was a testament to Tomlin's resourcefulness and coaching acumen. For instance, Bryant, the former fourth-round pick playing in Brown's absence, was brilliant with nine catches for 154 yards, primarily against All-Pro corner Aqib Talib.

With the ball on Denver's side of the field and the Steelers moving into field goal position, Roethlisberger handed the ball to Fitzgerald Toussiant, who was starting for Williams (who was starting for Bell). Toussiant, who entered the game with 42 yards rushing in five games with the Steelers and scored his first career touchdown in the first half, fumbled when cornerback Bradley Roby punched the ball loose. Linebacker DeMarcus Ware recovered at the Denver 35.

Up to that point, the Steelers, with the thirty-seven-year-old Harrison playing five years younger, had held quarterback Peyton Manning's offense in check. However, Manning capped a 65-yard march, handing off to C. J. Anderson for a 1-yard scoring run. An ensuing two-point conversion pass gave Denver a 20–13 lead with three minutes left.

Hoping for another playoff miracle, the Steelers came out of the two-minute warning in a fourth-and-5 hole. Instead of another big play, Ware came up big again for the Broncos, sacking Ben for a turnover on downs. After a field goal from Brandon McManus—his fifth of the game—put Denver up by 10, the Steelers were able to get Boswell in range for a field goal, with the hopes of getting the ball back on an onside kick. Anderson instead recovered the kick, and a kneel down from Manning sealed a 23–16 Denver victory.

Denver defeated New England in the conference title game and routed Carolina 24–10 in Super Bowl 50.

"I've been doing this [for] nine years," said Tomlin, who was moved to tears in front of his players after the playoff loss. "There's only one year where the conversation ended in the manner in which you want it to end."

* * *

After missing the playoffs two years in a row, the Steelers made back-to-back postseason appearances in 2014 and 2015. Losing by only a touchdown to Denver without several key starters energized the team entering Tomlin's 10th year in Pittsburgh.

Among the keys to a successful season was Bell's availability. Due to injuries and suspensions, Bell missed 13 of 48 potential starts—plus all three playoff games in his first three seasons. He opened 2016 on a sour note when he missed the first four games for violating the league's substance-abuse policy for the second time.

Despite Bell's absence, the Steelers won four of their first five games to start the season. It was their best record to open the season since a 5–1 start in 2010, when they last appeared in the AFC Championship Game.

A midseason lull resulted in four consecutive losses, including defensive breakdowns against Miami (30–15), New England (27–16), Baltimore (21–14), and Dallas (35–30). "The right team won at Heinz Field Sunday night," wrote *Post-Gazette* sports columnist Ron Cook. "The Dallas Cowboys were deserving winners against the Steelers for the following reasons: Better coaching. Better running back. Better tight end. Better offensive line. Better defense. Better kicker. It would have been a crime if the Cowboys hadn't won."

Cook addressed the Steelers' four-game losing streak: "The Steelers have hardly looked or played like a division winner—let alone a Super Bowl contender . . . Everyone, from Mike Tomlin to Roethlisberger to [Cameron] Heyward, talked about the Steelers' lack of attention to detail . . . Tomlin talks about refusing to live in his fears, but sometimes that gets in the way of his common sense. It was OK for the Steelers to go for a two-point conversion after Bell's two-yard touchdown catch early in the game for a 6–0 lead . . . But it made no sense to go for two again after Eli Rogers' three-yard catch late in the first period gave the Steelers a 12–3 lead. That attempt also failed. Wouldn't you have settled for a 13–3 lead? "We want to be aggressive," Tomlin said. How about being smart?"

Not to be deterred, as had been the case with Tomlin teams— and despite a steady stream of media critics—the Steelers finished strong and concluded their schedule with seven consecutive victories—the longest winning streak in the Tomlin era.

Roethlisberger, Brown, and Bell took the field together in a playoff game for the first time, hosting the wild-card game against Miami. Three months removed from their 15-point drubbing at the hands of the Dolphins in Week 6, the group that took the field looked (and played) completely different than what Miami had previously seen.

The offense flourished, with Bell rushing for 167 yards and two touchdowns, Brown adding five receptions for 124 yards and one score, and Roethlisberger averaging 15.2 yards per completion as the Steelers checked all the boxes in a 30–12 win. Pittsburgh's rejuvenated defense limited Miami to 52 yards rushing on 2.5 yards per carry while sacking quarterback Matt Moore five times. Harrison, the ageless wonder, chipped in with 1.5 sacks.

The following week, on the strength of six Boswell field goals—an NFL postseason record—the Steelers defeated Kansas City in the divisional round, 18–16. With the game delayed for more than seven hours because of ice, Tomlin's team maintained its composure to take the "W."

But even in victory, there are always things that can be improved upon. The team's red zone play was subpar, as they failed to score touchdowns on four trips inside the 20 and a fifth drive that reached the 20. "Obviously, we weren't perfect but we were good enough," Tomlin said after the game.

Bell was brilliant yet again, establishing a Steelers postseason rushing record with 170 yards after setting the previous record against Miami in the wild card game. Coach Butler's defense was stifling in limiting Kansas City to 227 total yards. And what to say about Harrison, now thirty-eight, who recorded a sack, three tackles for a loss, and two quarterback hits?

And what to say about Brown, who ruined it all when his Facebook Live post in the locker room after the game accidentally caught Tomlin spewing a few expletives about the New England Patriots, whom the Steelers faced next in the AFC Championship Game?

"We spotted those assholes a day and a half," Tomlin said in the locker room video. "They played yesterday. Our game was moved to tonight. We gonna touch down [back in Pittsburgh] at four o'clock in the fucking morning. So be it. We'll be ready for that ass. But you ain't gotta tell them we coming."

Unfortunately, Brown's video did just that.

For one of the few times in his tenure as head coach of the Steelers, Tomlin couldn't control the narrative. The entire football world heard what he said about the Patriots, even though his wording was no different than what most coaches say to their players about an upcoming opponent. What's more, Tomlin addressed his players using colorful language that's usually delivered behind closed doors. That's what some coaches do; they use coarse language to fire up the troops. It wasn't enough the Steelers had to travel to face a talented opponent that had dominated them throughout Tomlin's tenure, they now had to face that talented opponent with extra motivation thanks to Brown's video.

Tomlin was still livid when he addressed the Pittsburgh media at his weekly press conference two days later.

"I'll be bluntly honest here," Tomlin said. "It was foolish of him to do that, and it was inconsiderate of him to do that. . . . There are consequences to be dealt with from his perspective. We will punish him. We won't punish us. And we will do it swiftly, and we will do it internally."

Brown, who apologized on Twitter for his video, had seven receptions for 77 yards in New England's 36–17 blowout win over the Steelers. He became a footnote in the Steelers' worst loss in sixteen AFC title games.

"They played their type of game they normally play, and we didn't play the type of ball we normally play," Tomlin said. "They are the champions of the AFC. Rightfully so."

Brady continued his mastery over the Steelers, completing 32 of 42 passes for 384 yards and three touchdowns. In seven games against Tomlin and the Steelers (including the playoffs), Brady had thrown 22 touchdown passes without a single interception.

Bell, who rushed for 337 yards in his first two playoff games, injured his left groin in the first quarter and did not return. His day ended with 20 rushing yards on six carries. The Steelers' offense went with him.

Williams, Bell's replacement, averaged only 2.4 yards on 14 carries, resulting in Roethlisberger attempting 47 passes against New England. He completed 31 for 314 yards with one touchdown and an interception. With Bell hobbled and Brown held in check, Roethlisberger's main weapons weren't much help against an opponent that almost always seemed to have the Steelers' number.

"Not a lot went our way," Tomlin said. "Not only in terms of the final score, but just how the game was played."

For Tomlin and the Steelers, the worst was yet to come.

15

TROUBLE BREWING (HOW TO DEAL WITH DIFFICULT PEOPLE)

(2017–18)

"It's a fine line between drinking wine and squashing grapes."

NEXT to his locker at the Steelers' practice facility, Antonio Brown displayed a photo of himself and Roethlisberger smiling at each other in the locker room. It was titled "The Dynamic Duo" and signed by Roethlisberger, who wrote, "AB, we are unstoppable."

Then came Brown's Gatorade cooler toss.

In the fourth game of the 2017 season, the Steelers' 26–9 victory over the rival Baltimore Ravens was marred when Brown lost his cool. On the team's first drive of the second quarter, Brown proceeded to have a meltdown when Roethlisberger didn't throw him the ball when he was open, forcing a fourth down. Brown's frustration was obvious to everyone as he gestured excitedly on the field. Once on the Steelers' sideline, Brown tossed a Gatorade cooler and exchanged words with Haley.

Two days after Brown's outburst, Roethlisberger dressed down AB on his weekly radio show heard throughout Pittsburgh. "I think I was disappointed because it's not like I intentionally missed [Brown]," Roethlisberger said. "It's not like I intentionally didn't throw it to him. I was doing what my reads tell me to do. . . . It's unfortunate that it happened, and it's unfortunate that he acted and reacted that way."

It was a sign of things to come for Tomlin's Steelers—past, present, and future.

Nine months after Brown embarrassed Tomlin when his Facebook Live video captured the coach using profanity in the locker room following a playoff win at Kansas City, Brown—who was rewarded with a four-year, $68 million contract extension that made him the league's highest-paid receiver six weeks later—struck again.

Tomlin had harsh words for Brown's reckless, me-first behavior and fined him after the first incident. But when the Gatorade incident occurred after the Steelers' promising 3–1 start the following year, Tomlin softened his tone. "I'm not going to waste a lot of time talking to Antonio about throwing water coolers and so forth," Tomlin told reporters. "AB is a competitor. And we all know and understand that. It aids him, it aids us. But we gotta control 'it.' He has to control 'it.' If he does not it can work against him, it can work against us.

It doesn't need to happen. It shouldn't happen. Hopefully it won't moving forward."

Art Rooney II, who signed off on Brown's new deal, backed up his head coach. "As long as they stay little annoyances, you can always live through little annoyances. . . . AB is a big contributor to our success, has been for several years now, and I think he's capable of continuing to be that kind of player."

While some may balk at having a player who consistently causes "little annoyances," it's hard to overlook that Brown was coming off his fourth-straight season of 100-plus receptions and 1,000-plus yards.

In addition to putting his words—and money—behind the young wide receiver, Rooney also endorsed Tomlin's coaching performance in guiding the Steelers to three consecutive playoff appearances and a trip to the conference title game after missing the postseason two years in a row.

"I think we're playing at a high level," Rooney said. "You play in the AFC Championship Game, you're close to the highest level. I'm happy with the job he did."

In the short term, Tomlin's handling of Brown worked. The Steelers lost only two more games the rest of the season. Their 13–3 record was the team's best since they went 15–1 in 2004, and their first 13–3 record since 2001, earning them a first-round playoff bye for the first time since 2010.

In the long term, Tomlin's "I treat everybody fairly, but I don't treat everyone equal" point of view would come back to haunt him.

Brown was clearly a difference-maker on the field, so Tomlin didn't treat him the same as his teammates. It wasn't quite the same treatment that Roethlisberger received, but Brown was made to feel special, entitled. Tomlin's tolerance with Brown gained momentum during Brown's career year in 2015 (136 receptions, 1,834 yards, 13 touchdowns) when he downplayed his star receiver's excessive celebration penalties.

"It's funny to me sometimes that people think I can stop a grown man from doing that," Tomlin said. "What do you want me to do? Not play him?"

He also knew that the offense needed Brown, as his 101 receptions on the season were 43 more than the next-closest wide receiver, rookie JuJu Smith-Schuster (58).

Away from the field, the Steelers became their worst enemy. Every week, it seemed as though Tomlin had more than the next game on his mind. How he was able to maintain his sanity and keep his football team in the playoff hunt was anyone's guess.

The Steelers were the first NFL team to announce they would sit out the national anthem prior to their road game against Chicago. Tomlin and his players decided they would remain in the locker room following President Donald Trump's suggestion that players who don't stand for the anthem should be fired.

"We're not going to play politics," Tomlin told CBS before the game. "We're football players. We're football coaches. We're not participating in the anthem today. Not to be disrespectful to the anthem, but to remove ourselves from this circumstance. People shouldn't have to choose."

The week before the Baltimore win, Tomlin defended his decision to stand on the sideline for the national anthem in Chicago while most of his players remained inside a tunnel leading to Soldier Field. In speaking to his team prior to a players-only meeting the night before the game, Tomlin said that he would respect the players' decision on how they wanted to handle the current situation that was seen in headlines across the country, of Trump's criticism of NFL players who had begun kneeling during the anthem (in protest of police brutality of minority Americans). The players were reportedly divided over the issue, but when the anthem was played, the entire team—except for tackle Alejandro Villanueva, a former Army Ranger who was awarded a Bronze Star for his service—stayed inside the tunnel. Tomlin was joined on the sideline by three of his assistants: Haley, Mike Munchak, and James Saxon.

"We will not be divided by this," said Tomlin. "We got a group of men in there that come from different socioeconomic backgrounds, races, creeds, ethnicities, religions, and so forth. . . . But because of opposition, we get drug into bullshit, to be quite honest with you. . . . Some have opinions, some don't. We wanted to protect those that don't, we wanted to protect those that do."

Asked about Villanueva's decision to stand for the anthem, Tomlin told reporters, "I was looking for 100 percent participation, we were gonna be respectful of our football team."

Chicago defeated Pittsburgh 23–17 in overtime for the team's first defeat of the season. After allowing 148 yards combined over the first two games, the Bears had rushed for 220 yards.

"We truly lacked the focus we needed," linebacker Arthur Moats said on 93.7 The Fan, two days after the team's loss to Chicago. "We spent a lot of time from Saturday to Sunday morning to even today discussing the anthem issue and how we were going to handle it. I think the guys lacked a little focus when it came to playing in the game."

Tomlin didn't disagree.

"Good teams deal with distractions," Tomlin said. "There's a certain amount of fanfare that comes with being good. We embrace the distractions that come along with it. . . . Hopefully, we learn something from this past week's experience that allow us to be singularly focused in the midst of a potential storm that's out of our control."

Some disgruntled fans burned their Steelers jerseys in protest of the team's decision not to stand for the anthem. A volunteer fire chief in suburban Pittsburgh wrote on his Facebook page: "Tomlin just added himself to the list of no good N-words. Yes I said it." And yes, the fire chief later apologized (and "resigned" from his position).

The Steelers faced a life-threatening distraction four weeks later in Cincinnati when fourth-year linebacker Ryan Shazier was injured on the first drive of the game. After attempting to make a head-first tackle on receiver Josh Malone, Shazier stayed on the ground for some time before leaving the field on a stretcher. He was then taken by ambulance to the hospital.

"To lose one of your guys on the first series, you're a little shellshocked," said Cameron Heyward, who would lead the Steelers that season with 12 sacks. "You try to rally around each other and keep playing."

The Steelers trailed 17–3 at intermission.

"At halftime, we really tried to settle the guys down," Heyward said. "We said we had to get this W for 50 [Shazier]. We had to stick together."

The Steelers rallied for a 23–20 win on Chris Boswell's field goal as time expired.

Overcome with emotion, Tomlin told reporters, "I can't say enough about the mental toughness of that group in the locker room."

In speaking with Roethlisberger on his *Footbahlin'* podcast, Tomlin opened up about his thoughts the minute the play happened.

I knew it was really serious instantly by the way he rolled off of that tackle; the way the play came to an end. It was an unnatural look. And so, like, I knew instantly it was a real problem. I think—and just largely let me say this: it was probably the darkest professional day I've ever had, like, to have a guy laying like that . . . there's nothing worse as a coach. There's nothing worse.

But when I got to him, he was so conscious in communicating that I was naïve. I think a significant part of me said, "It's going to be OK." Because he was Ryan. He was like, "Oh man, coach. I can't feel my legs. Oh my God." I'm like, "Ryan, relax man." And because he could articulate it so well, it led you to believe, "OK, this is going to be some temporary paralysis."

When I got to him, he was communicating with me. And so that just created probably an unrealistic and probably inappropriate kind of comfort in me, in the big picture of things. And so even though I knew, man, this is real, this is a major deal . . . I just had an expectation that somebody was going to tap me on the shoulder and give me some positive update that I could share with the guys. You know, that's what I'm thinking as he left the stadium in the vehicle. The longer it went on and that did not happen, obviously the initial fear that I had returned, and by the end of the game, obviously, I was scared to death.

After the game my whole deal was to get to the hospital and, obviously, when I got to the hospital, then the worst fears was realized. Like, this is where we are, man. This is what we're dealing [with].

Shazier underwent spinal stabilization surgery and had to learn to walk again. After spending two full seasons on the physically unable to perform (PUP) list, he announced his retirement in 2020.

The Steelers won six straight after the Cincinnati win. Save for a surprising 30–9 home loss to Jacksonville in Week 5—a game in which Roethlisberger threw a career-high five interceptions, with two returned for touchdowns—the Steelers were virtually unbeatable.

As the Steelers' winning streak grew to eight games, it became apparent that the entire team—from Tomlin on down—believed the Steelers and New England would meet in the conference championship game for the second consecutive year, and that the winner would advance to the Super Bowl.

Appearing on NBC's *Football Night in America* with Tony Dungy on November 26—three days after Thanksgiving, and five games into the winning streak prior to a home game against Green Bay—Tomlin was asked "how good" can the Steelers be?

"Oh, we can win it all," replied Tomlin. "We should win it all. I sense that about the group. In terms of talent, in terms of having enough competition, depth, I think we check all those boxes. But checking the boxes doesn't run the race."

Looking ahead to a meeting with New England in three weeks, Tomlin told Dungy, "Man, I'm going to embrace the elephant in the room. It's probably going to be part one, and that's going to be a big game. But, probably, if we're both doing what we're supposed to do, the second is really going to be big. And what happens in the first is going to set up the second one, and determine the location in the second one."

Right after his opening comments assessing the Steelers' 31–28 victory over Green Bay on Chris Boswell's last-second 53-yard field goal for their sixth consecutive win, the Pittsburgh media went for the jugular on the very first question.

Welcome to Tomlin's world.

"Questions?" asked Tomlin. You betcha.

"Mike, you were quoted on NBC in a pregame there with Tony Dungy as saying, 'We should win it all' and that the Patriots game, the one coming up, would be probably part one. It's unusual to hear a coach talk like that. What compelled you to say those things?" asked *Pittsburgh Post-Gazette* sports columnist Joe Starkey.

What compelled you to say those things? Really? Starkey may as well have asked Tomlin, "How dare you speak so highly of your football team on national television?"

The media complains when coaches give routine, predictable answers to their questions. The media then complains when a Tomlin comes along and finally gives reporters substantial material to fill their notebooks and sound bites.

Somehow, Tomlin maintained his composure and gave a dignified response.

"He asked for non-coach speak. So I was having a conversation with an old friend," Tomlin replied, his face tight and unsmiling despite the big win. "You know I've got respect for this process. We've got a good football team. I've got a great deal of confidence in them. Everybody in America knows that's a big game, OK? We couldn't deny that if we wanted to. You guys are going to ask us about it between now and then. So I stand by the statement."

The Steelers started their winning drive against Green Bay at their 30 with only 17 seconds remaining. Brown set up the winning score with two catches for 40 yards, including an awe-inspiring 23-yard sideline toe-tapper right in front of Tomlin.

"We were really fortunate to get that ball into AB on the sideline," Tomlin said. "It was a heck of a catch and obviously a ridiculous throw."

Plays like that one from two of the Steelers' unique offensive talents may have given Tomlin and his players an overabundance of chutzpah. Roethlisberger was 33-for-45 (with six drops) for 351 yards and tossed four touchdown passes for the second week in a row. Brown had 10 receptions for 169 yards and two TDs.

Bell told reporters after the game, "I'm fully confident. I'm sure everybody in this locker room is confident. I don't think there's a doubt in my mind that we can win it all. There's not a team in this league that can beat us besides us." Bell's last sentence was oh so prophetic.

In Week 15, with the Steelers sitting at 11–2 and the Patriots at 10–3, the two teams would have their awaited regular-season match-up. However, it was not meant to be, as New England grabbed a 27–24 victory on the Steelers' home field when a touchdown catch by tight end Jesse James late in the game was ruled incomplete following an official review.[1]

It was the Steelers' fifth straight loss to the Patriots, a team they hadn't beaten since 2011. Hard-hitting safety Mike Mitchell couldn't care less.

---

1 After the season, the league adjusted the catch rule, eliminating the "going to the ground" portion. With the revised rule, James's catch would have counted for a touchdown.

"We're going to play [New England] again," Mitchell told *Sports Illustrated*'s Greg Bishop. "We can play them in hell, we can play them in Haiti, we can play them in New England . . . we're gonna win."

When the big day arrived against Jacksonville in the divisional playoffs, the Steelers, to the surprise of everyone attending the game (at what was then known as Heinz Field), weren't ready to play.

They fell behind 14–0 in the first quarter, and after a rushing touchdown by T. J. Yeldon (with the two previous TDs coming via Leonard Fournette) early in the second quarter, were down 21–0. Were they overconfident and too focused on getting revenge against New England the following week?

"This team whacked us good in October," Tomlin said after the Steelers' shocking 45–42 loss to the Jaguars. "You kidding me?"

The joke was on the Steelers who, despite Roethlisberger's five touchdown passes (including two to Brown), failed to live up to their own lofty expectations.

"We didn't play well enough," Tomlin said. "We didn't coach well enough. Just not enough detailed execution to win versus good people in January football. That's about the only way to cut it."

It was a squandered opportunity for a team whose franchise quarterback was on the downside of his illustrious career, throwing the majority of his passes to one of the best wide receivers of all-time whose sometimes questionable behavior endorsed by the team was beginning to overshadow his immense talent. To top it off, Bell, arguably the league's best running back—who played the season on the franchise tag—would never play another game for the Steelers.

So while New England played in its eighth consecutive AFC title game and appeared in its fifth Super Bowl since the last time it lost to the Steelers, Tomlin was left to ponder where to go from here.

* * *

The warning signs came early when Bell—who cautioned the Steelers before their playoff game against Jacksonville that he would sit out the 2018 season if the team once again gave him the franchise tag—turned down a five-year contract offer averaging more than $12 million annually.

The Steelers' offer was $3 million less than the $15 million per year Bell wanted, indicated by a line in his rap song "Focus": "I'm at the top," Bell rapped, "and if not, I'm the closest. I'm a need 15 a year and they know this."

Randy Fichtner, promoted to offensive coordinator after eight years as quarterbacks coach, wouldn't have the luxury of Bell in his backfield. Bell's loss was immense. He became the first player in NFL history to produce 4,000 rushing yards and 2,000 receiving yards in his first 50 games. Along with Brown, Bell was Tomlin's best value draft pick.

Even without Bell, who teased teammates that he would report to the team but never made good on his promise, Pittsburgh's offense remained formidable. It also says a lot into the way Tomlin handled the locker room. After the chance for Bell to return had passed, Tomlin spoke to the media in what he hoped would be the last time on the subject. "I'm sure that you guys will find a reason into bringing it up and continue to rehash it in some form or fashion. Even after today, so it's just part of being us on this journey," said Tomlin. "I think that we've all gotten extremely comfortable with that element of it, in regards to how we function in us. And that train has left the station."

In terms of his quarterback, Fichtner was Tomlin's concession to Roethlisberger, who never got over not having Arians in his ear and seemed to only tolerate Haley. With Fichtner, a more familiar sounding board in tow, Roethlisberger would have more control over play-calling entering his 15th season.

And voilá! Roethlisberger posted career highs in passing yards (5,129), passing attempts (675), completions (452), and touchdown passes (34).

On the rushing side of things, rookie James Conner stepped in for Bell and led the AFC in rushing and rushing touchdowns after 10 games. After a revenge win against the Jaguars, the Steelers were 7–2–1, good for first place in the division.

Despite the great start, the good feeling didn't last . . . mostly due to the fact that the Steelers were a team of fifty-three players traveling in different directions.

Normally, when a player of Bell's caliber is engaged in a contract dispute with management, teammates—almost to a man—throw their support behind the player. In a surprising role reversal, some of Bell's teammates on the offensive line turned against him.

"Here's a guy who doesn't give a damn, I guess, so we'll treat it as such," guard Ramon Foster said.

"Why play hide-and-seek?" said Maurkice Pouncey, the team's All-Pro center. "Just man up and tell us what you're going to do."

If it wasn't Bell holding out, Brown was unhappy because Smith-Schuster put up better receiving numbers and scored more touchdowns. Or was it Roethlisberger calling out Brown and fellow receiver James Washington following a loss at Denver in Week 12, tearing the team apart?

Roethlisberger's end zone interception sealed Denver's 24–17 win. The loss snapped a six-game winning streak and ignited a three-game losing streak, as the Steelers would finish the season at 9–6–1, missing the playoffs for the first time in five years.

On his weekly radio show, Roethlisberger criticized Washington for dropping a long pass. The quarterback also threw shade at Brown, his intended target on the interception.

"That's why I talked to [Brown] and said, 'AB, you have to come flat,'" Roethlisberger said. "You can't drift in the end zone because those undercuts can happen."

Speaking the next day at his weekly interview session, Roethlisberger defended his right to openly criticize teammates on his radio show.

"I think I have earned the right to be able to do that as long as I have been here," Roethlisberger said. "I'll be just as critical on myself as well as in front of you guys (reporters)."

Like Ronde Barber in Tampa Bay, Ryan Clark owes his career to Tomlin. In eight seasons with the Steelers under Tomlin, Clark went from journeyman to Pro Bowler to post-football television star. He values his friendship with Tomlin, but that doesn't prevent him from criticizing the Steelers on the air when the situation warrants. Asked if Tomlin surrendered power to Roethlisberger in the locker room, Clark told *Bleacher Report*, "I wouldn't say 'surrendered power' as much as 'empowered him.' He always wanted Ben to be the leader. I felt like he thought Ben had to be if the team was [going] to win."

Tomlin could only watch at this point and hope for the best. There was nothing he could do. The damage was done, and the wound was self-inflicted. His two best players were playing by their own set of rules. It was too late to put the toothpaste back in the tube.

"I just think the culture that was set by Mike Tomlin ... You walk around the building and 'the standard is the standard,' that's kind of the motto," Hines Ward told Pittsburgh's 93.7 The Fan. "Well, the shenanigans, the circus is not conducive to winning football, and that's not the standard of the Pittsburgh Steelers. . . . The way [Tomlin] handles certain players and try to treat players differently and stuff, I think you're opening up a can of worms."

When the Steelers were winning and dominating, it was easy for Tomlin to look the other way and play favorites. He was such a good coach that even when he encountered a season like this one, he still had his team in the playoff picture right up until the final weekend of the season. His standards were so much higher than just about everyone else this side of New England that even his so-called bad season at 9–6–1 was better than half the teams in the league.

"When you miss the playoffs, nobody gets absolved," Rooney said. "I think everybody knows we need to do better, including Mike."

The rift between Brown and Roethlisberger, which surfaced the year before when Brown had his moment with a Gatorade cooler, continued to grow with no conceivable end in sight. Brown did not play in the final regular season game against Cincinnati after another disagreement with his quarterback.

It all came to a head during that Wednesday morning's walk-through practice (prior to the regular afternoon practice) when

Brown threw a football in Roethlisberger's direction. Brown did not practice the rest of the week and skipped the Saturday morning walkthrough. He failed to attend the Saturday night meeting at the team hotel, yet showed up Sunday morning expecting to play against the Bengals. He was not permitted to dress for the game.

In what would be their final game together, in a 31–28 loss the previous week in New Orleans, Roethlisberger targeted Brown 19 times. Brown had 14 receptions for 185 yards and two touchdowns. In their nine seasons together, Brown had 804 receptions, 10,768 yards, and 78 touchdowns in 120 games. Brown had led all NFL receivers in receptions and touchdowns since 2013. He is also only one of two players in NFL history to have six seasons with at least 100 receptions and 1,000 receiving yards (the other being Brandon Marshall).

After the season ended and the players went their separate ways, tight end James compared the Steelers to the famous Kardashian family. "Ah, man, we are Kardashans," James told pennlive.com. "We have, I mean, we're something. It's Le'Veon Bell issues, you have more stuff popping up weekly . . . There's just people calling other people out. We were in front of the ticker on ESPN too much for reasons that weren't related to football and not for us playing great ball. It was more distractions." Following the season, James signed a free-agent contract with the Detroit Lions.

On February 19, 2019, just a few weeks after the Super Bowl, Brown went public with his displeasure, requesting a trade via Twitter: "If your squad want to win and your squad want a hungry receiver whose best in the whole world, someone hit my phone," Brown said while working out on an elliptical machine.

"Tell them I ain't doing no unguarantees. I ain't even gonna play myself no more for this NFL . . . I think I done everything. What y'all think? What's left for me to do? Win a Super Bowl? Gotta be the right team for that, right? . . . If your team got guaranteed money, they want to get to know me and work with me, tell them to call me." Brown also said he wanted to be known as "Mr. Big Chest."

Two years earlier, Rooney was willing to put up with Brown's off-field antics, but with a caveat: "As long as they stay little annoyances." That mind-set became ancient history when the Steelers decided that trading Brown was the best move for everyone.

"Mike knew that Antonio's high school coach was his father figure and he was able to push the right buttons to keep that perspective in place," Steelers radio announcer Bill Hillgrove said. "One thing about Antonio: He was the first one there and last one to leave. Nobody worked harder. But when his hard work between the lines started to become less and less because of the outside the lines stuff, I think [Tomlin] knew it was time."

During the same week in March, Brown and Bell joined new teams. The Steelers traded Brown to Oakland for third- and fifth-round picks in the upcoming draft. To make the deal work, the Raiders signed Brown to a three-year, $50.1 million contract that included $30 million guaranteed. Bell signed a four-year, $52.5 million free-agent contract with the New York Jets, with $35 million guaranteed.

Bell had high praise for his former Steelers coach who drafted him over more heralded Alabama running back Eddie Lacy.

"Coach Tomlin is probably the realest coach I've ever been around," Bell said in 2022, on the *No Jumper* podcast. "People like him so much because he's not afraid for you not to like him. He's like one of those guys who's real stern. He's gonna be real honest with you. He knows how to speak well. He can relate to me like no other. There's different styles of player coaches. He's more of a guy like he's on you but it's not to the point where it's uncomfortable to come up and approach him. Some people . . . You don't know how to approach them because they're always on you. Coach Tomlin has that perfect kind of medium: 'I'm on you but like I'm approachable too.'

"He kind of lets you do your thing," Bell continued. His rule he always goes by is don't be the guy. He's not going to sit around and make a whole bunch of rules: don't do this, don't do that. He always said if we sit around making rules we ain't getting to the shit we need to be getting to. Coach Tomlin, he's fair and a great coach. He's definitely one of those guys who deserves everything he got. Nothing bad I gotta say about Coach T."

In a wide-ranging video interview with *Sports Illustrated*, Bell, upon signing with the Jets, explained his reasons for not re-signing with the Steelers.

The first, he said, was based on former teammates' negative comments expressed to the media during his holdout.

"Originally, I was thinking I was just not going to come week one. That was my goal. Original plan in my head," Bell said. "But it just happened, like certain things leading up to Week 1. Certain things just like, 'Why would that happen? Why would you say that?' . . . Even after week one, it [was] kind of just like certain buildups. It's not making me feel comfortable."

Bell said Roethlisberger was another factor in his decision to leave.

"Quarterbacks are leaders; it is what it is," Bell said. "[Y]ou're still a teammate at the end of the day. You're not Kevin Colbert. You're not [Art] Rooney."

Appearing on HBO's *The Shop* in 2019, hosted by LeBron James and Maverick Carter, Brown responded to Roethlisberger criticizing him for his game-ending interception in Denver.

"All year, the dude called me out," Brown said. "We lose a game, he's like, 'Damn, AB should have run a better route.' . . . That's the type of dude he is. He feels like he's the owner."

In their five years together on the field, the Steelers' wannabe Triplets were an impressive 53–27. Their contributions led to four playoff appearances, three division titles, and one trip to the conference championship. Without a doubt, they could have accomplished so much more.

"It was no slight against those guys, but all journeys come to an end, and their journey in Pittsburgh did," Tomlin told ESPN about the departures of Brown and Bell.

It was time for a change in Pittsburgh.

16

STRUGGLES

(2019–21)

"You think my message is going to change? My message isn't going to change."

ROONEY viewed Tomlin's tenure with the Steelers as a marathon and not a sprint—the Steelers were one of four teams to reach the postseason in at least four of the previous five seasons. There was no need for Tomlin to look over his shoulder one year after the team posted its highest win total in thirteen years.

Rooney only spoke with the media after the season. During the season, he kept his opinions, compliments, and critiques about the coaching staff, front office, and players to himself. It made for a healthy working relationship built upon trust.

"Our fans judge us primarily on wins and losses," Rooney told 93.7 The Fan two weeks after Tomlin concluded his 12th season in Pittsburgh with a 9–6–1 record. "This team has won pretty consistently under Mike's tenure here. When you look at the season, we're disappointed we didn't make the playoffs, obviously, but we finished a half-game out of winning our division and were in it down to the last plays of the season.

"He has to be able to command the locker room and keep the attention of the players. That is the key to evaluating a coach, and I think Mike has done that," Rooney said. "Look, we didn't make the playoffs this year, and that is our first goal. We have to deal with that and figure out how to get better. . . . To be successful in the postseason, you've got to start with winning in the regular season."

Despite the Steelers' struggles in 2018—losing four of their final six games following a 7–2–1 start despite Bell not being in the lineup—Rooney cited a 17–10 win over New England and a 31–28 loss at New Orleans as evidence Tomlin never lost the locker room.

"Those were two of the better teams in the league that we went toe-to-toe with," Rooney told 102.5 FM. "The team was playing well, playing hard, and that tells me we didn't have a problem with Mike's communication with the team. They were playing hard down to the end."

Rooney pushed back on the narrative that two of the Steelers' star players—Ben Roethlisberger and Antonio Brown—were running the team, creating a culture problem exacerbated by Bell's holdout, with some of the running back's teammates publicly criticizing his decision not to play.

"I certainly don't think we have a culture problem," Rooney told 93.7 The Fan. "We won 13 games [in 2017], so if you have a culture problem, if you have a discipline problem on your team, those teams don't win 13 games in the National Football League. Those are the facts we have to deal with.

"The bottom line is when you point to [2017] and everybody talks about the drama, that team won 13 games. The first test to me is the performance on the field. Are we winning games? Do we have a winning culture? I think the record speaks for itself."

In April 2019, the Steelers reaffirmed their commitment to the last remaining member of the Triplets, locking up Roethlisberger, now thirty-seven, for three more years. It was a bit of a risk considering Roethlisberger started all 16 games only four times in fifteen seasons, was nearing forty, and would never be confused with Brady from the standpoint of keeping himself in tip-top shape. However, the Steelers determined long ago they would hitch their wagon to Roethlisberger. Given the departures of Brown and Bell, the Steelers were backed in a corner. Ben's new $80 million deal included a $37.5 million signing bonus, with $30 million in injury guarantees and averaged $34 million over the final two seasons. It placed Roethlisberger among the highest-paid players in the NFL.

"It has always been a goal to play my entire career in Pittsburgh," said Roethlisberger, coming off a season in which he led the league in passing attempts, completions, and passing yards. "I am as excited in Year 16 to be a Steeler as I was when they drafted me."

That same week, Tomlin spoke with ESPN's Trey Wingo during the NFL draft about the Steelers moving on from Brown and Bell. Without naming names, Tomlin said, "There's been a cleansing, if you will."

Then, when Roethlisberger injured his right elbow five months later—in the second game against Seattle—the Steelers, like their owner, didn't panic.

For the first time since Roethlisberger became a starter, the Steelers played most of the season without their franchise quarterback.

Despite what most teams would consider a major setback and a legitimate excuse to pack it in, Tomlin and Kevin Colbert sent a clear message they weren't giving up on the season. On the same day the Steelers announced that Roethlisberger was out for the year, the team also announced a major trade, acquiring safety Minkah Fitzpatrick from Miami for their 2020 first-round draft pick.

The move was unprecedented for the Steelers, who had not traded their first-round pick since 1967. But consider the alternative. At 0–2 and forced to rely on backup quarterback Mason Rudolph, the Steelers could be looking at their first losing season since 2003.

Instead, it was Colbert and Tomlin to the rescue.

The year after finishing 6–10 in '03, the Steelers went 15–1 and played in the AFC title game. The following year, they won Super Bowl XL.

In 2013, the Steelers lost their first four games. They rallied to win 8 of 12 and just missed the playoffs.

Would history repeat itself six years later?

"We are very excited to add Minkah to our defense," Colbert said. "We had him rated very high during the 2018 NFL Draft process and we thought he could be an impact player in this league."

"Obviously, you can tell they're not giving up," Steelers cornerback Joe Haden told reporters covering the team after the trade.

"The trade was great. . . . Minkah's a great player. Coach Tomlin comes in these meetings and is dead serious and very, very blunt. He wants us to perform the way we should perform."

Fitzpatrick stepped into the starting lineup in his first game at San Francisco and made his presence felt instantly, despite only one week of practice. He intercepted a pass and forced a fumble in his first 15 minutes of the game, and was soon calling signals and making checks in the secondary

With Fitzpatrick in the lineup, the Steelers won five of their next seven games, including a streak of four wins in a row. His four interceptions led the NFL at the halfway point of the season.

"Minkah needs no endorsement from me," Tomlin said. "The tape is his storyteller."

The Steelers coveted Fitzpatrick, the 11th overall pick from Alabama in the 2018 draft. Sitting at the 28 spot, the Steelers had no chance to get Fitzpatrick, but Tomlin and Colbert, doing their due diligence, continued to gather intel.

"I went to Tuscaloosa twice," Tomlin said. "There was a sense of readiness among us about his character and his football abilities."

Fitzpatrick provided the Steelers with another defensive play-maker to pair with outside linebacker T. J. Watt, their first-round pick in 2017. Watt, who somehow fell to the Steelers at No. 30, made the Pro Bowl in his second season and emerged as an elite pass rusher.

Watt spent two seasons under the tutelage of Porter, the former Steelers standout who set the standard for outside linebacker play and whose contract wasn't renewed after five seasons.

"These are difficult decisions when it comes to someone like Joey who has meant a lot to this organization both as a player and coach," Tomlin said. "I want to thank Joey for his coaching efforts on our defensive staff. We wish him the best in his future coaching career."

Porter's relationship with Tomlin remained strong after leaving the Steelers for the second time. Four years later, the Steelers selected Porter's son, cornerback Joey Porter Jr., in the second round of the draft.

"[People] thought that since I had to leave the job, it would put a strain on the relationship, but it didn't," Porter said. "He's still one of the closest people I have over there in the building.

"He took me under his wing, taught me a lot about football on the game-planning side, just how he's running it. It was like we had known each other the whole time even though we didn't until I got there. From that point on, it's been like, shoot, the long-lost brother I didn't know I had."

Ironically, the Steelers were counting on Rudolph to lead the offense in Roethlisberger's absence. One year earlier, Roethlisberger questioned the team's decision to draft Rudolph in the third round. "I was surprised they took a QB because I thought maybe in the third round you can get some really good players that can help this team win now," Roethlisberger said. "If he asks me a question, I might just have to point to the playbook."

Taking over for Roethlisberger, Rudolph started the next two games, including his first NFL win against Cincinnati in Week 4. He suffered a concussion in the next game against Baltimore and was replaced by undrafted Devlin "Duck" Hodges, who made the fifty-three-man roster after winning a practice squad tryout. After losing in overtime to the Ravens in Week 5, and with Rudolph and Hodges switching places in the lineup, the Steelers somehow won their next four games, which should have made Tomlin an automatic favorite for coach of the year.

"I have to say it was probably one of the craziest seasons in over fifty years of being around football," Rooney said. "When you wind up having three different starting quarterbacks over the course of the year, and particularly one who earned his way on the roster after starting out as a tryout in rookie minicamp, it's an unusual season."

It was about to get weirder.

The Steelers' winning streak came to a crashing halt after a 21–7 loss at Cleveland, with Rudolph throwing four interceptions and getting sacked four times. The Browns's defense, led by defensive end Myles Garrett, made Rudolph look like a backup quarterback. He couldn't rescue the offense the way Roethlisberger did against the Browns, as he won 23 of his first 25 starts against them. Rudolph and Hodges were game managers who lacked improvisation skills and didn't have the ability to go off-script. They were also young and inexperienced. And the defense, which held the Rams without an offensive touchdown the previous week, yielded three touchdowns to the Browns.

If that wasn't enough, Rudolph was clubbed in the head with his own helmet by Garrett in the final seconds of the fourth quarter. The brouhaha came about when Rudolph completed a short pass to Trey Edwards. After delivering the pass, Rudolph was wrestled to the ground by Garrett, who grabbed the quarterback's facemask rising from the pileup. Garrett proceeded to yank off Rudolph's helmet and, despite guard David DeCastro intervening, swung Rudolph's helmet at the charging quarterback, connecting squarely with his head.

The NFL suspended Garrett for the final six games of the regular season. Center Maurkice Pouncey was suspended two games for punching and kicking Garrett. Rudolph was fined $50,000 for his role in the melee.

During his appeals hearing for the suspension, Garrett told league officials Rudolph set him off when he called him a "stupid N-word," an accusation which Rudolph fiercely denied. An NFL spokesperson said the league investigated Garrett's accusation and "found so such evidence." Despite Rudolph's denials and unwavering support from his Steelers teammates, Garrett never backed down from his accusation.

"I know what I heard," Garrett said on Twitter.

After the season—Tomlin, a black head coach defending his white quarterback—released a statement when Garrett again accused Rudolph of using a racial slur on ESPN's *Outside the Lines*. "I support Mason Rudolph not only because I know him, but also because I was on the field immediately following the altercation with Myles Garrett, and subsequently after the game," Tomlin said. "I interacted with a lot of people in the Cleveland Browns organization—players and coaches. If Mason said what Myles claimed, it would have come out during many interactions I had with those in the Browns organization. I had a lot of expressions of sorrow for what transpired. I received no indication of anything racial or anything of that nature in those interactions."

Keeping his players singularly focused after the Cleveland loss, Tomlin's Steelers won three straight to improve to 8–5, including a revenge victory against the Browns two weeks later. Somehow, someway, the Steelers were still in playoff contention.

Although the defense kept the team in the postseason race until the final weekend, the offense went south over the last three games, totaling 30 points in losses against the Bills (17–10), Jets (16–10), and Ravens (28–10). Injuries—Hodges started the next-to-last game when Rudolph injured his shoulder—and especially instability at quarterback in Roethlisberger's absence—were too much to overcome.

"Maybe with a little more stability at the quarterback position, we could have gone a little further," Rooney said after the team finished 8–8 for the third time in Tomlin's tenure.

* * *

Entering his 14th season, the Steelers believed Tomlin had plenty of pop left on his fastball; that his message hadn't grown stale after so many years. It's not unusual for players to tune out their coach after hearing the same message over and over, necessitating the front office to consider seeking a new voice to deliver a different message. Not so with Tomlin.

Tomlin's message was endorsed by Roethlisberger, who missed 14 games the previous season after undergoing right elbow surgery. Tomlin and his franchise quarterback were eager to prove the Steelers made the right call when they gave him a three-year contract extension, making him one of the highest-paid players in the league. When Roethlisberger missed most of the previous season because of a career-threatening injury, the medical setback raised legitimate questions whether, at thirty-eight years of age, he still had what it took to lead the team.

"I said today I felt like I was in a train wreck. Hopefully tomorrow, it will feel like I fell off a bike," Roethlisberger said four days before the opener. "The good news is my arm is the only thing that doesn't hurt."

Roethlisberger's return was bad news for the NFL. Led by Big Ben's 25 touchdown passes, the Steelers opened the 2020 season 11–0 for the first time in franchise history.

In a 38–29 win over Philadelphia in Week 5, Roethlisberger tossed three touchdown passes—all to Chase Claypool, who became the third rookie wide receiver to record four touchdowns in a single game in NFL history.

There were cracks in the foundation during the winning streak, but the Steelers' big-play offense and stout defense—allowing the fewest points in the league—disguised them from the rest of the pack. After the team's first loss against Washington in which they were held to a season-low 17 points and blew a 14–3 halftime lead in Week 13, Tomlin delivered a positive message to his players via the media: "I'm excited about facing the adversity of losing with this group, man. Smiling in the face of it, preparing, getting ready for our next challenge."

For any number of reasons, Tomlin's best version of the 2020 Steelers became a distant memory. In spurts, running back James Conner and wide receiver JuJu Smith-Schuster could make Steelers fans forget about Le'Veon Bell and Antonio Brown, whom they had replaced. But despite the Steelers' decision to move on from two of the best-ever at their respective positions, they were never totally forgotten. Conner was an injury-prone runner who lacked Bell's elusiveness and cunning. Smith-Schuster wasn't a true No. 1 receiver and enjoyed his best season playing opposite Brown, who had gone off the deep end following his trade to Oakland and was now playing for his third team since leaving the Steelers. Claypool, virtually unstoppable early in the season, was held in check when defenses started keying on him.

Averaging 28.8 points in their first 11 games, the Steelers averaged only 19.8 points over their final five contests, stumbling into the playoffs with a 12–4 record.

Asked about the chances of the Steelers needing to play thirteen-straight weeks if they lost their initially scheduled bye week due to COVID-19, Tomlin told NFL Network reporter Aditi Kinkhabwala, "We do not care."

Tomlin's tough talk aside, the Steelers played their worst football down the stretch. Forced to play without a bye week because of the coronavirus, the Steelers played three games in twelve days, losing two straight and three of four.

The Steelers' late-season swoon coincided with another important learning lesson for Tomlin.

Smith-Schuster, now the No. 1 receiver in Pittsburgh, had assumed Brown's role as team diva. A social media phenomenon on TikTok, Smith-Shuster entertained his followers with pregame dances on the field. Prior to a 27–17 loss at Cincinnati in Week 15, Smith-Schuster danced on the Bengals' logo at the 50 yard line while Claypool filmed.

During the game, Smith-Schuster was crushed by safety Vonn Bell after catching a pass across the middle, and fumbled the ball. Cincinnati recovered and converted the turnover into a touchdown and a 10–0 lead in the second quarter. The Steelers trailed 17–0 at halftime on the way to their third consecutive loss.

Bell told reporters Smith-Schuster's pregame antics inspired Cincinnati's defense. Smith-Schuster's Antonio Brown–like response was troubling.

"I'm just having fun, doing myself," Smith-Schuster said. "At the end of the day, as long as we go out there and play . . . yes, we lost, they had a few words to say, and it is what it is. I'm not going to stop doing it."

Not unless Tomlin told him to stop.

Speaking at the NFL Combine during the same offseason that Brown and Bell left the Steelers, Colbert candidly admitted the team had "to do a better job of managing young players as they grow into mega-stars."

"Social media has changed things," Colbert said. "We're learning on the fly. It's more relevant this year because of Le'Veon's situation and Antonio's situation. But maybe the lesson is we have to catch these guys when they're young."

A week after claiming to be unaware of Smith-Schuster's pregame dancing, Tomlin said the day after the team's *Monday Night Football* loss at Cincinnati that he would talk to his twenty-three-year-old receiver.

Taking Tomlin's words into account, Smith-Schuster spoke with reporters the following day. "My coach is being asked this question," Smith-Schuster said. "There was no intention of disrespect. I'm big on social media, the positive. So, for the betterment of myself and my teammates, I'm going to stop dancing on the logos."

If only Smith-Schuster's *mea culpa* extended to his media interviews. Prior to the Steelers' playoff game against Cleveland, Smith-Schuster didn't try to hide his lack of respect for the Browns, who the team split their regular-season match-ups with and would be facing in the wild-card game.

"I think they're still the same Browns teams I play every year," Smith-Schuster said. "I think they're nameless, gray faces. They have a couple good players on their team, but at the end of the day, like, I don't know. The Browns is the Browns. They're a good team, but I'm just happy we're playing them again."

The Steelers' 48–37 wild-card playoff loss to Cleveland was eerily reminiscent of Pittsburgh's 45–42 wild-card playoff loss to Jacksonville three years earlier: both times the Steelers were heavy favorites, overconfident and not ready to play. Both times, they fell behind early. Against Jacksonville, the Steelers couldn't overcome a 21–0 first-quarter deficit. Against Cleveland, the Steelers trailed 28–0 in the first quarter.

Roethlisberger threw for 501 yards and four touchdowns, but was also nicked for four interceptions, including three in the first half when Cleveland essentially put the game away for its first playoff win since 1994.

The Browns' opening touchdown set the tone for the entire game. On the first play of the game, operating from the shotgun on the Steelers' 24-yard line, Pouncey inexplicably sailed the ball over Roethlisberger's head into the end zone. Browns defensive back Karl Joseph recovered to make it 7–0 only 14 seconds into the contest. Following Roethlisberger's first interception on the Steelers' next possession, Baker Mayfield's 40-yard touchdown pass to Jarvis Landry made it 14–0.

On paper, the Steelers made it look good, rallying to within 35–23 at the end of the third quarter. Early in the fourth, the Steelers were faced with fourth-and-one near midfield. A touchdown would cut the deficit to five points. Tomlin elected to punt (though they did try to get the Browns to jump, but ended up taking a delay of game penalty), and the Steelers never got any closer.

When asked about his team's readiness to play, Tomlin replied, "In terms of being all-in? You bet." On the other hand, Tomlin added, "We were a group that died on the vine."

During the Tomlin era, Pittsburgh's Fourth Estate never missed an opportunity to get its licks in.

Immediately following the playoff loss, *Post-Gazette* sports columnist Ron Cook acknowledged Tomlin's pros and cons while presenting the veteran coach with a win-or-else edict under the headline, "After yet another collapse, Mike Tomlin's seat is officially warming up."

It's easy to blame offensive coordinator Randy Fichtner, who could be fired over the fervent wishes of Roethlisberger, who is expected to return for one more season. But firing isn't necessarily going to fix the problem. When a team struggles the way the Steelers did down the stretch, the issue goes higher.

To the top.

To Tomlin.

. . . The Steelers have gone four seasons without a playoff win. They have just three postseason wins since the 2010 season when they made their most recent Super Bowl.

. . . The reaction around town has been predictable. It seems just about everybody wants to fire Tomlin . . .

. . . It's hard for me to fire a coach who just went 12–4 and unexpectedly won his seventh division title in 14 seasons despite not knowing if his quarterback's elbow would hold up all season. As the Steelers were going 9–0 and 10–0 and 11–0, Tomlin was the runaway favorite for NFL Coach of the Year . . .

That's why the Steelers should and will give Tomlin—and Roethlisberger, for that matter—one more shot to get it right.

And if they don't?

The Steelers will have to look for just their fourth coach since 1969.

When *all* of Pittsburgh just knew the Steelers were going to hire Russ Grimm in 2007, the Steelers instead hired Tomlin. And when *most* of Pittsburgh knew that Tomlin losing to Cleveland in the playoffs, at home, just had to be the final straw thirteen years later, Art Rooney II stood front and center in support of his head coach.

"All in all, Coach put us in a situation again where we had an opportunity," Rooney said on Steelers.com three weeks after the conclusion of the season. "He's done that most of the years he's been our coach. That's why we'd like to keep him as out coach."

* * *

Roethlisberger certainly couldn't recapture the strong-armed franchise quarterback who once cast 300-pound defensive linemen aside with the greatest of ease while flicking 50-yard touchdown passes. But Ben of old was still far better than any quarterback the Steelers brought in to compete for his job. The team's master plan was to milk one more year out of Ben before he rode off into the sunset.

Unlike the New England Patriots, who drafted Jimmy Garoppolo despite being in possession of arguably the best quarterback in league history, Pittsburgh never chose that route. Roethlisberger, who would be thirty-nine when the Steelers opened the season at Buffalo, had never been seriously challenged by any of his backups (though he did show some signs of annoyance after the team had drafted Rudolph).

Reduced to a sitting duck in the pocket with limited arm strength, Big Ben was still the Steelers' QB1 by a landslide.

Speaking to reporters following his team's playoff loss to Cleveland, Rooney said Roethlisberger was eager to return, but acknowledged he would have to play for less than his $41.25 million salary—the highest cap figure for any NFL player.

"Ben wants to come back," Rooney said on a conference call with beat reporters. "We've left that door open. We've been up front with Ben in letting him know that we couldn't have him back under the current contract. He understands we have some work to do there. I think it's fair to say this will probably be the most difficult salary cap challenge that we've had in a long time, maybe ever."

The Steelers needed to clear salary cap space to sign some of their key free agents, while possibly looking to add other available free agents. They needed to replace standout offensive linemen Maurkice Pouncey, who retired after being named to the Pro Bowl in all but one of his ten seasons; and David DeCastro, who also retired after being named to the Pro Bowl in each of his final six seasons.

Returning from elbow surgery, Roethlisberger threw 22 touchdowns and four interceptions in the first nine games of the 2020 season. His performance over the final seven games, including the playoffs, was concerning: 15 touchdown passes and 10 interceptions.

The Steelers were willing to overlook how Roethlisberger finished the season. "We know that Ben can still play at a high level and do special things for this team," said Colbert, who drafted Roethlisberger eighteen years earlier.

Roethlisberger signed a team-friendly deal, guaranteeing that 2021 would be his final season with the Steelers.

"I am grateful to be at this stage of my career and more than happy to adjust my contract in a way that best helps the team to address other players who are so vital to our success," Roethlisberger told reporters.

Once the Steelers committed to Roethlisberger for one more season, they were obligated to pledge to Tomlin as well—not just for Tomlin's final season with Roethlisberger, but also for his integral role breaking in a new quarterback the following season.

Seven weeks after signing Roethlisberger, the Steelers re-signed Tomlin to a three-year extension, locking him up through the 2024 season. It was Tomlin's largest extension since his original four-year deal.

"Mike is one of the most successful coaches in the National Football League," Rooney said, "and we are confident in his leadership to continue to lead our team as we work to win another championship."

Tomlin did some housecleaning, albeit painfully, when he replaced offensive coordinator Fichtner with Matt Canada, who became Roethlisberger's fifth offensive coordinator and fourth under Tomlin.

Fichtner's departure signaled the end of a partnership that originated in 1997, when Tomlin and Fichtner exchanged phone numbers during a college recruiting visit at a Memphis high school. Soon after their meeting, Tomlin left Tennessee-Martin to join Fichtner on Arkansas State's coaching staff.

When Tomlin became the Steelers' head coach, he hired Fichtner from the University of Memphis to coach wide receivers. Fichtner was promoted to quarterbacks coach, where he served from 2010 to 2017. He then took on the dual role of offensive coordinator/quarterbacks coach in 2018 and '19, and was the team's offensive coordinator for his final season in 2020. The Steelers' best year under Fichtner was in 2018, when the offense ranked fourth in total yards and sixth in points. In Fichtner's last year running the offense, the Steelers were 12th in scoring and 24th in total yards.

"Personally, Randy and I have been in Pittsburgh since I hired him in 2007, but our relationship began well before that," Tomlin said. "He has been a friend of mine for years and wish his family nothing but the best, and I am eternally grateful for our relationship both on and off the field."

Rip Scherer Jr., who helped Tomlin and Fichtner get coaching jobs at Memphis and knew both men personally, said Fichtner was caught off guard when Tomlin let him go.

"Randy, he was shocked" Scherer said. "He went in. It was like, 'Randy, I've got to do this.' Bang. It was done."

Following a 1–3 start to the 2021 season, the Steelers won four straight to improve to 5–3. A winnable home game against winless Detroit the following week turned into a nightmare when Roethlisberger tested positive for COVID-19 the day before the game, and was replaced in the lineup by Rudolph. A 16–16 tie ensued, followed by back-to-back road losses against the Los Angeles Chargers and Cincinnati Bengals, in which the Steelers yielded a total of 82 points (41–37 and 41–10, respectively).

Bouncing back, the Steelers won four of their last six, including a sweep of Baltimore, and qualified for the postseason for the second straight year. In their Week 18 match-up against the 8–8 Ravens, a 16–13 overtime victory, T. J. Watt tied Michael Strahan's NFL single-season record with 22.5 sacks. Watt became the third Steeler under Tomlin to be named NFL

Defensive Player of the Year, joining James Harrison (2008) and Troy Polamalu (2010).

In what was Roethlisberger's final home game of his career, fellow captains Cameron Heyward and Derek Watt fell back so that Roethlisberger could take the final coin toss at midfield by himself before the Steelers' 26–14 victory over Cleveland on *Monday Night Football.* Roethlisberger was the last Steelers player announced sprinting out of the tunnel.

Najee Harris broke Franco Harris's franchise rookie rushing record of 1,172 yards, gaining 188 yards on 28 carries and scoring a 37-yard touchdown in the final minute. "I'm just so thankful for these fans and this place. There's no place like it," Roethlisberger said during a postgame interview on ESPN.

The Steelers finished the regular season 9–7–1, maintaining Tomlin's amazing record of never experiencing a losing season in 15 years. The postseason was another story.

Kansas City throttled the Steelers, 42–21, with Patrick Mahomes passing for 372 yards and six touchdowns. Roethlisberger passed for two touchdowns in his final NFL game.

"He was 7," Tomlin said about sharing the field with Roethlisberger one last time. "It's been an honor and a pleasure. I don't have the words."

The Chiefs advanced to the AFC title game, losing to the Super Bowl–bound Bengals. Winless in the postseason since 2016 and failing to win a playoff game in five consecutive seasons for the first time since 1967–71, the Steelers regrouped in search of a quarterback for the next generation.

17

REPLACING BIG BEN

(2022)

"When you have red paint, you paint the barn red."

ROETHLISBERGER, the last remaining player from the Cowher era, was gone. The Steelers' franchise quarterback for eighteen years, Big Ben could best be described as Tomlin's millstone. The coach was forever linked to the quarterback who was already on board when he arrived in 2007. Their first meeting wasn't the greatest. Roethlisberger told his new coach he wasn't the players' choice, and that he would have to earn their trust. Yet all Tomlin did was win a Super Bowl in his second season.

Tomlin shielded and publicly supported his quarterback—sometimes to the detriment of team chemistry. Roethlisberger, the longest tenured player in franchise history, won big games for his head coach until he had nothing left to give. Still, you couldn't blame Roethlisberger for feeling some kind of way. His final season in Pittsburgh wasn't assured until Rooney made the decision to bring him back for one more year. After nearly two decades, the time had arrived for Roethlisberger to finally move on and for Tomlin to select his own QB1.

When asked to describe the relationship between Roethlisberger and his head coach, Willie Colon said, "I know both sides of the story. Me and Ben are close. Still are close. I was in his wedding. It's some stuff I can say I can't say. I like to speak frankly and, honestly, and I would be saying too much.

"I'll say this: There will be a 30 for 30 documentary (on ESPN) and we'll try to bring you behind the curtain. Mike Tomlin's in the business of winning. He's going to do whatever it takes to win at all costs."

It was also time for Tomlin to say goodbye to an old friend in Keith Butler, who retired after 23 NFL seasons. Butler's defense led or tied for the league lead in sacks five years in a row.

Butler influenced Tomlin's decision as a young college assistant coach to switch from offense to defense. As a graduate assistant at Memphis, Tomlin was drawn to Butler, the team's defensive coordinator where the pair worked together for one season. As fate would have it, Butler rejoined Tomlin at Arkansas State a year later. Feeling himself being pulled to the defensive side of the ball despite starting out as a wide receivers coach, Tomlin asked head coach Joe Hollis Sr. for permission to coach defensive backs under Butler. Altogether, including college and pro, Tomlin and Butler coached together for a total of eighteen years—fifteen with the Steelers.

"Keith and I began our friendship in 1996 at the University of Memphis and have remained close to this day," said Tomlin, who promoted secondary coach Teryl Austin to replace Butler. "He helped build some of the greatest defenses in the league during our time together in Pittsburgh."

Tomlin's 15th offseason would say a lot about his ability to reshape the Steelers. What style of quarterback did he prefer? Mobile or pocket passer? Veteran or rookie? Would he turn the offense completely over to his new coordinator? Would he give Austin carte blanche to run the defense the way he saw fit, or would he take over most of the play-calling as he did with Butler? With Kevin Colbert planning to step down after the draft, what did that mean for Tomlin's influence over personnel decisions? Would he have a role in choosing Colbert's successor? In doing so, would he maintain his sterling reputation around the league? Granted so much unchecked power and influence, would his career continue to serve as a proxy for all black NFL head coaches?

Tomlin was mindful of how he was perceived as a coach of color in a league nearly devoid of color in the head coaching ranks.

"I know that being a black guy, there are various forms of responsibilities for me," Tomlin said on the *Pivot* podcast. "Some of them I'm capable of meeting. Some of them maybe I'm not. I'm certainly not going to satisfy everybody all the time and really don't have a desire to. I've got to move in a space that I'm comfortable with. As long as I'm doing that, I can deal with whatever, wherever it comes from."

Some things are easier to deal with than others.

Tomlin offered an angry retort when a reporter framed a question a few months earlier around famous alum Carson Palmer's suggestion that Tomlin be considered for the USC head coaching job.

"I mean, that's a joke to me," Tomlin snorted. "I got one of the best jobs in professional sport. Why would I have any interest in coaching college football? There's not a booster with a big enough blank check."

Tomlin compared himself to other successful coaches with a Super Bowl victory on their resume.

"Anybody asking Sean Payton about that?" Tomlin asked. "Anybody asking Andy Reid about stuff like that?"

In some regards, Tomlin and Tony Dungy, who gave him his start in the NFL, were kindred spirits. They saw the league for what it was, but also for what it could be. If Dungy and Tomlin overcame immeasurable odds and won big at the highest level, others, given the same opportunity, can succeed as well.

Dungy literally talked the idea of deserving black men receiving head coaching opportunities in the NFL into existence. As he learned firsthand from Dennis Green, Dungy used his platform as Tampa Bay's head coach to hire Herm Edwards, Lovie Smith, and Tomlin, who went on to varying degrees of success as head coaches—just like their white counterparts. There's no presumption that when an NFL team hires a white coach, they must succeed. There's never been any uproar when an unsuccessful white coach is fired; the team simply hires another one. When a black head coach doesn't win, he's unlikely to become a head coach again, impacting other teams' reluctance to hire coaches of color.

"Most of the coaches hired are not successful. Hiring a coach is a risky venture. But there seems to be a prerequisite when it comes to black coaches that they be successful. That's not realistic," University of Miami sociology professor Jomills Braddock said in a 1987 award-winning series in the *Tampa Bay Times* that

I co-wrote with fellow journalists David Steele and Darrell Fry. The NFL Players Association commissioned Braddock in 1980 to author a study examining whether racism prevented former black players and black assistants from becoming head coaches. "It seems a little unfair and biased," Braddock continued, "that there should be a higher guarantee, or lower risk, if a black coach is hired."

The number of black coaches in the NFL increased from zero in 1980 to three in 2023.

"It is a global, collective failure, from my perspective," Tomlin said on HBO's *Real Sports with Bryant Gumbel* about the NFL's inability to hire more black head coaches in 2021. Seeking to fill Austin's opening with a quality candidate, Tomlin channeled his inner Dungy and hired Brian Flores as senior defensive assistant/linebackers coach just over a month after he was fired by the Miami Dolphins. Flores's hire came only eighteen days after he filed a class-action lawsuit against the NFL and three of its teams. The lawsuit alleged a pattern of racist hiring practices by the league and other forms of racial discrimination.

"I had an opportunity to get a quality dude that is a more than capable coach," Tomlin said on the *Pivot* podcast. "[W]hen he filed that lawsuit, I said, 'Man, I imagine people are moving away from this dude.' I just wanted him to know I'm not moving away from him. I shot him a text . . .

"I said, 'Hey, man, give me twenty-four hours. Let me kick this around a little bit. I go down the hall and walk into Art Rooney's office. I said, 'Art, I've been talking to Brian Flores . . . This dude wants to coach football and I want to hire him.' He's like, 'Great.' That's the extent of the conversation. I told [Flores], 'Give me twenty-four hours,' but I think I called him back forty-five minutes later. I didn't want to miss [the opportunity to hire Flores]."

A younger Tomlin, lacking the credentials that we were now in his possession, wouldn't have suggested to Rooney the idea of hiring a black coach who filed a discrimination lawsuit against his former employer.

Tomlin's impressive cache ensured he would play a huge role in selecting the Steelers' next franchise quarterback.

Would Mitch Trubisky, the former second overall pick in the draft selected ahead of Patrick Mahomes and now playing for his third team in six years, move the needle in Pittsburgh?

Colbert tossed cold water on that idea.

"Anything we did in free agency will not preempt us from taking another player at any of these positions," Colbert told reporters prior to the draft. "We've been at the top quarterback pro days because, for the first time in a long time, that may be a position we have to address. When we had the luxury of a Hall of Fame quarterback at our disposal, we may not have attended those type of pro days. Is that saying we're taking one? Possibly."

Trubisky, who started 50 games and made two postseason appearances with the Chicago Bears, signed a two-year, $14.2 million contract with the Steelers. He would get first crack at the starting job in Year 1 AB (After Ben).

Of the seven college quarterbacks to visit the Steelers before the draft, two players stood out: University of Pittsburgh's Kenny Pickett and Liberty's Malik Willis.

Tomlin appeared to reveal his hand when discussing the advent of mobile quarterbacks now popularized in the league. "Quarterback mobility is a more significant part of the game than it's ever been in today's game," Tomlin said. "It's because they're utilizing the quarterback as a runner. And so now you're playing 11-on-11 football. So do the math."

That would seem to favor Willis, who discussed dining with Tomlin the night before his pro day workout attended by both Tomlin and Colbert.

"It was cool. He's a normal dude. That's what you want," Willis told reporters attending his pro day. "He was eating his chicken wings, and I'm like, 'Mike Tomlin eats chicken wings?'"

"It's good to get back on the pro day circuit, see those guys in their college environments," Tomlin said. "We took every opportunity that was at our disposal to beat the bushes and engage with those guys."

Then there was Pickett, whom the Steelers first met as a college freshman. The Steelers and Pitt share the same practice facility, so the team knew everything there was to know about the four-year starter tutored by Pitt offensive coordinator Mark Whipple, a former quarterbacks coach under Cowher. Despite Pickett's impressive credentials, it seemed like all NFL types wanted to talk about was his small hands.

So who would it be? Willis, the new-age passer-slash-runner—perhaps a reincarnation of former Steeler quarterback Kordell Stewart—who was still learning the position? Or Pickett, the hometown favorite who possessed a wealth of playing experience?

Tomlin ended the suspense with a phone call prior to the Steelers making their selection at No. 20.

"Kenny, what's up? Hey, what you doing tonight? Y'all watching TV? What y'all got going on? You ready to come back to Oakland [where Pitt's campus is located]? We're about to make you a Pittsburgh Steeler, brother."

After making the selection, Tomlin told reporters, "We circled the globe, or at least the United States, the last several months, just exploring and researching. It's funny, we ended up with the guy from next door."

"Sometimes we're more critical of the Pitt guys because we watched them grow from freshmen on up," Colbert said. "We get a little too critical at times because some of the other players we catch them maybe in their sophomore year or junior year, you don't get to see them play as much. Kenny, he's special. He developed a lot. We watched him come in as a freshman, knew who he was and when he became a starter, just continued to watch him grow into the great season that he had."

Without naming any names, Rooney foretold the type of quarterback the Steelers were seeking prior to the draft. Pickett appeared to check most of the boxes.

"Certainly, mobile quarterbacks are the wave of the future, and having mobility at that position is something that would be desirable," Rooney said. "The other thing that's desirable is somebody that can read a defense and complete a pass downfield. There are a lot of pieces to the puzzle that you have to put together, and you might not get someone that meets every criteria you might want."

Pickett met enough of those criteria, according to Colbert, who completed his 22nd and final draft with the Steelers—15 with Tomlin. "We map it out, we get twenty guys lined up, and you just wait and hope," Colbert said. "To get that player at 20 was certainly a pleasant surprise."

Colbert, who joined the Steelers in 2000, had a sparkling draft record with twenty-one players making at least one Pro Bowl. All twenty of his first-round picks through 2019 started at least 32 games and played at least four seasons with the Steelers.

Going through the proper channels pertaining to the Rooney Rule, the Steelers hired front office fixture Omar Khan as their new general manager. Khan served as the Steelers' vice president/ football and business administration for twenty-one years. The Steelers interviewed at least four minority candidates, including Khan, whose father is a native of India and mother is from Honduras. Andy Weidl, a native of suburban Pittsburgh, was hired away from the Philadelphia Eagles to be the team's assistant general manager.

"To step in this job and know you're going to be working with coach Mike Tomlin is a dream come true," Khan said.

Similar to most teams that pick a quarterback in the first round, the Steelers did not draft Pickett to not play him. He was their quarterback of the future. Maybe Pickett would start as a rookie. Maybe not. Trubisky was insurance in case things went haywire. Only Trubisky didn't see it that way. He viewed Pittsburgh as an opportunity to jump-start his stalled pro career.

Trubisky considered himself the starter, and that was that.

"I've done a lot of great things so far and I really feel comfortable where I'm at and how I'm throwing the football and how I'm learning the playbook," Trubisky said during preseason.

"Just how I carry myself every day, what I've done on the practice field. . . . It's your whole body of work, everything I've done in my career, what I did in minicamp, the practices at Latrobe, the preseason games."

In the season opener at Cincinnati, Trubisky was 21-for-38 for 194 yards and one touchdown in a 23–20 overtime win over the Bengals. He didn't turn the ball over and managed the offense. Minkah Fitzpatrick opened the game with a pick-six interception and blocked an extra point for a defense that sacked quarterback Joe Burrow seven times. It was a great start for the Steelers, who were swept by Cincinnati the season before and had dropped three straight in the series. The pass rush took a hit when T.J. Watt was lost indefinitely with a pectoral injury.

Trubisky and the offense were held in check for the second straight week against New England. He passed for 168 yards, one touchdown and an interception in a 17–14 defeat. In two games, Trubisky's offense generated just two touchdowns.

The offense continued to struggle in a 29–17 loss at Cleveland, as Trubisky again failed to throw a touchdown pass. He was averaging a pedestrian 9.2 yards per completion.

Trailing 10–6 at intermission in the Steelers' next game against the New York Jets and their struggling quarterback, Zach Wilson, Tomlin pulled the plug on the Trubisky experiment.

It's rare for a rookie quarterback to receive his first NFL action in a competitive game at the start of the third quarter when the starter is healthy. Tomlin said he made an instinctive decision, something he never did when Roethlisberger was under center. "It's how I felt and how we felt in-game," Tomlin said. "We've also talked about when you're there, how do you know when you're there? And you just kind of know when you're there. And that's probably the perspective I had on the decision."

Pickett completed 10 of 13 passes for 120 yards and took the Steelers from four points down to a 20–10 lead. He became the first rookie quarterback to run for two touchdowns in his NFL debut. He also threw three interceptions; his last pick led to New York's winning touchdown.

Trubisky's benching had as much to do with a halftime locker room argument he had with receiver Diontae Johnson as did his play on the field. "We're sensitive to the situation Mitch is in," Tomlin said about benching his veteran QB.

Nevertheless . . .

"In an effort to be better and score more points, we decided to go to Kenny in the hopes he will provide a spark for us," Tomlin said. "We felt that, not only in terms of our ability to move the ball, but in terms of energy." Said Pickett, "I felt like I showed some emotion out there, but I felt like we needed it. So, it's like reading the room, reading the situation and fitting the [right] kind of leadership style and be myself."

"He pulled the trigger on Kenny when he absolutely knew it was the right time," said longtime Steelers broadcaster Bill Hillgrove who was also the broadcaster for Pickett's games at Pitt. "I thought, as I watched the season develop, Mitch Trubisky was playing not to lose. When you play not to lose, I think you set yourself up for failure. The worst thing you can do is turn a talented quarterback loose too soon—you could ruin him. Mike was making sure that wasn't going to happen."

Tomlin realized it was risky to start Pickett on the road against Buffalo and MVP candidate Josh Allen, but what did the 1–3 Steelers have to lose? "We have a level of concern about the environment we're taking him into," Tomlin said, "but you have a level of concern about any quarterback you take into that environment."

Despite Pickett failing to generate a touchdown in a 38–3 loss against the Bills, he passed for 327 yards and led the offense to a season-high 23 first downs. Trubisky never got his starting job back although he did see action from time to time.

When Pickett suffered a concussion midway through the third quarter against Tampa Bay, Trubisky completed 9 of 12 passes for 144 yards and a touchdown in the Steelers' 20–18 victory, snapping a four-game losing streak. Sure enough, Pickett was back in the lineup the following week.

The Steelers totaled only 23 points in back-to-back road losses against Miami and Philadelphia and failed to score more than 13 points for the third time in the past four games. Playing catch-up against the Eagles in an embarrassing 35–13 defeat, Pickett was sacked six times. "There's no excuse for the play we put out there," Tomlin said.

Sure there was. The Steelers were playing a rookie quarterback in a league that devours its young, first-year passers. That, barring injury, there was no reason sit Pickett. In Year 1 AB, why not see what the kid quarterback can do?

And, so, going into the bye, the Steelers were sitting at 2–6 for only the second time since Tomlin became head coach.

"There's a dysfunction in what we're putting on the field right now," Cameron Heyward told reporters following the 22-point loss to the Eagles, three weeks after an even more embarrassing 35-point defeat against Buffalo.

Harris took one for the entire team when he said, 'We lack a lot of experience, we lack a lot of discipline, accountability. We lack a lot."

The season was shaping up to be one big disaster. Not only were the Steelers sitting at four games under .500, they were counting on a rookie quarterback to turn the season around the way Roethlisberger did regularly. Good luck with that.

This was Tomlin's first time developing a rookie quarterback who the team needed to play rather than sit. Losing three of his first four games as a starter, Pickett threw two touchdowns and eight interceptions.

And it didn't help when Pickett complained to reporters after the Buffalo game about the team's study habits.

"We need to study more," said Pickett, taking a direct shot at Tomlin. "I don't think we study enough as a group."

Big Ben earned the right to say uncomplimentary things about his team after a loss. Clearly, Pickett hadn't earned that right. And based on his slow start, would he ever?

Tomlin was betting that he could. His response to Pickett's ill-advised comments was to remind his quarterback: Less talk, more action.

"I don't know what he was referring to there," Tomlin said two days later at his weekly news conference. "I'm not going to try to add any color to an opinion. I believe our guys study at an appropriate level, and I've seen that continually through the process. I'm not going to add any color to an opinion that I'm not highly familiar with."

Pickett tried not to intrude in the team's first game after the bye, a 20–10 home win over New Orleans. He passed for 199 yards, rushed for 51 more, and didn't throw an interception for the first time in his career. Sacked six times, he followed his coaches' instructions by not forcing throws, instead making the safe play. Tomlin didn't ask Pickett to win the game; the Steelers topped 200 yards rushing for the first time in six years. "Take care of the ball, give yourself a chance to win," Tomlin said. It was Pickett's first NFL victory in a game in which he started and finished. "You put your whole life into this," he said. "It's my first one all the way through."

Here's how much the AFC North had flipped: Cincinnati's 37–30 win over the Steelers was the fourth win in five tries for the Bengals against the team which beat them 11 straight times from 2015 to 2020. Pickett led the offense to a season-high

20 points in the first half, threw for 265 yards and a touchdown, and didn't have an interception for the second week in a row, but Burrow, his Cincinnati counterpart, was better, passing for 355 yards and four scores. Although improving, Pickett wasn't there yet. Neither were the Steelers, who fell to 3–7.

The Steelers continued to take the pressure off Pickett. In a 24–17 win at Indianapolis, the running game produced a season-high 172 yards. It was the third time in four games the Steelers rushed for more than 140 yards after topping that mark a total of three times in 2021. Pickett was 20 of 28 for 174 yards and didn't throw an interception for the third straight week. His commentary and Tomlin's response were long forgotten.

Ironically, Pickett first NFL season resembled Roethlisberger's rookie year. Relying on a safe passing game and strong ground attack, Pickett was 16 of 28 for 197 yards, one touchdown and no interceptions in a 19–16 victory at Atlanta. The Steelers were now 3–1 under Pickett since the bye.

Yet, all was not peaches and cream. Second-round draft pick George Pickens complained he wasn't getting enough looks from fellow rookie Pickett, who targeted him only twice in the Atlanta win. In Tomlin's defense, Pickens was third on the team in targets; second-year tight end Pat Freiermuth was second. "Everyone wants the ball," Pickens said. "Everyone wants to win." A former college receiver himself, Tomlin defended Pickens. "I want a guy that wants to be a significant part of what we do," Tomlin said. "The appropriate and mature way to express that? We're growing and working on it."

Trubisky replaced a concussed Pickett and threw for 276 yards and a touchdown in a disappointing 16–14 home loss to Baltimore, which played without starting quarterback Lamar

Jackson. Trubisky tossed back-to-back interceptions in the second quarter and a total of three picks after the offense had gone four straight weeks without an interception. The Steelers also had a field-goal attempt blocked in the three-point loss. "You do those things, you don't win," Tomlin said. Pittsburgh was now 5–8 with four games remaining, putting Tomlin's streak of never having a losing record in jeopardy.

With Pickett in concussion protocol, Trubisky redeemed himself by completing 17 of 22 passes for 179 yards and no interceptions in the Steelers' 24–16 win at Carolina. Trubisky split practice snaps with Pickett, but Tomlin stuck with the veteran, whose 1-yard touchdown sneak gave the Steelers a 21–7 lead in the third quarter. "I know what I can do in this league," Trubisky said. "The emphasis was on protecting the ball, and that's what I did today. It feels good to be able to get this opportunity and come through and have my teammates trust me."

In a game dedicated to Steelers Hall of Famer Franco Harris, who passed away earlier in the week, Pickett's clutch game-winning drive produced a 13–10 win over the Las Vegas Raiders in week sixteen. Every Steelers player entered the stadium on Christmas Eve wearing Harris's No. 32 jersey, which the team retired at halftime. Pittsburgh's come-from-behind win was fifty years and one day after "The Immaculate Reception"; Harris's improbable, final-play, playoff-winning touchdown catch against the Raiders.

Back in the starting lineup, Pickett was 26 of 44 for 244 yards, one touchdown and one interception—snapping his streak of not throwing a pick at 147 passes. Trailing 10–6 with 2:55 remaining, Pickett completed seven of eight passes to cap a 76-yard drive, throwing the game-winning, 14-yard touchdown pass to Pickens with 46 seconds remaining. After the game,

Tomlin praised his young offensive playmakers. "I didn't see big eyes," Tomlin said. "I saw sure eyes. I saw guys who were prepared to go do it."

With a potential playoff berth and Tomlin's unbeaten winning streak hanging in the balance, Pickett produced his signature NFL moment in a 16–13 victory at Baltimore for his second straight come-from-behind win. On the final drive resulting in the clinching 10-yard touchdown pass to running back Najee Harris with 56 seconds to play, Pickett completed passes of 20 and 28 yards. He ran for two more first downs. On the money play, Pickett, after being chased to his left, dropped in a pass to Harris behind linebacker Roquan Smith.

No wonder an emotional Tomlin greeted Pickett on the sideline appearing to say, "Kenny Effin' Pickett."

"I can't say enough about our young quarterback," Tomlin said after the team's Week 16 victory. "He smiles in the face of it. He's always ready to be that guy in the moments that we need him to be that guy." Addressing the Steelers' advantages of observing Pickett's college career in the same city, Tomlin said, "We benefitted so much from close proximity in the evaluation process. I don't think any of us are surprised by what he does from an intangible standpoint. The proximity to him at Pitt kind of gave us that comfort."

Pittsburgh's 28–14 home win over Cleveland in the season finale clinched Tomlin's 16th consecutive season without a losing record to start his career, an NFL record. It was the Steelers' largest margin of victory of the season. Pickett went 13 of 29 for 195 yards and a touchdown. In his eight starts after the bye, Pickett was 6–2, including a season-high four straight wins, with five touchdown passes and only one interception.

Tom Landry (21) and Bill Belichick (19) are the only coaches in league history with more consecutive seasons without a losing record.

"That was for Mike T," Harris said of the Steelers' 9–8 finish. "When we started 2–6, "[Tomlin] said, 'I'm not going to change the way I'm coaching. I'm not going to blink. I'm going to be the same guy.'"

While more of a media story, Tomlin was more focused on the Steelers missing the playoffs for the first time since 2019.

"I don't know if I pondered that," Tomlin said. "I was preparing for the potential of next week."

The Steelers turned their attention to next year, led by Pickett, their new starting quarterback.

"Even though we fell short of making the playoffs, I thought the second half of the season was encouraging," Rooney said in his end-of-the-season address to Pittsburgh reporters. "You want to see a team improve over the course of a season, start to finish, no matter what your record is.

"The fact we were breaking in new quarterbacks—two of them, in fact—was a factor with at least some of the difficulties we had early in the season."

Despite repeated calls throughout the season from newspaper columnists and on local sports talk shows to replace Matt Canada for being overly conservative and unimaginative, Tomlin remained loyal to his offensive coordinator.

"I thought he got better just as our team got better," Tomlin said. "That was encouraging."

Among those critics was former quarterback Doug Williams, the MVP of Super Bowl XXII, who worked in the Tampa

Bay Buccaneers front office when Tomlin was the team's secondary coach.

"I think Mike remained loyal to a fault. That's who he is, though," Williams said. "I think everybody in America probably felt like he should change the offensive coordinator. I'm not gonna lie. I was one of them. But his quarterback played well. I'm not going to argue with him because he stuck with him. I think this [2023] season will tell the tale whether or not he should have or shouldn't have. We've all got our way of thinking—what you feel. I'm a Mike Tomlin fan. I want Mike to do well. I do think his offensive coordinator weighed on him a little more than he should have. And I do think the average coach would have released his offensive coordinator. But Mike stuck with him. That's who Mike Tomlin is. I'm sure Mike had some sitdowns with his offensive coordinator and let him know what we got to do. And if that's the case, and his coordinator does what he needs to do, you've got to give Mike credit."

The Steelers ranked in the lower half in the league across the board in offensive performance: 26th in scoring offense, 23rd in total offense, 24th in passing offense, and 16th in rushing offense. Put into context, however, the Steelers produced their best running attack since finishing 14th in 2016.

As part of his decision to stick with Canada, Tomlin said he purposely dumbed down the offense for his young quarterback. "What you saw from us was what was appropriate, particularly in the second half of the year to engineer victory," Tomlin said. "It's our job as coaches to do what's required."

Rooney agreed with his head coach. "With a rookie quarterback, they seem to work well together," Rooney said. "To start over again with a new offensive coordinator, you could wind up back in the same situation again where the first half of the season, you're breaking in a new coordinator. We wanted to keep that group together."

* * *

Entering his 17th season with the Steelers—two years longer than Bill Cowher; six fewer than Chuck Noll—Tomlin has come full circle as a head coach.

He reshaped both the offense and defense in his image. Tomlin's influence extends to personnel decisions. Among his most important decisions was handpicking his new franchise quarterback, Kenny Pickett, in the first round of the 2022 draft to replace future Hall of Famer Ben Roethlisberger.

"He's maturing," Canada said about Pickett, who was 8–5 as a starter in his rookie season. "The speed of the game in Year One, he got thrown in. That was a fast-moving train. He got to the bye, continued to get better.

"The game is slowing down for Kenny. He's getting the ball to the right place at the right time. He's seeing things very well."

Tomlin can see clearly now that his quarterback is ready to take the next step. His prize pupil is growing up.

At his first news conference of the regular season—five days before the Steelers' 2023 home opener against the San Francisco 49ers—Tomlin let reporters know Pickett's role was upgraded to exalted status. It took Roethlisberger until his fifth season to become a team captain. Pickett made it his second year.

"I like the way that the group has worked in an intangible way," said Tomlin. "The development of the brotherhood, the mutual respect and understanding as we work cooperatively. The leadership that's been displayed can be reflected by our captain voting. Proud that this group selected Kenny Pickett on offense. Him being the captain on offense [is] probably more a reflection of everyone's feel of his growth and development. Not only as a player, but as a leader within this collective."

"Kenny has *it*," Steelers left tackle Dan Moore told the *Pittsburgh Tribune-Review* the same day Tomlin made his announcement. "I don't know what *it* is, but he has it."

Pickett's favorite receiving target is fellow second-year player George Pickens, a budding star in his own right who played on Georgia's 2021 national championship team. Pickett was selected in the first round; Pickens was the Steelers' second second-round pick. Loading up with two more players from Georgia's 2022 national championship squad in the most recent draft—tackle Broderick Jones and 6-foot-7 tight end Danell Washington were selected to open holes for 2020 first-round pick Najee Harris— Tomlin's Steelers are gearing up for a return to their glory years of offensive dominance featuring generational talents Antonio Brown and Le'Veon Bell.

Only Andy Reid of the Kansas Chiefs and Bill Belichick of the New England Patriots are ranked ahead of Tomlin in a power poll released prior to the start of the 2023 NFL season. Panelists including former NFL players, coaches, officials, talent evaluators, writers and broadcasters were asked: "If you owned an NFL team that was a legitimate Super Bowl contender in 2023, who would you want coaching that team?"

Reid received 103 of 184 votes for first place. Belichick finished second with 38 votes. Tomlin was third with 27 votes. All other finalists received single-digit support.

"Mike Tomlin has been around a long time," said power poll voter and Hall of Fame wide receiver Drew Pearson. "His no-nonsense approach with his players is a big reason why. But at the same time, he seems to understand today's players. The Pittsburgh Steelers are one of the most successful franchises in NFL history and the Rooneys trust him with their team. That's good enough for me."

But is it good enough for a demanding local media and fan base that prefers to overlook his .625 career winning percentage (including the postseason), and instead holds it against him that he hasn't won a playoff game since 2016?

Without question, Tomlin is a Hall of Fame head coach. He has more victories, a better overall winning percentage, and won as many Super Bowls as Cowher—the coach he replaced and is most compared with based on their Steelers coaching backgrounds. Cowher entered the Hall of Fame in 2021, fifteen years after coaching his final game.

"For the people who are like, 'Fire Mike Tomlin,' do you realize how quick he would be snapped up?" said award-winning NFL journalist Michael Silver. "And do you understand how hard it would be to then hire someone who is on his level magically? I do take heart in our inside football world of the people that really know the sport and play and coach and evaluate talent, *everybody* knows. I've never heard anyone who's in that world *not* get it. That is very validating."

Rick Minter hired Tomlin to be his secondary coach at the University of Cincinnati twenty-four years ago. Minter compared Tomlin to Seattle Seahawks head coach Pete Carroll, another future Hall of Famer perceived a certain way by the public whose level of NFL success rivals Tomlin's.

"Mike is like Pete Carroll," Minter said. "Pete and I worked together [at North Carolina State from 1980 to 1982]. He's a three-time NFL head coach who won a Super Bowl and is a wild and crazy guy on the sideline. And all he did was revolutionize USC football. He's not any different now. He's just gray-headed, he's seventy-one, but he's still the same Pete Carroll.

"Mike's the same way. People look at him and don't give him credit because they write it off by saying he's just a cheerleader. He's a guy that delegated well, but he just cheerleads. No, he loves his players. He supports his players. He's young at heart.

"I worked with both these guys," Minter continued. "I see similarities in their personalities that people don't know how to take those guys because they're not Nick Saban, they're not Belichick—those stoic looking guys on the sideline who make you think they're smart. I'm not taking anything away from Bill and those guys; they're brilliant coaches. But put Mike in that category too."

According to those who know him best, Tomlin is too unassuming for his own good. It's not in his DNA to bring attention to himself or his accomplishments. "His football acumen is off the charts. But he doesn't put it out there. He kind of keeps it under wraps," said former Memphis head coach Rip Scherer Jr., who hired Tomlin as his graduate assistant twenty-seven years ago. "Even when Dick LeBeau was there, Mike was much more involved on a day-to-day basis what they do defensively more than anybody would guess."

A noted orator among NFL coaches, Tomlin spoke at the Steelers' final team meeting in June 2023. He gave each player something to ponder—veterans and rookies alike—until they returned for training camp two months later.

Tomlin's brief yet forceful speech delivered in his unique baritone offered a succinct message: *If you're not getting better, you're getting worse.*

He titled his speech, "Reasonable Expectations."

In the growth and development of this thing, man, I'm talking to you about norms, expectations, mindsets. Mindsets that you should have. And it's always good to acknowledge reasonable expectations. I expect you to get better, man, whether it's the knowledge relative to what it is that you do, the preparation of your body, the understanding of the game. Etc., etc., etc.

You need to continually be a guy on the rise. That is a reasonable expectation. As opposed to just coming in here and putting in time. What do I mean by that? I mean the things that made you viable in the past aren't going to be the things that make you viable moving forward. You better be continually getting better. As long as you're sitting in rooms like this. I ain't doing my job if I'm not pointing that out.

You guys that have been here and know what it's about, man, we expect you to be significantly better. Hear the words. You were a young man, we might have tolerated mental errors a year ago. We'll have less tolerance for it moving forward. It's just a reasonable expectation.

So, let's just be really transparent, man, about expectations in this business, about how competitive it is. I never want you worrying about people on the outside. Even the man sitting next to you. This is a man versus himself battle. You've got to be continually pressing to get better. With that understanding that this is a highly competitive line of work that we're in.

BEING MIKE TOMLIN

What may be the most engrossing and distinctive quality about Mike Tomlin is the earnestness of his postulation in the merit of simplicity. He's no different than any other coach in that he assigns a value to each of his players; said value ultimately determines their worth to him and the team he's paid good money to lead. At the same time, Tomlin seems to be able to peel back the layers and examine beneath the surface to view his players on a multi-dimensional level.

Imagine at 5-foot-9 and 182 pounds, being told that you are too small to cash a paycheck in the National Football League. Some coaches might see right through you. Tomlin looks you dead in the eye.

"I love the 180-pound dude that plays in the National Football League," Tomlin said on the *Pivot* podcast. "I coached Cory Ivey.[1] Corey Ivey played at 5-foot-9, 182 pounds. Runs a 4.6. Played a decade in the National Football League. Them the dudes. There ain't a bunch of 325-pound people on the planet. There's a lot of men walking around 5-foot-9, 180, run 4.6. The will of that dude was so evident to me. I couldn't believe that others couldn't see it. [Those] stories turn me on. I want to be a

---

1 Ivey played in 113 NFL games, including four seasons with the Tampa Bay Buccaneers under Tomlin.

part of the fabric of somebody's life in that way. I want to speak the truth when I see it, like, 'That dude ballin'. And I don't care [by] what means he got here. He ballin'. That's football justice."

Football justice is Tomlin coaching the same team for 17 consecutive seasons after failing to secure his dream job as an NFL wide receiver.

Those who can't play, coach—and well . . .

"I love to hear coaches that resist the responsibility of coaching . . . That talk negatively about a dude that can't learn," Tomlin said on the *Pivot* podcast. "If everybody could learn, we'd need less coaches.

"I love reading draft [evaluations] and somebody's talking about anything other than pedigree," he continued. "Talking about how poor somebody's hand usage is. Well, that's coaching, right? I don't run away from coaching. I run *to* coaching. I love it."

You must be able to imagine in a certain way to see how Tomlin views himself as a former wide receiver castoff who made it to the big stage as a coach who doesn't mind calling out some of his peers—if not by name, then by their actions. He coaches with unbridled passion and grim determination to ensure the next Mike Tomlin gets to fulfill his NFL dream.

When Tomlin intimated a few years ago that he wasn't viewed the same as fellow NFL coaches Andy Reid and Sean Payton, when asked if he would be interested in becoming the head coach at USC, he didn't pick their names from a hat.

At the time, all three coaches had one Super Bowl title under their belt. And similar winning percentages.

As difficult as that may be for some people to grasp, Tomlin brought up the names of Reid and Payton—not by accident, or to point the finger at them—but to express his displeasure toward a system that would ask a black Super Bowl–winning head coach if he'd consider taking over a college program that hadn't been relevant in years (especially one who had yet to record a losing season in the NFL).

What was so different about Tomlin's resume than Reid's or Payton's? But they're not asking *them* that question. They're asking Tomlin.

If you're a successful NFL coach, there's no reason to take a college job. Name me the last high-profile NFL coach who did just that. You can't. Who's going to win a Super Bowl and then say, "Yeah, I'm going to leave this job to coach Mizzou?" (No offense to Mizzou, of course.)

Tomlin's critics say he hasn't been to a Super Bowl since 2010. Well, Payton hasn't been to a Super Bowl since 2009, and he's only been to one. Payton had three losing seasons in a row; Tomlin's *never* had a losing season. No one questioned what Payton did to deserve the Denver Broncos paying him $18 million a year, making him the second highest-paid coach in *all* of American sports. I'm not pocket watching, rather asking a question that has no answer.

How do you describe the perception that Tomlin encounters daily in his line of work? The indignity of former Steeler quarterback Terry Bradshaw once calling him a "cheerleader?" This after winning Super Bowl XLIII. You can't. You can't put your finger on it. You can't say what it is, or what you think it is, because you don't have anything tangible. You can only try to conclude what you think it is.

Why is Tomlin perceived differently from other coaches with the same number of Super Bowl rings? Bradshaw never called former Steelers head coach Bill Cowher a "cheerleader," even though Cowher won a single Super Bowl and was far more demonstrative and hyperbolic than his successor.

What's it like being Mike Tomlin? Being left with the realization that, no matter how well you speak or how many games you win, you'll never be viewed the same as your peers.

ACKNOWLEDGMENTS

It takes a village.

The undertaking of a book of this magnitude about a football coach for the ages wouldn't have been possible without the contributions of a multitude of experts, colleagues, peers, friends, family, football insiders, acquaintances—both old and new—as well as total strangers who became good friends over the course of telling a story that was long overdue.

My immeasurable appreciation goes to the shining lineup of individuals whose opinions, research, insight, humor, passion, honesty, and expertise helped turn a mere idea into my second book: Ronde Barber, Milton Barnes, Jomills Braddock, Derrick Brooks, Rick Brown, Reverend Dr. Aubrey Bruce, Curtis Bunn, Brad Childress, Andrew Conte, Mark Dominik, Herman Francois, Fred Goodall, Larry Fitzgerald Sr., DeJuan Gossett, Dan Hammerschmidt, Casey Hampton, Roger Headrick, Joe Hollis Sr., Michael Hurd, Gromer Jeffers, Ira Kaufman, Omar Kelly, Shawn Knight, Roland Lazenby, Joe Linta, Michael MacCambridge, Rick Minter, Brian Overstreet, Eric Pate, Joey Porter Sr., Dan Quinn, Donnie Ross, Rob Ruck, John Sauer, Rip Scherer Jr., Kevin Sherman, Michael Silver, Jeff Sperbeck, Kerry Stevens, Blaine Stewart, Ike Taylor, and Doug Williams.

Special appreciation to Tony Dungy, who took time out of his busy schedule to supply the foreword that appears at the beginning of this book, as well as Willie Colon, Cyrus Mehri, Ed Tomlin, and John Wooten. Without them, this project wouldn't be possible.

And to my editor, Jason Katzman, for trusting me to take on this project and guiding me from early conversations up to the very end.

SOURCES

PERIODICALS

Althon Sports

Billson, Marky: "Pittsburgh Steelers vs. San Diego Chargers Preview and Prediction," 10/12/15.

Associated Press

AP: "Rooney denies Steelers offered job to Grimm, then hired Tomlin," 1/23/07.

AP: "Steelers intrigued by new coach Tomlin," 2/10/07.

Behind the Steel Curtain

Hartman, Jeff: "Mike Tomlin refers to the departure of Le'Veon Bell and Antonio Brown as a 'cleansing,'" 4/28/19.

Bleacher Report

Freeman, Mike: "How Mike Tomlin's big three became just big Ben," 9/6/19.

Daily Press

DP: "Receiver for WM on a tear," 11/10/93.

ESPN

ESPN: "One season with the Vikings prepared Mike Tomlin to coach the Steelers," 9/16/17.

Fowler, Jeremy: "The Antonio Brown 21: What we learned from an epic draft fail," 4/21/17.

Fowler, Jeremy: "Steelers' 'perfect catch' turns 10: When Santonio Holmes won a Super Bowl," 2/1/19.

Fowler, Jeremy: "Steelers' Mike Tomlin isn't here to be understood," 7/17/19.

Garber, Greg: "Thanks to Rooney Rule, door opened," 2/1/07.

Holder, Stephen: "Inside Jim Irsay's tumultuous season as Colts owner," 1/31/23.

Keim, John: "Some Commanders players 'concerned' by Eric Bieniemy's intensity, Ron Rivers says," 8/8/23.

Pasquarelli, Len: "Whisenhunt hired as Cardinals' new head coach," 1/14/07.

Starkey, Joe: "Tomlin deflects controversy with easy manner," 5/14/07.

Logan Banner

Adkins, Paul: "Man's Lionel Taylor recalls his days with Pittsburgh's 'Steel Curtain' of the 70s," 11/17/21.

Los Angeles Times

Farmer, Sam: "Bruce Arians on Tom Brady's future with Bucs, coaching in 'Champa Bay' and more," 2/9/21.

National Football Post

Pompei, Dan: "NFP Sunday blitz," 6/16/13.

New York Times

Brown, Clifton: "Steelers' Tomlin expects to last and win," 8/8/07.

Freeman, Mike: "Pro Football: Notebook; project to introduce black coaches," 12/27/98.

Newport News Daily Press
Miller, Ed: "Whatever happened to . . . MW QB Shawn Knight," 7/30/14

Teel, David: "Sean McDermott third NFL head coach with William and Mary ties," 8/12/19.

Penn Live
Klinger, Jacob: "Jesse James calls 2018 Steelers 'Kardashians,' considers future with team," 12/31/18.

Pittsburgh Tribune-Review
Brown, Scott: "Cowher fearless of challenges," 1/7/07.

Brown, Scott: "Gailey, Steelers discuss coaching vacancy," 1/14/07.

Brown, Scott: "Is Rivera worth the wait?" 1/19/07.

Brown, Scott: "Grimm never got offer, Rooney says," 1/24/07.

Brown, Scott: "Hampton begins process of shedding weight," 7/29/08.

Harris, John: "Steelers interview Tomlin for second time," 1/16/07.

Harris, John: "Tomlin's capabilities evident from college years," 1/28/07.

Harris, John: "Taylor hopes Tomlin turns him into a Pro Bowler," 2/19/07.

Harris, John: "Big Ben leading the way," 9/7/08.

Harris, John: "Steelers fed Ben's sense of entitlement," 4/22/10.

Hasch, Michael: "Rooney unhurt in emergency plane landing," 8/1/02.

Kaboly, Mark: "Taylor: Wallace upset with contract status," 5/29/12.

Prisuta, Mike: "Cowher resignation a hiatus, not an ending," 1/6/07.

Prisuta, Mike: "Mike Prisuta: Steelers pick Grimm, sources say," 1/21/07.

Rutter, Joe: "Art Rooney II backs up belief that Steelers don't have a 'culture problem,'" 1/18/19.

Rutter, Joe: "In 2nd NFL season, QB Kenny Pickett elevated to role as Steelers captain," 9/4/23.

Pittsburgh Post-Gazette

Bouchette, Ed: "Grimm says he is ready for Steelers' top coaching job," 1/18/07.

Bouchette, Ed, and Dulac, Gerry: "Steelers pick Tomlin as head coach," 1/21/07.

Cook, Ron: "Cowboys display superiority in just about everything against Steelers," 11/13/16.

Copeland, Julia: "As a coach, Tomlin is said to have the gift," 7/22/07.

SBNation

Behind the Steel Curtain: "Art Rooney Looking Back at 2011 and Forward to the Future," 1/19/12.

Tampa Bay Times

"Qualified blacks are left outside hierarchy," 8/23/87.

USA Today

Myerberg, Paul: "From VMI to NFL, the shared origin of Mike Tomlin and Dan Quinn," 2/12/15.

Washington Post

Sell, Dave: "Terrapins make over secondary," 8/24/89.

West Central Tribune

WCT: "Williams weight no longer joking matter," 8/2/06.

William & Mary Alumni magazine

Ashley K. Speed: "Signature Threads," 1/8/19.

Williamsburg Yorktown Daily

Harris, Andrew: "Coach Laycock turned into NFL fan by former players turned pro," 1/19/08.

WTAE

Mayo, Bob: "Dick LeBeau resigns as Steelers defensive coordinator," 1/10/15.

BOOKS AND PUBLISHED WORKS

Halberstam, David: *The Breaks of the Game*, Random House, 1981.

Madden, Janet; Mehri, Cyrus; Cochran, Johnnie: "Black Coaches in the National Football League: Superior Performance, Inferior Opportunities," 9/30/02.

Rooney, Jim: *A Different Way to Win*, self-published, 2019.

PODCASTS

All Things Covered with Patrick Peterson and Bryant McFadden (6/22/21)

Bleav in Steelers (5/6/22, 5/9/22)

Catchin' Fades (8/4/21)

The Colin Cowherd Podcast (8/6/21)
Footbahlin' with Ben Roethlisberger (1/13/23)
Nittany Game Week (11/22)
No Jumper Podcast (3/12/22)
The Pivot Podcast (6/21/22)

ONLINE RESOURCES

Lombardi, Mike (via Twitter), 1/9/23.
Steelers.com
Video: "Not their first rodeo together,"
  steelers.com/video/not-their-first-rodeo-together, 8/2018.
Video: "Steelers President Art Rooney II on 2020 Season, Ben
  Roethlisberger, Free Agency, Coach Mike Tomlin," 1/28/21.

TELEVISION AND RADIO

93.7 The Fan
Koll, Matt: "McFadden on Clark-McGahee hit in '08 AFC title
  game: 'I thought he died,'" 12/2/20.
The Cook & Joe Show: "Hines Ward: AB is 'Accountable' but
  Tomlin to Blame Too," 1/31/19.
HBO: *The Shop*, 3/1/19.
HBO: *Real Sports with Bryant Gumbel*, "Black Coaches in the
  NFL," 2/25/21.
Ike Taylor Radio Show

TOMLIN COACHING CAREER

College Coaching Career (1995–2000)

Season	League	School	Role	Wins	Losses	Winning %
1995	College (I-AA)	VMI	Wide Receivers	4	7	.364
1996	College (I-A)	Memphis	Graduate Assistant	4	7	.364
1997	College (I-A)	Arkansas State	Wide Receivers	2	9	.182
1998	College (I-A)	Arkansas State	Defensive Backs	4	8	.333
1999	College (I-A)	Cincinnati	Defensive Backs	3	8	.273
2000	College (I-A)	Cincinnati	Defensive Backs	7	5	.583
		Totals		24	44	.353

NFL Assistant Coaching Career (2001–06)

Season	League	Team	Role	Wins	Losses	Winning %
2001	NFL	Tampa Bay Buccaneers	Defensive Backs	9	7	.563
2002	NFL	Tampa Bay Buccaneers*	Defensive Backs	12	4	.750
2003	NFL	Tampa Bay Buccaneers	Defensive Backs	7	9	.438
2004	NFL	Tampa Bay Buccaneers	Defensive Backs	5	11	.313

Continued

Season	League	Team	Role	Wins	Losses	Winning %
2005	NFL	Tampa Bay Buccaneers	Defensive Backs	11	5	.688
2006	NFL	Minnesota Vikings	Defensive Coordinator	6	10	.375
		Totals		**50**	**46**	**.521**

NFL Head Coaching Career (2007–2022)

Season	League	Team	Role	Wins	Losses	Ties	Winning %
2007	NFL	Pittsburgh Steelers	Head Coach	10	6	-	.625
2008	NFL	Pittsburgh Steelers*	Head Coach	12	4	-	.750
2009	NFL	Pittsburgh Steelers	Head Coach	9	7	-	.563
2010	NFL	Pittsburgh Steelers**	Head Coach	12	4	-	.750
2011	NFL	Pittsburgh Steelers	Head Coach	12	4	-	.750
2012	NFL	Pittsburgh Steelers	Head Coach	8	8	-	.500
2013	NFL	Pittsburgh Steelers	Head Coach	8	8	-	.500
2014	NFL	Pittsburgh Steelers	Head Coach	11	5	-	.688
2015	NFL	Pittsburgh Steelers	Head Coach	10	6	-	.625
2016	NFL	Pittsburgh Steelers	Head Coach	11	5	-	.688
2017	NFL	Pittsburgh Steelers	Head Coach	13	3	-	.813
2018	NFL	Pittsburgh Steelers	Head Coach	9	6	1	.563

Continued

Season	League	Team	Role	Wins	Losses	Ties	Winning %
2019	NFL	Pittsburgh Steelers	Head Coach	8	8	-	.500
2020	NFL	Pittsburgh Steelers	Head Coach	12	4	-	.750
2021	NFL	Pittsburgh Steelers	Head Coach	9	7	1	.530
2022	NFL	Pittsburgh Steelers	Head Coach	9	8	-	.529
Totals				163	93	2	.632

* Super Bowl champions.
** AFC champions.

INDEX

Mendenhall, Rashard, 239,
268, 281, 288, 289, 293,
298, 301, 316, 318
Metrodome, 116
Metz, Eric, 177
Miami Dolphins, 21, 102,
126n1, 127, 160, 164, 168,
169, 175, 204, 205, 270,
280, 317, 322, 329, 344,
345, 346, 372, 393, 400
Miami Herald, 168
Miami University (OH), 272
Michigan State University, 318
Mid-American
Conference, 279
Milledgeville (GA), 270–271
Miller, Heath, 245, 253, 286,
287, 294, 337, 339
Minneapolis (MN), xxi, 75,
102, 110, 168
Minnesota Vikings, x, xi,
xiii, 20, 24, 73, 75, 90, 92,
94, 97–118, 125, 127, 133,
136–137, 147, 167, 179, 181,
187, 218, 195, 203
Minter, Rick, 56–58, 61–63,
64, 66, 72, 175, 187, 198,
409–410, 417
Mitchell, John, 186–187, 274
Mitchell, Mike, 358–359

Monday Night Football, 116,
238, 315, 380, 387
Montana State University, 18
Montgomery (AL), 152
Montgomery, Scottie,
278, 279
Moore, Dan, 408
Moore, Matt, 345
Moore, Mewelde, 239,
241, 280
Mora Jr., Jim, 101
Morris, Raheem, 72,
92–95, 214
Moss, Randy, 222, 235,
273n1
Moss, Santana, 235
Motor City Bowl, 59
Mularkey, Mike, 169
Munchak, Mike, 330, 353
Mundy, Ryan, 305
Myles, Godfrey, 143

NAACP, 151–152
NAIA, 142–143
national anthem, 352
National Baseball Hall of
Fame, 152
National Basketball Hall of
Fame, 132
National Football Post, 72